T0248438

THE INVENTION OF OSCAR WILDE

THE INVENTION OF
OSCAR WILDE

NICHOLAS FRANKEL

REAKTION BOOKS

Published by
REAKTION BOOKS LTD
Unit 32, Waterside
44–48 Wharf Road
London N1 7UX, UK
www.reaktionbooks.co.uk

First published 2021

Printed and bound in Great Britain
by TJ Books Ltd, Padstow, Cornwall

A catalogue record for this book is available from the British Library

ISBN 978 1 78914 414 7

CONTENTS

For Susan

'. . . all that's best of dark and bright
Meet in her aspect and her eyes'

– Lord Byron

Oscar Wilde, photo-portrait by Napoleon Sarony, 1882.

Introduction

'I have put my talent into my works, but I have put all my genius into my life,' Wilde told his friend André Gide. To be sure, Wilde put his genius into his written works as well. Today his plays are among the wittiest and most frequently performed in the English stage repertoire, and together with his stories, essays, dialogues and poems, they helped bring down the curtain on an outmoded Victorianism.

But if Wilde gave rein to his imagination in his works, his invention and commitment to art were such that his life now reads like the greatest of his works. One should either wear a work of art or be a work of art, he declared. As we shall see, even as a young man he was determined to approach life on his own terms, and he remained an antinomian till his dying day, seizing at experience and unsettling the preconceptions of his fellow Victorians. In what he said and did – and even in the way he dressed, no less than in what he wrote – his life embodied a provocation and a rebuke to the pious conformism, cruelty and hypocrisy of Victorian England. Indeed he was never at home in England, where he spent the most successful years (1874–95) of his life and where he was always viewed as a rare exotic. Born in Ireland in 1854, he found the more open, tolerant atmosphere of

France and the United States more conducive to his temper and sexuality, and he vowed to take up citizenship in France long before his final exile there following his release from an English prison in 1897.

If he was always at odds with England, however, he nevertheless lived among the English with rare passion, conviction and imagination, treating life as if it were the greatest of all arts. He was determined to put into practice Walter Pater's injunction that 'to burn always with this hard, gemlike flame, to maintain this ecstasy, is success in life'. In *The Picture of Dorian Gray*, he called for a new spirituality of the senses; and like the eponymous hero of his own novel, Wilde's object was nothing less than 'to recreate life, and . . . save it from . . . harsh, uncomely puritanism'. Imprisoned for 'gross indecency' in 1895, he famously said that the company of male sex workers and blackmailers was like 'feasting with panthers. The danger was half the excitement,' and he emerged from prison under the pseudonym Sebastian Melmoth more determined than ever to follow his own path. It has been said that in his plays and stories Wilde dramatized the emergence of what the Situationist philosopher Guy Debord called a 'society of the spectacle', a world of conspicuous material consumption in which even language operates like a commodity or visual fetish. But Wilde's greatest spectacle was himself: renowned in his own day for his sparkling conversation and wit no less than for his impeccable grooming and couture, he lived with self-conscious deliberateness and flamboyance – a living paradox, at once a creature of this world and apart from it. And if his written works stand in judgement on Victorian England, heralding the modern period that he helped bring into being, so too does Wilde's uncompromising and novelistic life.

He succeeded in creating a cult of himself long before he published anything of note. Even as an undergraduate he developed that personal style and sartorial elegance for which he later became internationally famous. In 1882 the American celebrity photographer Napoleon Sarony paid $1,500, the same sum he paid to the actresses Sarah Bernhardt and Lillie Langtry, for exclusive American rights to Wilde's photographic image, and it is not insignificant that one of the resulting photo-portraits was the subject of a landmark court case whereby photographs came to enjoy the same privileges as painted artworks in American law. Sarony's photographs, timed to capitalize on Wilde's 1882 tour of North America, are as ubiquitous in our own time as they were in Wilde's day. With his long, flowing locks, clean-shaven face and love for soft, colourful clothing fabrics ('Men should dress more in velvet . . . as it catches the light and shade,' he said), Wilde represented a new kind of masculinity, and he had more in common with iconic male figures of the 1960s and 1970s – with Jim Morrison, Mick Jagger, David Bowie and The Beatles – than the heavily bewhiskered, moustached or bearded Victorian masculine ideal that peers out from so many Victorian portraits.

Rumours about Wilde's unconventional sexuality accompanied these visual representations, corroborated by homoerotic strains in Wilde's poetry and (later) his fiction. These rumours grew to a clamour in the early 1890s when his affair with the reckless Lord Alfred Douglas became the subject of gossip, culminating in his conviction and imprisonment for gross indecency in 1895. While Wilde's sexuality cannot be made to fit easily into the modern categories of homosexual, heterosexual and bisexual, categories which are now as much markers of personal identity as of sexual taste, Wilde was unapologetic and defiant about his love for men, and today he is rightly seen as a ground-breaking figure for modern homosexual men.

But Wilde's strong sense of personal style and elegance were not merely signs of an unconventional masculinity and sexual orientation. 'Thou art not fit/ For this vile traffic-house,' Wilde says to his own soul in his early poem 'Theoretikos', while turning contemptuously away from a world in which 'wisdom and reverence are sold at mart'. The world of commerce and industry 'mars my calm: wherefore, in dreams of Art/ And loftiest culture I would stand apart'. Born at the height of the Pre-Raphaelite movement, Wilde early on declared a personal allegiance to art and beauty that is as clear in his surviving portraits as it is in his writings. While still a young man, he surrounded himself with fine paintings and objects, advising his listeners to transform their lived environments into small palaces of art. His earliest writings are works of art criticism, or imitations of Classical and Romantic poetry, and as W. P. Frith's famous painting *A Private View at the Royal Academy, 1881* shows, Wilde himself was a compelling object of fascination no less than the artworks he criticized or endorsed with his pen.

It is often said that he was the greatest dandy of his – or any – age. But if Wilde was 'a Man whose trade, office and existence consists in the wearing of Clothes', to employ Thomas Carlyle's definition of a dandy, this should not be mistaken as implying a thoughtless self-indulgence or self-absorption. In his visual and sartorial self-invention, Wilde exemplified Baudelaire's concept of the dandy as 'the supreme incarnation of the idea of beauty transported into the sphere of material life'. In an age of gross materialism, industry and commerce, his personal artistry and

Oscar Wilde, photo-portrait by W. & D. Downey, 1889.

elegance stood as a rebuke to the dominant values of his age, harking back to such figures as Byron and Beau Brummell even as they insisted on what Wilde called 'the absolute modernity of Beauty'.

We can now see that Wilde's dandyism and love of art masked his unconventional sexuality, as his aphorism 'to reveal art and conceal the artist is art's aim' may tacitly acknowledge. Forced to defend *The Picture of Dorian Gray* in court in 1895, he insisted that far from depicting male same-sex love, his intentions in writing the novel had been thoroughly artistic, much like those of the painter Basil Hallward, whose painting of Dorian Gray represents the 'visible incarnation' of an unseen, Platonic ideal. But in dramatizing Hallward's artistic motivations in the revised book-length version of *Dorian Gray* published in 1891, one year after the novel's appearance in *Lippincott's Monthly Magazine*, Wilde simultaneously occluded motivations that were more frankly personal and sexual in earlier versions, almost certainly because scandalized reactions to the serial version raised fears of prosecution in the minds of author and publisher. 'There was love in every line [of the portrait], and in every touch there was passion,' Hallward confesses in the uncensored text of the novel that Wilde submitted for publication in April 1890. 'I have worshipped you with far more romance of feeling than a man usually gives to a friend,' he tells Dorian Gray in a phrase that Wilde's first editor altered to the more censorious 'more romance of feeling than a man should ever give to a friend' (in the first published version) and that Wilde cut entirely from the book version. Hallward's confession might easily have been made by Wilde himself, whose 'worship' of numerous young men is palpable in his correspondence and who later confessed that

'Basil Hallward is who I think I am.' It uncannily foreshadows Wilde's own worship of Lord Alfred Douglas, the preternaturally youthful-looking young aristocrat whom Wilde once called 'the supreme, the perfect love of my life' and whose shadow looms over the final turbulent years of Wilde's life.[1]

'All art is at once surface and symbol,' Wilde declared, and 'Those who go beneath the surface do so at their peril.' To many in his own day, Wilde was the embodiment of a new movement for the triumph of art and beauty as ends in themselves that did much to shape the avant-garde movements of the early twentieth century. But today we view Wilde's love of art through a double lens, celebrating the beauty, wit and inventiveness of his language while remaining keen to the personal and political energies that course just below its surface. And if Wilde's elevation of art embodied a paradox, this is no less true of other aspects of his life. A self-declared socialist who believed in the supremacy of the individual; a Christian who once proclaimed that 'the faith that others give to the unseen, I give to what one can touch and look at. My Gods dwell in temples made with hands, and within the circle of actual experience';[2] an Irishman who schooled himself in the poetry of Keats and the Pre-Raphaelites and for whom Queen Victoria was one of the three greatest women in history; a decadent who produced some of the greatest stories ever written for children; a married paterfamilias and dutiful son who, like Jack and Algernon in *The Importance of Being Earnest*, enjoyed secretly 'bunburying' in London's West End or in Paris with a panoply of young male lovers; an international celebrity who courted public attention while pursuing a double life in the homosexual underworld of late Victorian London. Wilde was a living paradox. Indeed he was an *artist* of the paradox, incorporating its form and structure into his writings and sayings, determined on unsettling the truth claims that his contemporaries took to be self-evident. He died in 1900, on the cusp of the twentieth century, a social pariah and outcast, bankrupt and bereft of the fame that had spurred his greatest works. But his life, like his works, embodies an inventiveness that continues to shape the world that came in his wake.

ONE

The Birth of 'Oscar Wilde'

When one is unknown, a number of Christian names are useful, perhaps needful . . . I started as Oscar Fingal O'Fflahertie Wills Wilde. All but two of the names have already been thrown overboard. Soon I shall discard another and be known simply as 'The Wilde' or 'The Oscar'.

WILDE, to Coulson Kernahan, *c.* 1891

Oscar Fingal O'Fflahertie Wills Wilde was born on 16 October 1854 at 21 Westland Row, a medium-sized terraced residence on a busy Dublin street. Ten months after his birth, the family moved into a grander Regency home at 1 Merrion Square, where Wilde was to grow up and where he would always claim he was born. As Wilde's full name suggests, his Irish inheritance was important to his parents: 'Oscar' and 'Fingal' came from Irish legend and 'O'Fflahertie' (spelt in the Norman fashion, with the distinctive double 'f') linked him with the ferocious O'Fflahertie clan of Galway, from whom he was descended through his maternal grandmother. 'Wills' was a late addition, proudly touted by Wilde in his youth and adopted in deference to his cousins, who included James Wills the poet and W. G. Wills the dramatist.

Wilde's childhood home, Merrion Square, Dublin.

Wilde's parents were among Ireland's leading intellectuals, though also widely renowned for their hospitality and repartee. While Wilde was growing up they regularly opened their doors to Dublin's leading artistic, scientific and literary lights. On Saturday afternoons they hosted large receptions while at night they presided over glittering and lavish dinner parties, where the repartee flowed as easily as the wine. Both parents were also fiercely nationalist, although they distanced themselves from the militant republican Fenianism that erupted in the late 1860s. Wilde's father, Sir William Wilde, was a leading eye and ear surgeon as well as a highly skilled amateur archaeologist, folklorist and demographer. When still a young man he founded St Mark's Ophthalmic Hospital, the most advanced eye and ear hospital in Ireland, and he pioneered a number of modern medical procedures (even today, eye and ear surgeons use the terms 'Wilde's incision', 'Wilde's cone of light' and 'Wilde's cords').[1] In 1863 he was made Surgeon Oculist to Queen Victoria in Ireland, and he was knighted in 1864, in part for his work as Assistant Commissioner of the Irish Census for 1851 and 1861. Along with a medical textbook on aural surgery, still a classic in its field, he authored numerous books on Irish history and legend. His catalogue of the Irish antiquities housed in the National Museum of Ireland is still in use, while his book *Irish Popular Superstitions*, which he dedicated to his wife on its appearance

Sir William Wilde, early 1870s.

in 1852, has been frequently reprinted. Sir William would often collect superstitions, charms, legends and magical 'cures' in lieu of medical fees from his peasant patients; their traces can be felt in his younger son's short stories and prose poems, and after Sir William's death, this body of folklore was edited and gathered by his widow into the two-volume *Ancient Legends, Mystic Charms, and Superstitions of Ireland*, where it had a profound effect upon W. B. Yeats, among others.

Wilde's mother, Lady Wilde, born Jane Francesca Elgee, was no less accomplished. She was familiar with Greek and the Classics, and she mastered German, Italian and French at an early age. In the late 1840s, she published Irish revolutionary poetry in *The Nation* under the pen-name 'Speranza', and when

Lady Wilde as a young woman, when she published poetry as 'Speranza'.

her editor, Gavin Duffy, was tried for treason by the English, she published two militant prose editorials in his defence, including 'The Hour of Destiny', in which she announced that 'the long pending war with England has actually commenced,' and the incendiary 'Jacta Alea Est [The Die Is Cast]', in which she cried 'O for a hundred thousand muskets glimmering brightly in the light of heaven.' When Duffy was pressed about these editorials in court, she proudly took ownership of them from the public gallery, later writing that 'I express the soul of a great nation. Nothing less would satisfy me, who am the acknowledged voice in poetry of all the people of Ireland.' From this point on, Speranza was a great favourite with the citizens of Dublin and her carriage was regularly cheered in the streets. She was also a skilled translator and essayist: her translation of Meinhold's *Sidonia the Sorceress* was much loved by the Pre-Raphaelites; it inspired Burne-Jones's painting *Sidonia von Bork* and it was later printed in 'Golden' type by William Morris at the Kelmscott Press. With some justification Wilde was to write from prison, less than four years before his death:

> She and my father . . . bequeathed me a name they had made noble and honoured not merely in Literature, Art, Archaeology and Science, but in the public history of my own country in its evolution as a nation.[2]

But there was a darker side to Wilde's parents. While still a bachelor, Sir William fathered three illegitimate children by at least two different women, and after his marriage these children mingled freely with his legitimate children and their mother. As the biographer Richard Ellmann explains, 'in the Dublin of this time, the old Regency permissiveness lingered.'[3] The oldest son, named Henry Wilson, grew up to be an eminent eye surgeon like his father, first as Sir William's assistant and eventually his successor as Senior Surgeon at St Mark's. While an undergraduate in the 1870s, Wilde regularly socialized with his illegitimate half-brother, and when Wilson died unexpectedly four days after they last dined together, in June 1877, Wilde confessed that he had been 'very much attached' to Wilson and was 'very much down in spirits and depressed'.[4] The two illegitimate daughters, meanwhile, adopted by Sir William's brother as his wards, kept the name Wilde. When these two daughters perished in a fire in 1871, the entire family was distraught. And when Sir William himself was dying, in 1876, Lady Wilde tolerated the daily visits to his bedside of a mysterious veiled woman – presumably the mother of at least one of his illegitimate offspring – on the grounds that, as Oscar Wilde himself later put it, 'she knew that my father loved the woman and felt that it must be a joy and comfort to have her there by his dying bed.'[5]

One serious upshot of Sir William's sexual licentiousness came from his involvement with an attractive, laudanum-addicted, female patient by the name of Mary Travers, who was briefly a nanny to the Wilde children. At first Lady Wilde welcomed Travers into her home. But Travers's behaviour became increasingly erratic and inflammatory, perhaps with good reason, and she began to hint that Sir William had administered chloroform and raped her in his consulting room. She went public with her insinuations, then accepted from Sir William the fare money to emigrate to Australia (but failed to embark), and eventually she published a scurrilous pamphlet in which she attacked the Wildes while repeating her insinuations of rape. When Lady

Wilde found that Travers had employed newspaper boys to distribute this pamphlet from her own front hall at Merrion Square along with copies of William Wilde's letters to Travers, she could stand it no longer and wrote the following ill-advised letter to Mary's father:

> Sir, you may not be aware of the disreputable conduct of your daughter . . . [who] consorts with all the newspaper boys . . . employing them to disseminate offensive placards, in which she makes it appear that she has had an intrigue with Sir William Wilde. If she chooses to disgrace herself, that is not my affair; but as her object in insulting me is the hope of extorting money, for which she has several times applied to Sir William Wilde, with threats of more annoyance if not given, I think it right to inform you that no threat or additional insult shall ever extort money for her from our hands. The wages of disgrace she has so basely treated for and demanded shall never be given her.[6]

Upon reading this letter Mary Travers sued Lady Wilde for libel, naming Sir William as a co-respondent.

The resulting court case – a cause célèbre in Dublin, heard over five days in December 1864 – is one of the defining events of Wilde's childhood, and in many respects it uncannily foreshadows the libel case that would wreak havoc on Wilde's life and family in 1895. Travers won a legal victory, although the jury took a dim view of her behaviour and awarded her only a farthing in damages. The Wildes did not acquit themselves well either and had to pay £2,000 in costs. Sir William's decision not to take the stand in his wife's defence was widely considered a point against him, while Speranza's answer under oath to the question of why she hadn't answered Travers when the latter had written complaining of her husband's attempt upon her virtue (Speranza replied only 'because I was not interested') was a major error. 'The only thing for a woman to do' in the face of scandal, contends Lord Goring in Wilde's play *An Ideal Husband*, is to 'stand by her husband'. Speranza's reply, however, was widely interpreted as condoning her husband's infidelity, and her behaviour in this respect makes a sharp contrast with that of Wilde's own wife, Constance, who, following his criminal conviction and imprisonment in 1895, was to change her last name along with that of her children while instituting a legal separation that severely restricted her husband's future conduct and rights.

It has been said that the failed libel suit left Sir William a broken man, and while this may be an exaggeration, there is no doubt that Sir William spent increasing amounts of time henceforth away from Dublin, at Moytura, the villa he was building on the edge of Lough Corrib in the west of Ireland. Along with the sudden death of Wilde's sister Isola in 1867, an event later commemorated touchingly by Wilde in his poem 'Requiescat', followed closely by that of Sir William's illegitimate daughters in 1871, the Travers case placed immense strain on the family.

When the Travers case unfolded, Wilde was a ten-year-old boarder at Portora Royal School at Enniskillen, where nearly sixty years later Samuel Beckett was a pupil too. If he was aware of the case at all, Wilde must have known of it only indirectly at first, by gossip and by letters from home. No trace of the scandal remains in the only letter surviving from Wilde's years at Portora, dated nearly four years after the libel case, in which

Wilde affectionately thanks both parents for a hamper and 'for letting me paint'. Portora, one of five schools in Ireland founded by Royal Charter in 1608, has been described as 'the Eton of Ireland' and a site for the production of an Anglo-Irish colonial class.[7] It was one of Ireland's foremost Anglo-Irish educational institutions, and Wilde was to remain a student there until 1871. As his thanks for 'letting me paint' imply, his first academic love was art: he won a school prize for art, and the Irish biographer Davis Coakley speculates that the Wildes' friendship with the school art teacher, William Wakeman, may have been a significant factor in their decision to send Wilde and his brother to Portora. However, he quickly developed a reputation among his fellow students for his ability to read with phenomenal speed and retentiveness, and it was at Portora that his reputation as a talker and his interest in dress first flourished: for a wager, he would read a three-volume novel so rapidly and closely as to give an accurate summary of its plot within half an hour, he later told the American writer Eugene Field, while he was 'more careful in his dress than any other boy', his schoolfellow Louis Purser later recalled.[8] In his final years at Portora, he started to distinguish himself academically as well, making deft and mellifluous translations from Plato, Thucydides, Virgil and Aeschylus. (Translations from Aeschylus and Aristophanes were to be among Wilde's earliest published poems.) In 1869 he won a third prize in Scripture, and the following year he won the Carpenter Prize for Greek Testament, eclipsing even his fellow pupil Purser, later the Distinguished Professor of Latin at Trinity College, Dublin. It was little surprise when, along with Purser and another boy, Wilde was awarded a Royal Scholarship to Trinity College, Dublin, in 1871.

The three years Wilde spent at Trinity were even more distinguished academically, culminating in his being awarded the Berkeley Gold Medal in Greek, the blue ribbon of Classical scholarship. He made the most of the opportunities Trinity afforded, and if he had decided to stay at Trinity, he would almost certainly have been elected to a fellowship. He particularly endeared himself to his tutor John Pentland Mahaffy, whom Wilde was much later in life to call 'my first and best teacher' and 'the scholar who showed me how to love Greek things'.[9] Wilde worked closely with Mahaffy, one of the most distinguished Classicists of his day, assisting him with his 1874 book *Social Life in Greece*.[10] Mahaffy was also renowned as one of the most brilliant wits and

John Pentland Mahaffy, Wilde's Trinity College tutor, whom Wilde many years later called 'my first and best teacher'.

talkers of his day, and he helped Wilde develop the art of repartee for which his pupil too would shortly became famous. Many years later, Wilde described Mahaffy's 1887 book *The Principles of the Art of Conversation* as written expressly to encourage the 'delightful art of brilliant chatter', calling it 'a social guide without which no debutante or dandy should ever dream of going out to dine'.[11] Like his protégé, Mahaffy was a 'diner-out' of the first order, and it is little surprise that when Wilde was awarded a Classics Demyship to Magdalen College, Oxford, following a competitive examination in June 1874, Mahaffy is reputed to have quipped: 'You're not quite clever enough for us here, Oscar. Better run up to Oxford.'

Wilde arrived at Oxford in October 1874 carrying high academic expectations, and ultimately he did not disappoint. At first he cultivated an air of insouciance, seeking a reputation for scholarly brilliance without zeal. In November 1874 he failed an elementary examination in Classical Literature and mathematics, and in March 1875 he was formally admonished by the President of Magdalen College. But after this he applied himself with greater zeal, and when the first important examinations, Honours Moderations, came around in June 1876, he scored an impressive First. His Oxford Notebooks and Commonplace Book, published and annotated in 1988, show that he was a dedicated and talented student. At first, he discipled himself to John Ruskin, Slade Professor of Fine Art and England's leading art critic, who remained a close friend until his unbalanced mind entailed his withdrawal from all social commitments in the late 1880s. He dined with the great linguist and philologist Max Müller, while also coming under the sway intellectually of the Oxford Hegelians, particularly William Wallace and Benjamin

Jowett, as well as Herbert Spencer and W. K. Clifford, in whose writings Wilde found a tantalizing marriage of evolutionary science, moral philosophy and innovative sociology that had a profound impact on his thought.

Wilde's biggest intellectual influence at Oxford, however, was the Classicist and aesthete Walter Pater, a fellow of Brasenose College, whose *Studies in the History of the Renaissance* was published to loud controversy one year before Wilde's arrival. The book's Conclusion, omitted from the second edition and not restored until 1888 on the grounds that 'it might possibly mislead some of those young men into whose hands it might fall', proved especially inflammatory. In it Pater declared that life is 'a drift of momentary acts of sight and passion and thought', that 'not the fruit of experience, but experience itself is the end', and that 'to burn always with this hard, gemlike flame, to maintain this ecstasy, is success in life.' Although Wilde is not known to have attended Pater's lectures and did not personally meet Pater until his third year at Oxford, he read *The Renaissance* in his first term and thereafter always spoke of it as 'my golden book', describing it in *De profundis* as 'that book which has had such a strange influence over my life'. With its elevation of 'art for its own sake' and insistence on passion at any cost, *The Renaissance* more than any other book shaped the course of Wilde's life and work.

Academically Wilde was a superstar at Oxford. His First in Honours Moderations was followed in 1878 by a First in Literae Humaniores (Ancient History and Philosophy), a rare 'Double First', as well as by the award of the Newdigate Prize for poetry, previously won by John Ruskin, Matthew Arnold and John Addington Symonds, among others. The biographer Richard Ellmann tells us that at the viva voce for his final exams, the

Wilde as an undergraduate, April 1876.

dons spent their time complimenting Wilde instead of questioning him and revealed that his was the best examination of his year. But his time at Oxford was not without controversy. He showed a markedly independent streak, and this is probably why he was not offered a fellowship to pursue his academic career further. (He applied unsuccessfully for a fellowship at Trinity College, Oxford, and in late 1879 also applied unsuccessfully for an 'archaeological studentship'. As late as 1885, he wrote: 'I often think with regret of my Oxford days and wish I had not left Parnassus for Piccadilly.') He treated the dons with insolence and refused to attend the lectures of those who did not interest him.[12] Instead he cultivated and quickly achieved a reputation as an aesthete and a dandy, taking great care over the decor of his college rooms and making a name for himself for his purported remark that he found it 'harder and harder to live up to his blue china'. The remark, widely reported in the papers and satirized in *Punch*, was denounced from the pulpit by the vicar of St Mary's, the university church.

He threw himself into the social whirl of undergraduate life and was evidently keener on joining the Masonic Lodge or becoming a convert to Roman Catholicism than on joining the hallowed halls of academe. He travelled in Italy in the summer of 1875 with his old Trinity tutor Mahaffy and again in the spring holiday of 1877, this time venturing as far as Greece, where they visited the excavations at Olympia, among other major historical sites. Wilde had known that he would miss the start of the summer term at Oxford, but when he was rusticated (suspended) from the university and his Demyship suspended, on his return to Oxford, he was appalled. His argument that 'seeing Greece is really a great education for anyone . . . and Mr. Mahaffy is such a clever man that it is quite as good as going to lectures' fell on deaf ears.[13] 'I was sent down for being the first undergraduate to visit Olympia,' he was to quip in later years.[14]

Wilde's Oxford years are notable too for his first flirtations with Roman Catholicism. According to his friend Lord Ronald Gower, at this time his 'long-haired head [was] full of nonsense regarding the Church of Rome' and his rooms were 'filled with photographs of the Pope and Cardinal Manning'. Around the time of his first trip to Italy with Mahaffy, in 1875, he began entertaining the idea of conversion to Catholicism; and when a shortage of funds meant returning home without visiting Rome, where he had hoped to 'see . . ./ The only God-anointed King,/ And hear the silver-trumpets ring/ A triumph as He passes by', he expressed his disappointment in his poem 'Rome Unvisited'.

Two years later, at the start of his second visit to Italy with Mahaffy, he was still set on the idea of visiting Rome, in order to immerse himself in the full pomp and circumstance of Catholicism at its source. David Hunter-Blair, a college friend and a recent convert, had entered the Benedictine Order in Rome and had arranged a private audience with the Pope. It seems more than likely that Wilde was considering converting to Catholicism under Hunter-Blair's aegis. 'This is an era in my life, a crisis,' he told a friend just before setting out; 'I wish I could look into the seeds of time and see what is coming.'[15] Wilde had planned to leave Mahaffy at Genoa and travel on to Rome, but Mahaffy insisted that he should visit Greece with himself instead, reputedly saying: 'we cannot let you become a Catholic, but we will make a good Pagan of you instead.' As a result Wilde postponed visiting Rome once again and opted for visiting Greece with Mahaffy. The struggle Wilde experienced as he debated between the competing exhortations of Hunter-Blair and Mahaffy – between Roman Catholicism and Hellenic Paganism – is expressed between the lines of his 'Sonnet Written during Holy Week':

I wandered in Scoglietto's green retreat;
The oranges, on each o'erhanging spray,
Burned as bright lamps of gold to shame the day.
Some startled bird, with fluttering wings and fleet,
Showered the milk-white blossoms; at my feet
Like silver crowns the pale narcissi lay;
And the curved waves, that streaked the sapphire bay,
Laughed i' the sun, and life seemed very sweet.
Outside a little child came singing clear,
'Jesus, the Blessed Master, has been slain –
O, come and fill his sepulchre with flowers.'
Ah, God! ah, God! these sweet and honied hours
Had drowned all memories of Thy bitter pain –
The Cross, the Crown, the Soldiers, and the Spear.

Genoa, 1877[16]

Mahaffy and Greece won this struggle, although on his return from Greece Wilde finally visited Rome, where Hunter-Blair saw to it that the promised private audience with the Pope took place. But the damage was done. As Hunter-Blair later recognized, 'he had become Hellenized, somewhat Paganized, perhaps, by the appeal of Greece . . . and Rome retired into the background.'[17] Although flashes of a revived interest in Catholicism obtrude into works published many years later, such as 'The Sphinx', *The Ballad of Reading Gaol* and *De profundis*, and some believe that he experienced a deathbed conversion in his final moments (see Chapter Ten), Wilde was to remain an unapologetic Pagan for the rest of his life.

Wilde's Oxford years are notable above all, however, for the beginnings of the Wilde we think we know today. If Oscar Fingal O'Fflahertie Wills Wilde was born in 1854 in Dublin, 'Oscar Wilde' was born between 1874 and 1878 at Oxford, for it was at Oxford that he started his literary career and created an aura about himself suggesting that he was *himself* a great imaginative invention. While still an undergraduate, he published reviews of the 1877 and 1879 Grosvenor Gallery exhibitions that are still frequently cited in art scholarship today. He was especially determined to make a name for himself as a poet. Between 1875 and 1878, when he took his degree, he wrote more than fifty poems, no fewer than 23 of which he also published during this period. With one or two significant exceptions,[18] these poems appeared in Irish serials, generally under the name 'Oscar F. O'F. Wills Wilde', 'Oscar O'F. Wills Wilde' or the initials 'O. F. O'F. W. W.' (although occasionally the first 'F' disappeared). His preferred sites were the *Dublin University Magazine*, *The Month and Catholic Review*, *The Irish Monthly* and *Kottabos*, the last of which was closely associated with Trinity College. But in 1877 he started signing his publications 'Oscar Wilde' as well as identifying Oxford as the site of their composition. Richard Ellmann tells us that, while at Oxford, Wilde 'remade his speech', ridding himself of his Irish accent in favour of 'a distinct and stately English'.[19] ('My Irish accent was one of the many things I forgot at Oxford,' Wilde later quipped.) As Wilde himself explained many years later,

> a name which is destined to be in everybody's mouth must not be too long. It comes so expensive in the advertisements. When one is unknown, a number of Christian names are useful, perhaps needful. As one becomes famous, one sheds some of them, just as a balloonist, when rising higher, sheds unnecessary ballast, or as you shed your Christian name when raised to the peerage. I started as Oscar Fingal O'Fflahertie Wills Wilde. All but two of the names have already been thrown overboard. Soon I shall discard another and be known simply as 'The Wilde' or 'The Oscar'.[20]

It was the beginning of a process of self-division, the deliberate creation of a public persona at odds with his private self, that was to have tremendous ramifications for the rest of Wilde's life.

TWO

The Poetry of Englishness

By nothing is England so glorious as by her poetry

MATTHEW ARNOLD, 1879

By jettisoning his Irish names, Wilde was not merely creating himself as an Englishman. He was also indicating that 'Oscar Wilde' was a cultural construction, a persona predicated on fame and a large audience. Unsurprisingly perhaps, print media were essential to the success of this new persona.

While still a student at Oxford, Wilde harboured great ambitions for his publications. An article on the Irish artist Henry O'Neill (*Saunders's News-Letter*, 1877) was written so that 'an Irishman of genius, and a heroic devotion to art, may be rescued from undeserved want'. A review of the first Grosvenor Gallery exhibition (*Dublin University Magazine*, 1877), Wilde's first prose publication, was effectively a dry run for proclaiming what he was later to call 'The English Renaissance of Art', and it was instrumental in bringing about Wilde's friendship with Walter Pater. In it Wilde praised the leading lights of contemporary English painting, including Watts, Burne-Jones, Millais and Whistler (at that time long-resident in London), and concluded by saying that the Gallery's owner, Sir Coutts Lindsay, was doing much to advance 'that revival of culture and love of beauty which in great part owes its birth to Mr. Ruskin, and which Mr. Swinburne, and Mr. Pater, and Mr. Symonds, and Mr. Morris, and many others, are fostering and keeping alive, each in his own peculiar fashion'. Wilde reserved some of his warmest praise, however, for a now-neglected painting by Spencer Stanhope, *Love and the Maiden*, and dwelt rhapsodically on the 'boyish beauty' of Stanhope's depiction of love:

> A rose-garland presses the boy's brown curls, and he is clad in a tunic of oriental colours, and delicately sensuous are his face and his bared limbs. His boyish beauty is of that peculiar type unknown in Northern Europe, but common in the Greek islands, where boys can still be found as beautiful as the Charmides of Plato. Guido's *St. Sebastian* in the Palazzo Rosso at Genoa is one of those boys, and Perugino once drew a Greek Ganymede for his native town, but the painter who most shows the influence of this type is Correggio, whose lily-bearer in the Cathedral at Parma, and whose wild-eyed, open-mouthed St. John in the 'Incoronata Madonna' of St. Giovanni Evangelista, are the best examples in art of the bloom and vitality and radiance of this adolescent beauty.

The note of homoeroticism here is also apparent in 'The Tomb of Keats' (*Irish Monthly*, 1877), a personal essay commemorating Wilde's visit to Keats's grave during his passage through Rome in April 1877. Here Wilde declares a personal allegiance to the English poet Keats that would run through much of his early writing. He calls Keats 'a Priest of Beauty slain before his time' and likens him to St Sebastian, 'pierced by arrows, raising his eyes with divine, impassioned gaze towards the Eternal Beauty of the opening heavens'. (Wilde had seen one of Guido Reni's painted depictions of St Sebastian at Genoa; the image (see illus. 34) was burned into his mind, and an echo of it survives in the pseudonym, Sebastian Melmoth, that Wilde was to adopt on leaving prison in 1897.) He ends 'The Tomb of Keats' with a sonnet, 'Heu Miserande Puer', dedicated to Keats's memory, which ends as follows:

> O proudest heart that broke for misery!
> O sweetest lips since those of Mitylene!
> O poet-painter of the English Land!
> Thy name was writ in water – it shall stand:
> And tears like mine will keep thy memory green,
> As Isabella did her Basil-tree.

When Wilde submitted 'The Tomb of Keats' to the *Irish Monthly* for publication, 'the English Land' was worded 'our English Land', leading Matthew Russell S. J., the magazine's editor, to ask of his fellow Irishman: 'we speak English and we fortunately understand Shakespeare as one of our own – but is the English land *ours*?' Wilde replied that 'it is a noble privilege to count oneself of the same race as Keats and Shakespeare,' although he nevertheless changed 'our English Land' to placate Russell, saying he 'would not shock the feelings of your readers for anything'. On republishing the sonnet as 'The Grave of Keats' in *Poems* in 1881, Wilde altered the revealing phrase back to 'our English Land'.

A sea-change came over both Wilde's publication and personal arrangements when he left Oxford for London after taking his degree in late 1878. All but one of his poems up to this point had been published in Ireland (or, in the case of three poems published in the Boston *Pilot*, for American readers with Irish sympathies), and he had returned to Dublin during each college holiday. But in early October 1878 he took a final leave from Dublin, saying that he would be returning to England for good this time. From April 1879 until his departure for America in late 1881, all except one of his poems appeared in high-profile English publications. He was now determined to make a name for himself in London.[1]

This shift towards England may have been motivated partly by romantic disappointment. In late 1876 he had become romantically involved with a pretty young Irishwoman, Florence Balcombe, whom he accompanied to church on at least one occasion and to whom he gave a small gold cross inscribed with his name. As the biographer Richard Ellmann writes, 'it is hard to gauge the intensity of his feelings, which he exaggerated and she later minimized.' Possibly Wilde considered marrying her, even though she possessed 'not a sixpence of money'.[2] But in September 1878, just before returning to Oxford for his final term, Wilde learned that 'Florrie' was engaged to be married to Bram Stoker (the marriage took place in Dublin in December 1878). The news elicited three letters to Balcombe, written hot on the heels of one another, in which Wilde took a painful parting from her as well as from Ireland more generally. In the first of these, Wilde asked Balcombe for the return of the gold cross, saying that it 'will serve to remind me of the bygone days', and asked to meet her one last time, adding that he 'cannot leave Ireland without sending you my wishes that you may be happy'.[3] He hinted that he had been hurt by the news of her engagement, and said that the gold cross would always remind him 'of two sweet years – the sweetest of all the years of my youth'. Although they now stood apart, he said, and would 'never meet again, after I leave Ireland', he would nonetheless 'always remember [Florence] at prayer' and would 'never be indifferent to [her] welfare: the currents of [their] lives flowed too long beside one another for that'.

But Balcombe evidently took exception to Wilde's request for the return of the gold cross and thought that Wilde was seeking a clandestine meeting, ill-befitting her new status as Stoker's fiancée. She in turn asked for the return of all her letters. Wilde's final two letters to her betray notes of bitterness and impatience: while promising to send back all her remaining letters on his return to Oxford, he enclosed a 'scrap' she had written eighteen months previously, saying that he had always carried it with him and 'how strange and out of tune it all reads now', before ending with finality 'Goodbye, and believe me yours very truly, Oscar Wilde.'

Possibly Wilde was genuinely hurt by Florence's engagement. As Davis Coakley observes, however, 'he also relished the drama of the situation.'[4] And if Wilde's break with Ireland owed something to romantic disappointment, it owed at least as much to his ambition to conquer London. 'All things come naturally to London,' Wilde was to tell an American interviewer in 1882; there was no lack of culture in Ireland, he explained, but there it was 'nearly all absorbed in politics', whereas in London he could dedicate himself to the artistic life.[5]

Early in 1879 he was approached by the editor and magazine proprietor Edmund Yates, who had written to Wilde's brother Willie: 'I wish you would put me *en rapport* with your brother, the Newdigate man, of whom I hear so much and so favourably.'[6] Yates, a pioneer of the so-called New Journalism and once a protégé of Dickens, was one of the most important journalists in London. In 1874 he had founded a gossipy Society weekly, *The World*, advertised in its subtitle as 'a journal for men and women'. This weekly magazine proved so successful that in 1879 Yates started a monthly magazine as well, titled *Time: A Monthly Miscellany of Interesting and Amusing Literature*. *The World* was to prove one of Wilde's favourite publishing sites for the next eight years, not least through its publication of a series of witty telegrams – later gathered into that masterpiece in the art of controversy, *The Gentle Art of Making Enemies*, by the painter James Abbott McNeill Whistler – in which Wilde carried out his highly competitive friendship with Whistler.

But it was in his new monthly *Time* that Yates first published Wilde. The opening number, published with great fanfare in April 1879, featured a ten-stanza narrative poem by Wilde titled, appropriately enough, 'The Conqueror of Time'. The poem, indebted to Rossetti's 'The Burden of Nineveh', is undistinguished from a literary standpoint, and its allusions to 'that gaunt House of Art which lacks for naught/ Of all the great things that men have saved from Time' – particularly to the acquisition of an Egyptian mummy 'dead ere the world's glad youth had touched its prime' – seem deliberately geared to Londoners' fascination with the British Museum and the current craze for Egyptian relics. At the end of the poem, however, Wilde speaks stridently as a peer to his English audience, warning them that 'we mar our strength in barren strife/ With the world's legions led by clamorous care' and that 'we live beneath Time's wasting sovereignty.' It is not simply the collective English voice that is of interest here, for the poem also contains a revealing personal metaphor: it describes how a seed, found clasped in the mummy's hand after the linen bands have been removed, sprouts 'starry blossoms' and spreads 'rich odours through our springtide air' when 'sown in English ground'. The seed is the 'conqueror of time' or 'child of all eternity', because it 'never feels decay but gathers life'. As the poem's punning play with the magazine's title implies, the seed is an important metaphor for Wilde's own ambitions in England.

Those ambitions were on display in other English publications as well. In the summer of 1879 *The World* published two sonnets over the signature 'Oscar Wilde' honouring the actresses Sarah Bernhardt and Ellen Terry, followed by a second sonnet honouring Terry in January 1880. Each sonnet was titled after a dramatic character that the actress had recently performed on the London stage;[7] and when Wilde republished them in his collection *Poems* in 1881 under the collective title 'Impressions de Théâtre', together with new sonnets commemorating Sir Henry Irving and Ellen Terry, he made their real subject – theatre – explicit. Other poems published around this time seem similarly geared to a large and fashionable audience: in 'The New Helen', a poem heavily beholden to Gautier and Swinburne and first published in Yates's *Time*, Wilde likens England's best-known professional beauty (and the Prince of Wales's mistress), Lillie Langtry, to Helen of Troy. In 'Sen Artysty; or, The Artist's Dream', the speaker dreams of feeling 'the mighty pulse of Fame' and hearing 'the sound of many nations praising me'. Once again, the poem is more notable for its appearance in a publication aimed at a fashionable theatre-going readership and its association with a distinguished actress (the poem's subtitle tells us that it is Wilde's translation from the original Polish of the actress Helena Modjeska) than for any inherent literary value.[8] 'I am really only the reed through which her sweet notes have been blown,' Wilde said of his association with Modjeska.

Wilde sought to advance his position in London by other means as well. The actresses and professional beauties whom he honoured publicly in poetry became close friends. They appeared with him at fashionable openings and became regular visitors to the cramped apartments that he shared with the portrait artist Frank Miles, first at 13 Salisbury Street, off the Strand (Wilde called the place 'Thames House'), and then, from August 1880 onwards, at No. 1 Tite Street, Chelsea (renamed 'Keats House' by Wilde). Guests were invited for 'Tea and Beauties at 3.30', and the professional beauty was as much the invitation's object as its subject. Wilde loved to be associated with 'very beautiful people' and 'clever beings', he said, because it enabled him to attract others to his presence. Even the Prince of Wales asked to be introduced, saying: 'I do not know Mr. Wilde, and not to know Mr. Wilde is not to be known.'[9]

Wilde's capacity to attract bright young things of both sexes was later satirized in *A Private View at the Royal Academy, 1881*, the large oil painting by W. P. Frith that took pride of place at the Royal Academy's Summer Exhibition of 1883. Here Wilde is depicted admiring the art on the gallery walls, accompanied by professional beauties such as Langtry and Terry, with 'clever beings' such as the fashionable sculptor Joseph Boehm and the illustrator George Du Maurier standing less admiringly a little way off. Even Wilde's critical publications were forms of self-advancement, as is clear from the beginning of his 1877 review of the first Grosvenor Gallery exhibition, in which Wilde brags about the pleasures of his London existence as follows:

William Powell Frith, *A Private View at the Royal Academy, 1881*, photogravure, 1885, after Frith's oil painting of 1883.

> surely those who were in London last May, and had in one week the opportunities of hearing Rubenstein play the Sonata Impassionata, of seeing Wagner conduct the Spinning-Wheel Chorus from the Flying Dutchman, and of studying art at the Grosvenor Gallery, have very little to complain of as regards human existence and art-pleasures.

Wilde was rapidly becoming an English celebrity, in part by virtue of his own relentless self-promotion. When Bernhardt arrived in England in May 1879, Wilde was there to greet her at Folkestone and cast an armful of lilies at her feet. His efforts to boost the up-and-coming Lillie Langtry, herself on the verge of a fame matched only by his own and Bernhardt's, were also efforts at boosting himself, and the lily was his symbol. Each day, says Langtry, he would buy a single lily and stroll down Piccadilly, carefully carrying the solitary flower before delivering it to her door. The 'scribblers construed this act of homage as a pose', says Langtry in her memoirs, and she herself conferred upon him the title of Apostle of the Lily. Later the pose was immortalized in Gilbert and Sullivan's comic opera *Patience*, when Bunthorne sings: 'you will rank as an apostle in the high Aesthetic band/ If you walk down Piccadilly with a poppy or a lily in your medieval hand.' Langtry writes that as he became a target for the gossip columns of the newspapers and weeklies, Wilde was quick to realize that they could be turned to his advantage and proceeded forthwith to develop personal mannerisms and affectations 'so audaciously that it became impossible to ignore them'. When he wore a daisy in his button, thousands of young men did likewise. When he proclaimed the sunflower adorable, it was found to be in every drawing room. When he said that plain and flowing garments were the only becoming coverings for the female form, 'every young woman, and many elderly ones, [went] scampering off to their *modistes* with delirious suggestions for Grecian draperies.'[10] He was a tastemaker of the very first order, despite not having more than a handful of poems and reviews to his name. When attending fashionable gallery or theatre openings, he often upstaged the eminent painters, writers, aristocrats and politicians in attendance, and he is known to have worn a specially tailored coat shaped like a cello, designed by himself, to at least three such openings.[11] Frith's satiric painting of 1883 underscores what Wilde's review of the Grosvenor exhibition had implied six years earlier, that Wilde himself was a work of art no less than the paintings on the gallery walls, albeit one that walked, talked and held the beau monde spellbound at fashionable Society events.

In pursuit of social and artistic cachet, Wilde cultivated friendships with fashionable painters such as Whistler, Millais and Frank Miles as eagerly as he did well-known actresses. The friendship with Whistler was especially important. Whistler courted controversy and was determined to test the limits of Victorian art. Wilde knew that by praising this 'great dark master' in print, he was identifying himself with an artist who was at the forefront of modern art. In his first Grosvenor Gallery review, he called Whistler's paintings 'the most abused in the whole exhibition', and although, like most other critics of his time, he expressed reservations about Whistler's Nocturnes, he acclaimed the painter's works of portraiture highly. 'I wish my full remarks on Mr. Whistler to be put in,' he peremptorily instructed the editor of the *Dublin University Magazine* as the review was in press; 'I know he will take them in good part, and besides they are really clever and amusing.'

Whistler's response to Wilde's review of the 1877 Grosvenor Gallery exhibition is not known, but by the time of Wilde's second Grosvenor Gallery review, in 1879, Wilde's identification with Whistler, as well as with the Grosvenor Gallery more generally, was stronger. Where the Royal Academy was associated merely with English art 'at its most commonplace level', he declared, the Grosvenor Gallery represented 'the highest development of the modern artistic spirit'. Now Whistler was a 'wonderful and eccentric genius', better appreciated by the French than by the English; in the art of etching Whistler was 'the consummate master', while the paintings he had sent in for display were 'very wonderful', 'delightful', and even one of his Nocturnes was an 'extremely good example of . . . the "Impressionist point of view"'.

Nonetheless there was a competitive edge to Wilde's personal identification with Whistler. Around the time he became friendly with the painter, Wilde began publishing a series of

'Impression' poems in which he attempted to surpass in poetry the special effects of tone, atmosphere and colour to be found in Whistler's landscapes and cityscapes. (Whistler, who had trained in Paris and painted *en plein air* with Courbet before moving to London, was at this time associated with the newly denominated 'Impressionist' school.) The most important of these poems is 'Impression du Matin', first published in *The World* in March 1881, in which Wilde self-consciously invokes Whistler's 'Nocturnes' and 'Harmonies':

> The Thames nocturne of blue and gold
> Changed to a Harmony in grey:
> A barge with ochre-coloured hay
> Dropt from the wharf: and chill and cold
>
> The yellow fog came creeping down
> The bridges, till the houses' walls
> Seemed changed to shadows and St. Paul's
> Loomed like a bubble o'er the town.

The poem is at once a form of homage to and competition with the painter, the first round in a lengthy and very public battle for artistic superiority that was to unfold between Wilde and Whistler over the course of the 1880s. It is also an important, early example of a desire to bring language to the condition of visual art that was to become more pronounced in Wilde's work of the early 1890s.

If Wilde's 'Impression' poems and Grosvenor Gallery reviews associated him widely with leading developments in the visual arts, it was the publication of a very different kind

James Abbott McNeill Whistler, *Nocturne: The River at Battersea*, 1878, lithograph.

of poem – titled 'Ave Imperatrix', meaning 'Hail, Empress!', and subtitled 'A Poem on England' – in October 1880 that more than anything cemented his position as a force to be publicly reckoned with. The poem – intended for *Time*, although Wilde was persuaded by Yates to publish it in *The World* on the grounds that there he could reach 'a far larger and better audience' – was timely. Queen Victoria had been declared Empress of India in 1877, the British had invaded Afghanistan in 1879, and memories of the First War of Indian Independence (1857–9), in which hundreds of Indians as well as dozens of British colonists and soldiers had died, were still fresh in British memories. The poem invokes these and other recent colonial ventures in which British lives were lost in the questionable cause of Empire, to conclude:

What profit now that we have bound
    The whole round world with nets of gold,
If hidden in our heart is found
    The care that groweth never old?

What profit that our galleys ride,
    Pine-forest-like, on every main?
Ruin and wreck are at our side,
    Grim warders of the House of pain.

Where are the brave, the strong, the fleet?
    Where is our English chivalry?
Wild grasses are their burial-sheet,
    And sobbing waves their threnody.

O loved ones lying far away,
    What word of love can dead lips send!
O wasted dust! O senseless clay!
    Is this the end! is this the end!

Peace, peace! we wrong the noble dead
    To vex their solemn slumber so;
Though childless, and with thorn-crowned head,
    Up the steep road must England go,

Yet when this fiery web is spun,
    Her watchmen shall descry from far
The young Republic like a sun
    Rise from these crimson seas of war.

The political message is avowedly republican, anti-imperialist and pacifist, as if Wilde were determined to counter the central touchstones of English political life. Yet the poem is decidedly lifeless and studied when considered as a political poem, and one comes away from it wondering whether its political sentiments, like the lily and the sunflower, were also a form of public 'posing'. The poem was immediately popular in America, however. E. C. Stedman remarked that this 'lyric to England' was 'manly verse – a poetic and eloquent invocation', and New York's *Century Magazine* remarked 'how an Englishman can read it without a glow of pride and a sign of sorrow is beyond comprehension'.[12] From the standpoint of Wilde's fellow Irishmen, however, the most interesting thing is once again the pronoun 'we' with which Wilde announces and assumes his kinship with the English. It is a feature that he was to sharpen when he revised the poem for publication in his 1881 *Poems*.

Like his personal mannerisms and public appearances, Wilde's poetry was becoming increasingly difficult to ignore, and it was only a short matter of time before he was being caricatured in comic verse as well as on stage and in pen-and-ink. The great caricaturist George Du Maurier had been lampooning the Aesthetic movement visually in the pages of the satirical magazine *Punch* for some time, but in 1880 his cartoons became sharper when he started to incorporate Wilde into them in the persona of the lily-toting dilettante and aesthete 'Jellaby Postlethwaite'. In 'An Aesthetic Midday Meal' (*Punch*, 17 July 1880), Postlethwaite is pictured seated at a table in a restaurant, staring at a lily in a glass of water, while the caption below reads 'At the Luncheon hour, Jellaby Postlethwaite enters a Pastrycook's and calls for a glass of water, into which he puts a freshly-cut lily, and loses himself in contemplation thereof.'

AN ÆSTHETIC MIDDAY MEAL.

At the Luncheon hour, Jellaby Postlethwaite enters a Pastrycook's and calls for a glass of Water, into which he puts a freshly-cut Lily, and loses himself in contemplation thereof.

Waiter. "SHALL I BRING YOU ANYTHING ELSE, SIR?"

Jellaby Postlethwaite. "THANKS, NO! I HAVE ALL I REQUIRE, AND SHALL SOON HAVE DONE!"

George Du Maurier, 'An Aesthetic Midday Meal', *Punch*, 17 July 1880.

Wilde was to be an object of satiric attack in *Punch* and elsewhere, both visually and poetically, for many years to come. He was often favourably impressed by these attacks, writing in 1889 that 'parody, which is the Muse with the tongue in her cheek, has always amused me; but it requires a light touch and a fanciful treatment, and oddly enough, a love of the poet whom it caricatures.'[13] Around 1893 he would become close friends with the satirical writer Ada Leverson, who authored at least two

Linley Sambourne, 'Punch's Fancy Portraits – No. 37' (caricature of Wilde), *Punch*, 25 June 1881.

Punch parodies of Wilde's works. Long before his friendship with Leverson, however, Aesthetic and anti-Aesthetic movements had become a mutually reinforcing dialectic, and such satires as Du Maurier's and (later) Leverson's served the interests of both satirist and his/her object. 'Which one of you invented the other?' Whistler is purported to have asked Wilde and Du Maurier, when encountering the two men in conversation with one another at an art opening. Even Wilde's own editor, Edmund Yates, got in on the act: as early as April 1880, Yates published in *Time* a parody of Wilde's 'The New Helen' titled 'The Bard of Beauty' under the comic pseudonym 'Oscuro Mild', while a little over a year later, following the appearance of Wilde's poem 'Libertatis Sacra Firmes' in *The World*, Yates penned a poetic parody titled 'Ego Upto Snuffis Poeta', also for publication in *The World*.

In the summer of 1881 Wilde gave the satirists a boost with the publication of his first major volume, *Poems*. It wasn't his first book,[14] but Wilde intended it to signal his arrival as a poet on the English scene. It was a vanity publication, for which Wilde personally assumed all the costs, and upon publication he immediately sent presentation copies to Robert Browning, Matthew Arnold, Algernon Swinburne and W. E. Gladstone, among other major English figures. Although the collection contained a number of interesting new poems, including the shockingly sensuous 'Charmides' (Wilde's personal favourite), based on one of Lucian's *Essays in Portraiture*, about a youth who falls passionately in love with a statue of Aphrodite, over half the collection consisted of poems that had appeared previously in serial publications. The volume's division into five distinctly titled sections showed that Wilde recognized the distinctions between

Alfred Thompson, 'The Bard of Beauty' (caricature of Wilde), *Time: A Monthly Miscellany*, April 1880.

the different phases of his career so far. The sonnets to actors and actresses were grouped as 'Impressions de Théâtre'. The poems previously published in Ireland, many of them giving evidence of Wilde's youthful interest in Catholicism and in Italian settings, were grouped under the title 'Rosa Mystica'; 'Ave Imperatrix' was grouped with a number of new poems on political subjects under the heading 'Eleutheria', the Classical Greek term for 'Liberty', while sections titled respectively 'Wind Flowers' and 'Flowers of Gold' housed new poems celebrating English landscapes or expressing Wilde's devotion to the spirit of Keats and Shelley, as well as new poems indebted to the Pre-Raphaelite poetry of Rossetti, Swinburne and Morris.

Equally striking are five new longer poems that conclude each of the book's five sections. Here Wilde makes his Romantic and Pre-Raphaelite allegiances especially clear. The critic Rodney Shewan finds these poems to be modelled on the poetry of Keats, Shelley and Wordsworth, and discerns running through them a determination to adopt the poetic persona of 'the last Endymion' or 'the disaffected sentimentalisch artist'. But it is not significant merely that Wilde borrowed from Romanticism; it is more important that he borrowed from a Romanticism that was by late Victorian times strongly identified with the canon of an English cultural tradition. As in the sonnet to Keats that had troubled the editor of the *Irish Monthly*, Wilde's latest poems merged the spirit of Romanticism with Englishness as such, so decided is his assumption of an English poetic 'voice' and his celebration of English pastoral landscapes.

But for readers who expect poetry to be original, unique and directly personal, Wilde makes his debts to his English forebears too evident, and *Poems* was immediately and roundly condemned in England on publication on the grounds of artificiality, insincerity and even Wilde's plagiarism of previous English poets. 'Imitation of previous writers goes far enough seriously to damage the claim to originality,' wrote one reviewer; the book is 'a cento of reminiscences' from other poets, complained another; it is 'entirely devoid of true passion, with very few vestiges even of genuine emotion, and constituted entirely out of sensuous images and pictures strung together', complained a third.[15] The most notorious reaction came from the Oxford Union, which loudly declined the presentation copy of *Poems* that Wilde sent, on grounds articulated by the young Oliver Elton, later Professor of English at Liverpool and a distinguished historian of English literature:

> It is not that these poems are thin – and they *are* thin: it is not that they are immoral – and they *are* immoral: it is not that they are this or that – they *are* all this or that; it is that they are for the most part not by their putative father at all, but by a number of better-known and more deservedly reputed authors. They are in fact by William Shakespeare, by Philip Sidney, by John Donne, by Lord Byron, by William Morris, by Algernon Swinburne, and by sixty more . . . [of] whose works . . . the Union Library already contains better and fuller editions.[16]

Although Elton exaggerated the extent of Wilde's poetic debts to other poets, his is a charge that has haunted Wilde's poetry right up to our own day, notably in Harold Bloom's epochal 1973 study *The Anxiety of Influence*. In the view of Bloom, who begins *The Anxiety of Influence* with Wilde's poetry, Wilde epitomizes the 'weak' poet, without the strength and originality to surpass his poetic forebears. As an American critic of Wilde's own day noted, 'Mr. Wilde's volume could have been written by any one who should set himself to reproduce the impression of certain English poets.'[17] It is important to emphasize, however, that such accusations as Elton's and Bloom's are premised on an ideologically inflected notion of literary originality or 'sincerity', inherited from the self-expressive poetry of the Romantic period, to which a self-consciously 'cultured' writer like Wilde stands adamantly opposed.

In fact it was precisely on a reproduction of 'the impression of certain English poets' that some commentators saw the cultural well-being of the English nation to depend. In 1869 Matthew Arnold had argued that English 'culture is of like spirit with poetry'.[18] By 1881 Arnold was making much greater claims for the need to study and imitate the classics of English poetry. In 'The Study of Poetry', published just one year before Wilde's *Poems*, Arnold argued that 'The future of poetry is immense, because in poetry . . . our race, as time goes on, will find an ever surer and surer stay.'[19] Arnold saw English poetry as a spiritual replacement for religion, and he demanded that students and would-be poets study only the best English poets in order to realize their excellence for themselves. Such poets represented English cultural touchstones, and for Arnold, the spirit of English poetry was to be found in the Romantic poetry of Wordsworth and Keats in particular: it was in the context of his 1879 preface to the poetry of Wordsworth ('one of the very chief glories of English poetry') that Arnold issued his famous dictum 'by nothing is England so glorious as by her poetry.' Arnold's call for an academic, *studied* English poetry finds its direct correlative in Wilde's exercises and experiments with English modes, helping us to see that Wilde – whose influences always lie on the surface, naked to the eye – applied the same academic principles he had previously used for his Greek translations, while a student, to his practice as a poet in the English tongue.

When read in the light of Arnold's theory of poetic touchstones, Wilde's poetry can be seen clearly as a fierce attempt to display the signs of cultural *distinction*. English poetry represented important cultural capital, as Arnold had been among the first to realize. By openly displaying his poetic techniques, Wilde was remaking his national identity into a distinctive and self-consciously English one, thereby bearing out Arnold's own recent argument, in an essay on England's 'Irish problem', that if 'the Irish [were] to acquiesce cordially in the English connection', they must first learn to simulate the Englishman.[20] So far as Wilde's English contemporaries were concerned, however, his poetry was simply 'self-conscious', 'artificial', 'insincere' or, still worse, 'plagiarism'; and to the satirists – who after the publication of *Poems* accelerated their poetic satires of Wilde as 'Oscuro Wildgoose', 'Drawit Milde' and 'the Wilde-Eyed Poet' – it cemented the idea that Wilde was an alien figure, outside the mainstream, as well as a creature of ridiculous personal affectation.

This is also the implication of two important satirical plays that opened in London in 1881. In *The Colonel*, a farce by Du Maurier's colleague (and *Punch*'s editor) F. C. Burnand which opened at the Prince of Wales Theatre in February, Wilde was satirized as the fake poet Lambert Stryke. The play promulgated the notion that Wilde was a cultural oddity, but at least it kept him before the public eye. It was the first play in over twenty

A. S. Seer, 'Bunthorne' in *Patience*, 1881, woodblock print.

years to receive a Royal Command Performance, and after seeing it Queen Victoria commented that it was 'a very clever play, written to quiz and ridicule the foolish aesthetic people who dress in such an absurd manner . . . carrying peacock's feathers, sunflowers and lilies'. Wilde himself found *The Colonel* a 'dull farce' and he was much more favourably impressed by Gilbert and Sullivan's comic opera *Patience*, which opened at the Opera Comique in April 1881, and in which he was satirized as the lily-toting, oddly costumed Aesthetic poet Bunthorne. He 'attended the opening night and had all manner of fun', he later said, proclaiming it 'very pretty . . . with some charming music', although he thought its satire was 'the veriest twaddle' and said he 'was not to be laughed out of my theory'.[21]

Wilde probably knew that such gentle-humoured satire as Gilbert's and Du Maurier's was good for business. He had aspirations to be a dramatist himself, and over the course of 1881 he was making plans to have a play, written the previous year, produced on the West End stage. This was *Vera; or, The Nihilists*, a serious four-act political drama set in modern-day Russia, which Wilde called 'my first attack on Tyranny'.[22] It expressed both Wilde's fascination with and revulsion at the proletarian anarchist-revolutionary forces that were to succeed in assassinating Tsar Alexander II in March 1881, about six months after Wilde finished the play. By December 1881 *Vera* was scheduled to be performed at the Adelphi Theatre with Mrs Bernard Beere in the title role, under the direction of Wilde's friend and fellow Irishman, the playwright Dion Boucicault. But by this date politicians, public and the play's cast alike were averse to its subject, and three weeks before the scheduled first performance, *The World* announced that 'considering the present state of political feeling in England, Mr. Oscar Wilde has decided on postponing, for a time, the production of his play *Vera*.'[23]

Vera's cancellation may have had another cause besides political untimeliness. In late September 1881 Wilde had received an offer he could not refuse. *Patience* had recently opened to great acclaim in New York, and the opera's producer, Richard D'Oyly Carte, proposed bringing Wilde to America to undertake a lecture tour. As the original of Bunthorne, Wilde's presence would help promote the opera, but, just as importantly, money could be made by allowing Wilde, as D'Oyly Carte put it, to 'illustrate in a public way his idea of the aesthetic' and promulgate 'a true and correct definition and explanation of this latest form of fashionable madness'.[24] Wilde realized that the offer could easily be turned to his own advantage. Some months before the announcement of its cancellation in London, he had said that *Vera*'s 'democratic note' made it 'unthinkable to act it in London', and he had been seeking for a while to have the play produced in New York, where he felt it would be received more favourably. As importantly, D'Oyly Carte's offer gave him the opportunity to put himself and his ideas about art before a massive new public. He did not hesitate to agree, provided the offer was 'good'. It *was* good – Wilde's expenses were to be covered, and he was to receive half of all profits – and within days he was making arrangements to embark.

THREE

'Nothing to Declare Except My Genius'

I have nothing to declare except my genius

WILDE's purported quip to a U.S. Customs agent on arriving in North America, 1882

Wilde embarked for New York on the steamship *Arizona* on 24 December 1881. Over the previous weeks he had prepared carefully for his departure: he had read up on Charles Dickens's two lecture tours of the U.S., he had taken private elocution lessons from the American actor Hermann Vezin, and he had paid close attention to how he would appear before Americans. His tailor had concocted an 'Aesthetic' costume, including knee-length breeches and patent-leather pumps, closely resembling that of Bunthorne in Gilbert and Sullivan's *Patience.* He had had a London furrier create a massive bottle-green overcoat, trimmed in otter fur, with a matching round sealskin hat called a 'Polish cap', and after he was seen emerging from the furrier's dressed in this new outfit, he was mercilessly mocked by Whistler, who published the following open letter in *The World*:

Wilde dressed in 'aesthetic' garb, photo-portrait by Napoleon Sarony, 1882.

> Oscar – How dare you! What means this unseemly carnival in my Chelsea! Restore those things to Nathan, and never let me find you masquerading the streets in the combined costumes of a degraded Kossuth and Mr. Mantalini![1]

The coat and hat – essentially props, as Whistler implied – were to feature in newspaper reports and in the publicity photos that were to circulate widely during – and long after – Wilde's lecture tour. Wilde became so attached to the coat that he still missed it in prison nearly sixteen years later, after it had been pawned or sold by his brother, writing that 'It was all over America with me, it was at all my first nights, it knows me perfectly, and I really want it.'[2]

Wilde's ship docked in New York Harbor on the evening of 2 January 1882, one week before he was scheduled to speak at Chickering Hall. During the crossing he had composed his first lecture, but the journalists who swarmed onto the ship as it lay at anchor off Staten Island were more interested in Wilde himself than in the theories he had come to expound. 'His outer garment was a long ulster trimmed with two kinds of fur, which reached almost to his feet,' reported the *New York World*; 'he wore patent-leather shoes, a smoking-cap or turban, and his shirt might be termed ultra-Byronic . . . His hair flowed over his shoulders in dark-brown waves, curling slightly upwards at the ends . . . His teeth were large and regular, disproving a pleasing story which has gone the rounds of the English press that he has three tusks or protuberants.' His face presented 'an exaggerated oval of the Italian face carried into the English type of countenance', the *World* reporter continued, while his 'manner of talking' was 'somewhat affected . . . his great peculiarity being a rhythmical

Wilde dressed in his beloved fur-trimmed coat, photo-portrait by Napoleon Sarony, 1882.

chant in which every fourth syllable is accentuated'. 'The dress of the poet was not less remarkable than his face', declared the *San Francisco Chronicle*, 'and consisted of a short velvet coat, rose-colored necktie and dark-brown trousers . . . cut with a sublime disregard of the latest fashion.'

Like modern tabloid journalists, they peppered him with questions both flippant and straight: what time did he get up in the morning? Did he like his eggs fried on both sides or just one? Did he trim his fingernails in the style of the Empress of Japan? Was he here to secure copyright in his play? If Wilde was thrown by this barrage of questions, he did not betray it. A fellow passenger told a reporter that five days into the crossing, Wilde had told him that he was 'not exactly pleased with the Atlantic' because 'it was not so majestic as I expected.' Wilde's disappointment was soon widely reported on both sides of the Atlantic. So too was his purported retort to a Customs agent when asked if he had anything to declare: 'I have nothing to declare except my genius.'[3] On arriving in New York City proper, Wilde encountered blocked streets and required policemen to clear a way through. He could now understand why the Prince of Wales was always in a good humour, he remarked bemusedly to a mutual friend back home: 'it is delightful to be a *petit roi*.'[4]

From one standpoint, the attentions of the press and the cult of celebrity surrounding Wilde in America are more important than the message he intended delivering in his lectures. Wilde in person was a rare exotic, at once a creature of elaborate artifice and consummate self-possession, and it is hardly surprising that American reporters fuelled a wider interest in him as the living incarnation of a new kind of man. He was the first modern celebrity, a transatlantic superstar whose self-created public image went before him, and his lecture tour went hand in hand with a media frenzy accompanying his every move. Between January and March 1882 there were 314 items about him in the *New York Times* alone. His ideas and convictions, and still more his personal appearance, history and ambitions, were eagerly reported in the American press, initially with some scepticism. But Wilde quickly became adept at turning the press to his own advantage, and within weeks he had won journalists over, resulting in a series of interviews, often syndicated, that were increasingly fawning and star-struck. Mass appeal followed as quickly: when he got down from the train in Oakland on 26 March, a reporter for the *San Francisco Examiner* noted that 'wherever he moved, the crowd, guided by a large, wide-brimmed, white slouch hat that he wore, followed . . . quietly and respectfully.' 'On the train and the boat', observed a reporter for the *San Francisco Morning Call*, 'he was the observed of curious hundreds, many of whom had apparently made the trip across the bay purportedly to see him.' In Denver, a 'large crowd of unaesthetics . . . gathered about the platforms' waiting for a glimpse of the arriving celebrity. When his train finally arrived, they 'trod upon the heels of the aesthetic apostle, . . . blockaded his way and surrounded his carriage, till the pressure of the crowd became disagreeable and even an annoyance'. Wilde said that he encountered such crowds at almost every station and ascribed his fans' frenzy to 'idle curiosity', adding that it was 'evidence of an unfinished civilization'.[5] His American travelling companions 'complained bitterly of the rudeness of the crowds at small stations', and in Corinne, Utah, 'a grotesquely accoutred crowd, with a band' sought to invade the car in which he was travelling.

This cult of celebrity embraced the private realm as much as the public. 'I, for one, desire that the best homes may be open to him, and that he may have the opportunity of seeing and conversing with our best people,' wrote the prominent Boston abolitionist (and author of 'The Battle Hymn of the Republic') Julia Ward Howe, near the start of his tour. At nearly every turn, Wilde was greeted by civic dignitaries, given private tours and welcomed into the homes of the rich, the powerful and the famous, where he swiftly overcame any diffidence with his charm, wit and style. While many in the American establishment remained wary of him, the list of those who met or hosted him reads like a *Who's Who* of post-bellum America: Louisa May Alcott, Sam Ward, Julia Ward Howe, Walt Whitman, Jefferson Davis, Ulysses S. Grant, Robert Lincoln, George B. McClellan, Eugene Hale, Frances Hodgson Burnett, Oliver Wendell Holmes Sr, Charles Eliot Norton, Henry Wadsworth Longfellow, Henry Ward Beecher, Joaquin Miller. Much of the cultural work of Wilde's lecture tour was accomplished not when he was formally lecturing, but when Americans invited him into their homes, businesses and offices. With one or two conspicuous exceptions, notably the poets Walt Whitman and Bret Harte, American men seem to have been wary of him at first, but Wilde quickly disarmed any hostility or suspicion, and in their homes and workplaces his interlocutors could appreciate him and his ideas with a directness and immediacy impossible in the lecture hall.

Perhaps the most memorable of these incursions into the private realm was Wilde's trip by bucket to the bottom of the 'Matchless' silver-mine in Leadville, Colorado, accompanied by the mine's administrator and the town's mayor. At the bottom of the mine, Wilde was the guest of honour at an impromptu banquet, 'the first course being whiskey, the second whiskey, and the third whiskey', where the miners cheerily pronounced him to be 'a bully boy with no glass eye'. After the banquet, Wilde was presented with a silver drill and invited to open a new bore, subsequently named 'The Oscar' in his honour.

To be sure, Wilde's message was rather different in such settings from the one he presented, for a price, by evening in the lecture hall. Ostensibly he had come to America to lecture on matters to do with art and aesthetics. 'You have listened to *Patience* for a hundred nights and you have heard me for only one,' he told his New York audience; 'it will make, no doubt, the satire more piquant by knowing something about the subject of it, but you must not judge of aestheticism by the satire of Mr. Gilbert.'[6] At first he lectured on 'The English Renaissance', a title soon expanded to 'The English Renaissance of Art', by which he meant developments in nineteenth-century English culture, centred chiefly on the Romantic and Pre-Raphaelite movements, that were akin to those of the Italian Renaissance in their 'desire for a more gracious and comely way of life, . . . passion for physical beauty, . . . exclusive attention to form . . . [and their search for] new subjects for poetry, new forms of art, new intellectual and imaginative enjoyments'. But the lecture, which borrowed heavily from Ruskin, Morris and Pater, often verbatim, was too long and theoretical. American audiences were often bored by it and showed it.

Within a month he had abandoned 'The English Renaissance' in favour of a shorter, simpler lecture titled 'The Decorative Arts'. Here Wilde argued more concisely that

> what you want here [in America] is not that higher order of imaginative art of the poet and painter, because they will take care of themselves, but . . . the art that will hallow the vessels of everyday use, exerting its influence in the simplest and humblest of homes.

In sentences that seem to have ushered in America's so-called Gilded Age, Wilde told Americans that 'if you develop art culture by beautifying the things around you, you may be certain that other arts will follow in the course of time.' Once again he drew heavily on William Morris, the leader of the Arts and Crafts movement, whose own lectures on the politics of decorative art appeared in book form around this time. But his new lecture was calculated to appeal to the democratic and pacifistic impulses of Reconstruction-era America:

> The victories of art can give more than heroes yield or the sword demands, for what we want is something spiritual added to life. And if you wish for art you must revolt against the luxury of riches and the tyranny of materialism, for you may lay up treasures by your railways, or open your ports to the galleys of the world, but you will find the independence of art is the perfect expression of freedom. The steel of Toledo and the silk of Genoa did but give strength to oppression and add lustre to pride. Let it be for you to create an art that is made by the hands of the people, for the joys of the people, too, an art that will be an expression of your delight in life. There is nothing in common life too mean, in common things too trivial, to be ennobled by your touch; nothing in life that art cannot sanctify.

A third lecture, added in March 1882 for towns and cities where Wilde was engaged to lecture twice, was even more prescriptive and practical in orientation: 'I do not address those millionaires who can pillage Europe for their pleasure,' Wilde declared at the beginning of 'The House Beautiful', 'but those of moderate means who can, if they will, have designs of worth and beauty before them always and at little cost.' Art does not depend upon extravagance of luxury, he explained, doubtless recalling the triumphs of interior decoration that he had managed on a student budget while at Oxford, 'but rather the procuring of articles which, however cheaply purchased and unpretending, are beautiful and fitted to impart pleasure to the observer as they did to the maker'. He dispensed practical advice about how middle-class homes should be carpeted, furnished and decorated: 'if you are having a house built, contract with the builder to have the main rafters of the ceiling exposed in outline' so that 'the light may play constantly upon it, and not lie in a dead way'. If a room contains limited or light furniture, then 'the design should be light and simple.' If you have big windows, 'let a portion of them be filled with stained glass . . . with little bright spots of pure colour which give a more subdued light.' Also, 'I advise you to have Queen Anne furniture,' he told Americans, but 'do not send to . . . England for it: it could be made here, and to that end a good school of design should be established.' 'Have nothing in your house that is not useful or beautiful,' he intoned, in an almost verbatim repetition of William Morris's mantra 'Have nothing in your houses that you do not know to be useful or . . . beautiful.' He ended the lecture on a lofty note that could not fail to inspire Americans anxious about the despoliation of their land and the growth of industry:

> Today more than ever the artist and a love of the beautiful are needed to counteract the sordid materialism of the age. In an age when science has undertaken to declaim against the soul and spiritual nature of man, and when commerce is ruining beautiful rivers and magnificent woodlands and the glorious skies in its greed for gain, the artist comes forward as a priest and prophet of nature to protest, and even to work against the prostitution or the perversion of what is lofty and noble in humanity and beautiful in the physical world, and his religion in its benefits to mankind is as broad as the sun.

It is hard today to gauge the effectiveness of Wilde's American lectures. Any positive effects were not immediate. Audiences were restless and bored listening to 'The English Renaissance', and even after switching to 'The Decorative Arts', Wilde's East Coast and Midwest lectures generally did not go well. His lecture was 'scholarly but pointless', remarked the *Fort Wayne News*, 'as instructive as a tax-list to a pauper, and scarcely as interesting'. His delivery was 'flat and insipid', observed the *Minneapolis Tribune*, and 'he kept up the same unvarying endless drawl, without modulating his voice or making a single gesture.' In Philadelphia the audience 'listened at first with interest and then with sullen despair', while in Indianapolis his lecture was met with 'tumultuous silence'. In Boston, Wilde only narrowly avoided being upstaged when sixty Harvard undergraduates trooped late into the theatre, dressed mockingly in the High Aesthetic manner, like Gilbert's Bunthorne, each bearing a sunflower. In Rochester, a full-blown riot erupted when local students booed, hissed and cat-called throughout, leading to the arrival of police, a general melée and a dispersal of the disgusted audience when the lights were extinguished. In Chicago, where Wilde first delivered 'The Decorative Arts', his message was drowned out by Chicagoans' shocked response to some ill-considered, impromptu remarks on the ugliness of the city's

'Oscar Wilde, The Apostle of Aestheticism: An Aesthetic Reception' (artist unknown), *Frank Leslie's Illustrated Newspaper*, 21 January 1882.

castellated water-tower, the only edifice to have survived Chicago's great fire of 1871 and a symbol of civic pride. As Wilde's interrogation by local journalists the following day proved, his 'sentences fell numbly on the ears of the audience', and 'the insult to the water-tower protruded beyond all.'

According to the *San Francisco Daily Report*, 30 per cent of Wilde's audience arrived 'determined not to be convinced' and another 13 per cent came only 'because wife insisted', compared to 10 per cent 'willing to be convinced', 3 per cent 'anxious to be convinced' and just 1 per cent who were 'honest admirers of Oscar'.[7] Another 9 per cent 'wanted to see and hear the Damphool on general principles', added the *Report*, 7 per cent came 'to please "her"' and 8 per cent 'came to keep up the reputation of the city'. But there were many in Wilde's audience who were receptive to what he had to say, while still others absorbed his ideas indirectly or through the press. This was especially true of women and the young, whose receptivity to Wilde's ideas was not fully represented in the hostile, generally cynical, printed reviews. In the latter half of 1882, Anna, Comtesse de Brémont, encountered Wilde at a New York dinner party, 'one of many given him at that time . . . as a protest to the attitude of misrepresentation and ridicule assumed by the press'.[8] The party 'was entirely composed of ladies well-known for their beauty and wit in the society of Boston and New York', says de Brémont, and many of the women 'had donned aesthetic robes of charming design' as a mark of their admiration. Even if they did not attend Wilde's lectures as such, female American artists and writers such as Candace Thurber Wheeler and Celia Thaxter, already dedicated to the pursuit of beauty and art, found important affirmation in Wilde's pronouncements as reported in the press.

As importantly, Wilde gave fresh impetus to an effort to reconceive the American home along more thoroughly artistic lines that was already underway among middle-class white American women – represented, for instance, in the 'picturesque' home of the Cincinnati ceramicist Mary Louise McLaughlin. As the historian Mary Blanchard has written,

> the little-known or neglected female artists of American aestheticism realized the deeper promise of the aesthetic movement . . . [They] understood that the aesthetic quest pointed out by Oscar Wilde offered women a way out of the dead ends of conventional life . . . an escape from Calvinist orthodoxy, an evasion of tyrannical fathers and ineffective husbands, and an opportunity to advance in the social and business worlds . . . In America, aestheticism was the story of the feminine and domestic world.[9]

This silent absorption of aesthetic ideas in the lives, homes and work of American women went hand in hand with a much louder extension of Aestheticism into the daily lives of Americans. On arriving in New York, Wilde immediately sat for a series of photo-portraits by the celebrity photographer Napoleon Sarony, who had previously photographed Sarah Bernhardt and many other celebrities. The resultant photographs of Wilde in artfully staged poses, variously in dinner dress, in 'Aesthetic' garb including knee-length breeches and patent-leather pumps, in a long cape with a felt hat, or in his fur-trimmed coat, circulated widely and are still ubiquitous today. Sarony paid handsomely for exclusive rights to Wilde's photographic image in America – rights Sarony was prepared to defend in court – and no other

Thomas Nast, 'Something to "Live up" to' (caricature of Wilde), *Harper's Bazaar*, 10 June 1882.

photographs of Wilde from his year in America are known to exist.[10] Endlessly reproduced in print on both sides of the Atlantic, Sarony's photo-portraits instantly brought Wilde a fame (and Sarony a profit) that he could never have quickly achieved through his writing or lecturing alone. 'In the eastern cities his photograph was most conspicuous,' observed a reporter for the *Manchester Examiner and Times*, 'and Mr. Wilde told me that the demand for it far exceeded any possible supply.'

Sarony's photographs also cemented Wilde's absorption into American popular culture through the inspiration they gave to caricaturists such as Thomas Nast, who repeatedly caricatured Wilde in *Harper's Bazaar* much as Du Maurier had done in London's *Punch*, as well as to commercial designers and advertisers, who shamelessly and openly fed the Aesthetic 'craze' by incorporating Wilde's form and name into packaging and advertising for an array of household products. One of Sarony's photo-portraits was even the subject of a landmark court case, in which the U.S. Supreme Court extended copyright protections to photography: when a New York department store, Ehrich Bros., used an unauthorized reproduction of Sarony's '*Oscar Wilde, No. 18*.' to trumpet a line of hats, Sarony successfully sued for damages and established photography as a creative endeavour akin to painting and literature in the eyes of the law. Wilde's response to Sarony's lawsuit is not known, but unquestionably Wilde was aware of the power of Sarony's photo-portraits to cement his broad appeal: in March 1882 he told Richard D'Oyly Carte, 'I think if some large lithographs of me were got it would help business . . . The photograph of me with head looking over my shoulder would be the best – just the head and fur collar.'

As these photographs and caricatures proved, the message of the lectures was inseparable from Wilde himself as a flesh-and-blood creature. Although he consistently attempted to steer journalists' attention to the ideas he propounded in his lectures, the media circus surrounding him was far more interested in

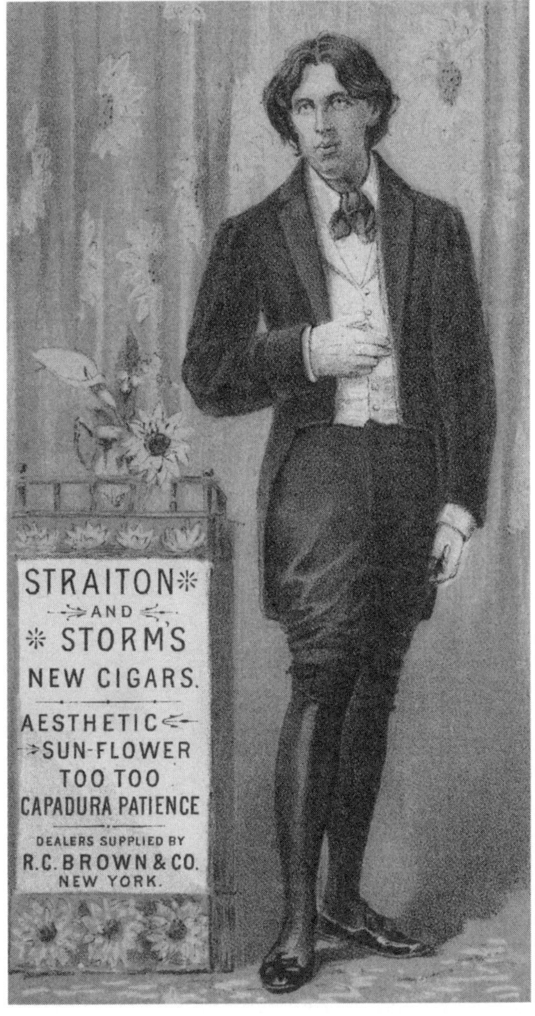

Trade card for 'Straiton and Storm's New Cigars' featuring an image of Wilde based on a Sarony photo-portrait, *c.* 1882.

the ideas he incarnated in his person, and for this reason surviving press reports and interviews return repeatedly to matters of Wilde's personal appearance, dress and mannerisms. 'He is scholarly, studiedly polite, a gentleman, shrewd, fearless, self-possessed and of poetic temperament,' observed the *Sacramento*

Napoleon Sarony, photo-portrait no. 18, 1882.

Record-Union; 'he is, however, ludicrously odd to the American eye in personal appearance; is eccentric (or affected) in this regard.' One of the subtexts here was that Wilde embodied a new kind of masculinity, sharply distinct from the bearded or moustachioed, faintly military, heroic ideal that had dominated constructions of American manhood since the beginning of the American Civil War. He 'lacks the manifestations of manliness in his countenance, and frequently in his manner', went on the

Trade card for Ehrich Brothers (hatters), based on Sarony's portrait no. 18. Sarony's successful suit against the Burrow Giles Lithographic Co., makers of this card, established the extension of copyright protection to works of photography.

Sacramento Record-Union. 'He wears no beard or mustaches,' remarked the *Denver Rocky Mountain News*, 'and the lips are as full and bright-colored as a girl's.' His face possessed a 'womanly air', observed the *Cincinnati Gazette*, partly by virtue of the 'thick locks . . . falling on either side of the cheeks'; his 'overfull features . . . are almost effeminate in apparent lack of vigor and force,' observed the *Sacramento Record-Union*. Similarly, the *Dayton Daily Democrat* commented on his 'soft effeminate flesh' and 'graceful form', while the *Toronto Globe* remarked upon his 'effeminate face'. As Mary Blanchard has observed,

> Wilde's flamboyant dress, his breaking of gender codes, spoke to a nation that was beginning to explore style, not to expose social nonconformity but to create alternate identities . . . The reaction to Wilde in the popular press indicated an emergent anxiety not only about the new aesthetic ideology but, more dangerously, about the celebrated and stylized masculine self.[11]

That anxiety is clearly and loudly on display in a February 1882 article titled 'Unmanly Manhood', by the Boston Brahmin (and Emily Dickinson's mentor) Thomas Wentworth Higginson – ostensibly a review of Wilde's *Poems*, but one that quickly devolves into an attack on Wilde personally. 'A young man comes upon us', says Higginson, 'whose only distinction is that he has written a thin volume of very mediocre verse, and that he makes himself something very like a buffoon for notoriety and money.'[12] Nonetheless, complains Higginson, 'women of high social position receive him at their houses and invite guests to meet him; in spite of the fact that if they were to read aloud to the company his poem of "Charmides," not a woman would remain in the room.' Like other Victorian homophobes, Higginson hid his personal aversion to Wilde's threat behind a putative concern for the moral well-being of women: 'Is it manly to fling before the eyes of women page upon page which no man would read aloud in the presence of women?' he asked in outrage. Yet it was not merely Wilde's poetry or his purportedly corruptive effect upon women that lay at the root of Higginson's hostility. Wilde also failed the 'test of manhood' that 'lies in action'. He 'has had his opportunity of action and waived it', fulminated Higginson. Wilde's own mother had 'written poems upon the wrongs of Ireland that are strong and fervid enough . . . to enlist an army'. But 'is it manhood for her gifted sons to . . . cross the Atlantic and pose in ladies' boudoirs or write prurient poems which their hostesses must discreetly ignore?'

Implicitly Higginson registers that Wilde embodied a new kind of masculine sexuality and gendering: Wilde threatened traditional concepts of manhood, but he was also bringing the modern homosexual into being, as his trials and conviction in 1895 would only loudly underscore. The same point is implied too by the *Brooklyn Daily Eagle*'s snide comment that Wilde would on 'any fair day on Fifth Avenue' find 'a school of gilded youths eager to embrace his particular tenets'[13] (Fifth Avenue was akin to London's Piccadilly in being 'a favorite area at the time for male prostitutes'[14]), and again by a link made by the *Washington Post* between Wilde, Aestheticism and 'young men painting their faces . . . with unmistakable rouge upon their cheeks'.

Something of the fillip that Wilde gave to new and expanded concepts of masculinity is implicit in the witty essay he wrote celebrating the American man, over four years after the end of his lecture tour, where he remarks on the 'bright handsome eyes' of American men and says with tongue firmly in cheek that 'there is no doubt but that, within a century from now, the whole culture of the New World will be in petticoats.' While in America he sought to liberate American men and women from the restrictive clothing that had hitherto defined as much as confined their genders: 'the present evening dress of gentlemen is the most objectionable possible,' he told the *Salt Lake Herald*, comparing conventional men's clothing to his own 'pearl-grey' velvet coat and 'Venetian green' necktie, 'and I should be glad to do something towards introducing a better.' 'Mr. Wilde believes that there will be a complete revolution in gentlemen's wearing apparel within the next few years,' remarked the *Denver Rocky Mountain News*. When he left New York in January, Wilde was even promised a party on his return at which 'all the gentlemen shall discard the odious trousers of dull respectability and assume the more becoming costume of the aesthetic future.'[15]

The 'more becoming costume of the aesthetic future' was as feminine as it was masculine. As we shall shortly see, Wilde did not begin formally lecturing on 'Dress' and 'Dress Reform' until his return to Britain, over a year after the end of his American tour. But the bare bones of his later lectures and articles on dress are discernible in 'The House Beautiful', where he excoriates present trends in both men's and women's clothing and, looking forward to the paisley cottons of the 1960s, predicts that 'the dress of the future . . . will use drapery to a great extent and will abound in joyous colour.' Nothing can be beautiful, he observes, thinking of the tight corsets favoured by Victorian women, if it is 'destructive of health'. Both women's and men's clothing should 'follow out the lines of the figure' and 'should be free to move about in, showing the figure'. So far as women alone were concerned:

> if one could fancy the Medician Venus taken from her pedestal in the Louvre to Mr. Worth's establishment . . . to be dressed in modern French millinery, every single beautiful line would be destroyed, and no one would look at her a second time.

And as for men:

> the only well-dressed men I have seen in America were the miners of the Rocky Mountains; they wore a wide-brimmed hat which shaded their faces from the sun and protected them from the rain, and their flowing cloak, which is by far the most beautiful piece of drapery ever invented, may be dwelt upon with admiration. Their high boots too were sensible and practical. These miners dressed for comfort and of course attained the beautiful.

EXCEPT FOR SHORT rest periods spent in New York, Wilde lectured constantly from mid-January until mid-October 1882, often giving as many as six lectures a week, covering every corner of the United States except for the Pacific Northwest, as well as the principal Canadian cities of Ontario, Quebec and the Maritime States. He delivered over 150 lectures in total, travelling over 24,000 kilometres (15,000 mi.) by train in the process.[16] The tour was 'an achievement of courage and grace', writes Richard Ellmann: despite the satire and with his obvious propensity for self-advertisement, Wilde succeeded in naturalizing the word 'aesthetic', and 'however effeminate his doctrines were thought to be, they constituted the most determined and sustained attack upon materialistic vulgarity that America had seen.'

The tour also left important traces upon Wilde himself and his future writings. At the crudest level, it made him temporarily wealthy and famous as a global 'brand'. 'We, of Tite Street and Beaufort Gardens, joy in your triumphs and delight in your success,' trumpeted Whistler in an open letter in the London

World, before cattily adding: 'but we are of opinion that, with the exception of your epigrams, you talk like "Sidney Colvin in the provinces"; and that, with the exception of your knee-breeches, you dress like 'Arry Quilter'. (Sidney Colvin and Harry Quilter were prominent Victorian art critics of whom both Whistler and Wilde were contemptuous.) 'You are still the talk of London,' Wilde's mother wrote as late as September 1882; 'the milkman has bought your picture, and in fact nothing seems celebrated in London but you.'

But America also wrought subtle changes in Wilde's understanding, broadening his sense of himself as a citizen of the world. When Henry James called on Wilde in his Washington hotel and remarked that he was nostalgic for London, Wilde replied stonily, 'Really? You care for places? The world is my home.' Although Wilde found plenty in America to object to, and on returning to England was quick to reassure Britons that he could not 'picture America as altogether an Elysium', he nonetheless found Americans 'the best politically educated people in the world', and he celebrated America as 'a country which can teach us the beauty of the word "freedom" and the value of the thing "liberty"'. He told a Philadelphia reporter that 'one of the most delightful things I find in America is meeting people without prejudice – everywhere open to the truth. We have nothing like it in England.' Moreover, there was 'an air of comfort in the appearance of the people' that contrasted sharply with British towns and cities, where 'too often, people are seen in close contact with rags.' In America, he told British audiences, 'one learns that poverty is not a necessary accompaniment to civilization', and it was a country 'that has no trappings, no pageants and no gorgeous ceremonies'. It was also a country where 'every man when he gets to the age of twenty-one is allowed to vote.'

Given what he perceived to be America's greater egalitarianism, it is not surprising that after seven years in which Wilde largely effaced his Irish accent and remade himself as an English poet, America enabled him briefly to reclaim and reaffirm his dormant Irish identity. To be sure, journalists throughout America celebrated Wilde as 'the young English poet and apostle of aestheticism', 'the English aesthetic poet' or 'the great English exponent of aestheticism', and Wilde was quick to self-identify as English on numerous occasions: the stiff reception afforded his poetry was 'an ordeal which every English poet has had to go through', he told the *Philadelphia Inquirer*.[17] Yet many Irish-Americans saw in Wilde not the English poet or the costumed aesthete, but the son of Speranza, a poet of considerable stature among Irishmen. In cities with large Irish populations, such as St Louis and St Paul, Minnesota, where his mother's reputation went before him, he spoke eagerly, if informally, of his support for Irish independence in the form of Home Rule or an Irish Parliament. In San Francisco in early April 1882 he went further by lecturing not merely on matters of decoration and art, as elsewhere, but also on 'Irish Poets and Poetry of the Nineteenth Century'.

This lecture, expressly written for an audience receptive to the Irish cause, and the third (of three) he gave in San Francisco,[18] constitutes the single most important, sustained declaration in Wilde's lifetime of his allegiance to Irish nationalism. 'Since the English occupation,' Wilde began, 'we have had no national art in Ireland at all, and there is not the slightest chance of our having it ever until we get that right of legislative independence so unjustly robbed from us, until we are really an Irish nation.' Art 'sickens in slavery', said Wilde, 'grows languid in luxury, but reaches its full fruition under the fostering care of liberty'. There was, however, 'one art which no tyranny can kill, and no penal laws can stifle, the art of poetry'. The poetry of the Irish people, he said, 'ever kept alive the fires of patriotism in the hearts of the Irish people'. The bulk of the lecture concerned his admiration for a plethora of contemporary Irish poets, many of whom he had met as a child at his parents' receptions and dinners. But Robert Pepper, who edited the lecture in 1972, speculates that the surviving manuscript represents only two-thirds of the lecture as delivered and omits passages that were fervently pro-Irish and anti-English. Either Wilde destroyed the most incendiary pages, says Pepper, or, having delivered the lecture hurriedly from rough notes, he simply omitted incendiary parts when writing out a fair copy. In either event, the surviving manuscript 'almost certainly represents Wilde's circumspect second thoughts'.

If America enabled Wilde to reaffirm a dormant Irish identity, it also exemplified a greater openness than Britain in matters of gender and sexuality. Some years after returning from America, he celebrated the sexual and social freedoms allowed to American women in particular. Young American women were 'pretty whirlwinds in petticoats', he declared, whom 'one soon gets to love'. Admittedly 'their eyes have no magic nor mystery in them, but they challenge us to combat; and when we engage, we are always worsted.' 'The American man marries early,' he remarked, while 'the American woman marries often, and they get on extremely well together.' The great success of marriage in the States, he added, perhaps thinking of the warm social reception awarded him in America by such women as Julia Ward

Howe, Mrs Paran Stevens and Mrs S.L.M. Barlow, was due 'partly to the fact that no American wife is considered responsible for her husband's dinners' and 'in America, the horrors of domesticity are almost entirely unknown.' Even the 'American freedom of divorce . . . has at least the merit of bringing into marriage a new element of romantic uncertainty'. Years before his first recorded homosexual love-affair, Wilde celebrated American women for possessing a freedom in marriage that he would himself later assume to his cost. He too would 'marry early', barely a year after returning from America, but when a few years later he sought sexual and emotional satisfaction in the company of young men rather than in the arms of his wife, it was not 'freedom of divorce' that resulted. It was prison.

FOUR

'Married . . . in Consequence of a Misunderstanding': London 1883–6

I have only been married once. That was in consequence of a misunderstanding between myself and a young person.

LANE, in *The Importance of Being Earnest*, 1895, Act One

'The Oscar of the first period is dead,' Wilde is reputed to have said shortly after returning from America in January 1883. Just days after arriving home, he left London again to begin a three-month stay in Paris, determined to conquer the French capital much as he had conquered New York and Boston. 'I discarded my eccentricities of costume and had my hair cut,' he told a friend; 'All that belonged to the Oscar of the first period. We are now concerned with the Oscar of the second period, who has nothing whatever in common with the gentleman who wore long hair and carried a sunflower down Piccadilly.'[1]

But the Oscar of the first period was not quite as dead as Wilde maintained. When his lecture tour ended in October 1882, Wilde stayed on in New York for another two and a half months, determined to make a name for himself in the city as a dramatist. He had been revising *Vera* as early as March, as well as making plans with Richard D'Oyly Carte to stage the play with Clara Morris or Rose Coghlan in the title role. In the summer of 1882 D'Oyly Carte had an acting edition of the play printed, and in September D'Oyly Carte's tour manager had this edition copyrighted in America and distributed to leading figures in the theatre world.

Vera was not the only play with which Wilde planned to make his theatrical debut. For two years he had also had in mind the writing of a blank-verse tragedy in five acts to rival the Jacobean tragedies of Webster. In September 1882 he set about courting the American actress Mary Anderson to star in this as-yet-unwritten tragedy. He promised her a 'tragedy [that] will take the world by storm' and that the play 'created for you, and inspired by you, shall give you the glory of a Rachel, and . . . me the fame of a Hugo'.

Once his lecture tour was over, now ensconced in New York, he put the finishing touches to arrangements for both plays. Along with the actor-manager Steele Mackaye, he formed a plan for both plays to inaugurate an innovative new 'dream theater' that Mackaye was planning to open at 33rd and Broadway,[2] and in early November Mackaye introduced him to Marie Prescott, the actress who would subsequently star in *Vera*. By 1 December he had secured an agreement with Mary Anderson stipulating that for a down payment of $1,000 he would finish and submit *The Duchess of Padua* by 31 March. She in turn committed to paying him another $4,000 upon completion provided she was satisfied with the finished play, also promising to 'get it up grandly, costumes and scenes after [Wilde's own] drawings and paintings, within a year'. At the same time, Wilde was negotiating with Prescott to produce *Vera*. When he embarked for London on 27 December, these negotiations were still unresolved, Prescott having recently told him: 'I hope you will not go to England before I see you again.'[3] By 9 January, when Wilde was back in London, he had secured her agreement to produce the play in New York the following season, in August 1883, for $1,000 plus a royalty of $50 per performance.

When Wilde embarked for Paris at the end of January 1883, then, he held hopes that he would have two plays mounted on the New York stage within a year, both starring well-known actresses, and he had already begun making plans to return to America. 'I look forward with much interest to a second visit to America,' he told Prescott, 'and to the privilege of presenting to the American people my first drama. There is, I think, no country in the world where there are such appreciative theatrical audiences as . . . the United States.' But while Prescott was largely happy with *Vera*, *The Duchess of Padua* was yet to be written and its acceptance by Anderson still uncertain. By going to Paris, he could escape his social and family commitments in London and thereby find the time and means to write the play on time.[4] Once ensconced in the stylish Hôtel Voltaire on the Left Bank, he got down to the task of composing *The Duchess of Padua*. On 23 March he sent Anderson a 'Titan' of a letter giving a lengthy 'scientific analysis' of the now-finished play and describing it as 'the masterpiece of all my literary work, the *chef d'oeuvre* of my youth', clearly in expectation of seeing Anderson perform it on the New York stage.[5]

But Paris offered much more than an opportunity to write a play for American audiences: it was inevitable that Wilde would throw himself into the social and intellectual life of the city. On his arrival he sent copies of *Poems* – recently reprinted in a revised edition – with accompanying letters to numerous French artists and authors. He was 'not disdainful of the indispensable arts for fostering social advancement', says his friend and first biographer Robert Sherard, who met and saw a great deal of him at this time, and 'the advances which were made to him by distinguished people in Parisian society had been carefully attracted by himself.' Somewhat fawning letters survive from this period from Wilde to the poet Maurice Rollinat, the critic Théodore Duret, the writer and collector Edmond de Goncourt and the painter Jacques-Émile Blanche. Duret introduced Wilde to Émile Zola, and Blanche introduced him to the wealthy hostess Charlotte Baignères, whose distinguished salon was later attended by André Gide and Marcel Proust, among others. On a visit to the house of the Greek model and sculptor Maria Zambaco, who had been the muse of the painter Edward Burne-Jones, Wilde met Sherard for the first time, as well as the critic Paul Bourget and the painter John Singer Sargent. All three became good friends of his. Days later Sherard took Wilde to visit Victor Hugo, where his fellow guests listened enraptured as he spoke about Swinburne (although the elderly Hugo remained asleep by the fire). Sherard also accompanied Wilde on two visits to Sarah Bernhardt, in whose house the playwright Alexandre Parodi 'showed much deference' to Wilde, while at the house of Giuseppe de Nittis Wilde talked of art to a number of fellow guests including Degas, Jean-Charles Cazin and the Pissarros, remarking upon leaving that he had been 'quite amazing'. Goncourt was also a guest and recorded in his diary that Wilde seemed '*au sexe douteux*' (of dubious sexuality).

Sherard observes that 'with his usual skill in advertising himself, [Wilde] had prepared carefully for his Parisian campaign.' If he abandoned the velvet jacket, breeches, neckties and shoulder-length hair of his 'Aesthetic' period, he affected instead 'the

Photo-portrait taken by Robert W. Thrupp, 1884, possibly representing Wilde's 'Nero-like' look.

elegances of a Lucien de Rubempré, and modelled the arrangement of his hair after a bust of Nero in the gallery of the Louvre'. He also wore a red waistcoat in tribute to the writer Théophile Gautier.[6] On first meeting Wilde, Sherard found him

> such a strange apparition . . . in his Count D'Orsay costume, with his turned-back cuffs, his coloured handkerchief, his *boutonnière*, his noticeable rings, and his mass of banked-up and artificially curled hair, that I could not restrain a burst of almost hysterical laughter.

But if the Oscar of the second period was as self-advertising and strikingly dressed as the first, in literary matters Wilde made a cleaner break.

The French *décadent* movement was at its height. His new friend Paul Bourget was writing a book on the subject, and Sherard says that during Wilde's stay 'we interested ourselves in Gerard de Nerval and the children of sorrow who, like him, trod the path of letters to a very evil goal.' In his composition habits and literary paraphernalia – including the wearing of an ostentatious white dressing-gown when writing, in imitation of Balzac – Wilde was attempting to 'school himself into labour and production'. But at a deeper imaginative level, he was fascinated by the new school of *décadent* poetry exemplified by de Nerval, Baudelaire and Verlaine (whom he met), as well as by the American Edgar Allan Poe, who had done much to inspire the French *décadents*. The influence of Poe and Baudelaire is especially pronounced in the two poems that Wilde is known to have largely composed in Paris, 'The Harlot's House' and 'The Sphinx'. These are among Wilde's best poems, much more successful and carefully wrought than *The Duchess of Padua*, written around the same time, and their composition may have compensated somewhat when Anderson declined the play in early April, saying that 'in its present form . . . [it] would no more please the public of today than would *Venice Preserv'd* or *Lucretia Borgia*.' If Wilde was disappointed at receiving Anderson's rejection by telegram in Sherard's presence, he only remarked: 'Robert, this is very tedious. We shan't be able to dine with the Duchess tonight.'

Both 'The Harlot's House' and 'The Sphinx' are stylistic and technical tours de force, the most powerful and successful demonstrations we possess of Wilde's ideas that 'the morality of art consists in the perfect use of an imperfect medium' and that rhyme 'in the hands of a real artist becomes not merely a material element of metrical beauty, but a spiritual element of thought and passion also'. Written at a time when French poets were inching towards *vers libre*, both poems exemplify the importance that Wilde attached to rhyme. He later wrote:

> rhyme gives architecture as well as melody to verse; it gives that delightful sense of limitation which in all the arts is so pleasurable, and is, indeed, one of the secrets of perfection; it will whisper, as a French critic has said, 'things unexpected and charming, things with strange and remote relations to each other,' and bind them together in indissoluble bonds of beauty.[7]

Wilde's architectural metaphor here is significant, because the consistent rhyme scheme and metre ('architecture') of 'The Harlot's House' stand in stark contrast to the abruptly abandoned music emanating from the 'house' or brothel described in the poem. The poem is itself a built environment of enticing sensuous pleasure, whose waltz-like prosody deliberately undermines its apparent message about the dangers of overtly sensuous music. Wilde worked especially hard at producing ingenious rhyme schemes, and by printing the carefully constructed quatrains of 'The Sphinx' as couplets in the first edition, he created astounding internal rhymes as well as startling end-rhymes. While he recognized that prose too had its 'rhythmical value', he would do no further work in prose, he wittily told Sherard, until he had 'sung my Sphinx to sleep, and found a trisyllabic rhyme for "catafalque"'.

Yet behind their carefully sculpted verbal artifice, both poems also express Wilde's new fascination with decadent style and behaviour, especially illicit and perverse sexual behaviour. In this respect as much as in their stylistic self-consciousness, they bear the influence of such archetypal decadent poems as Baudelaire's 'Le Chat' and 'Femmes damnées', or Verlaine's 'Femme et chatte', and when Wilde eventually published 'The Sphinx', he dedicated it to the French writer Marcel Schwob in homage to its French roots. Wilde was now clearly trying to remake himself as a decadent writer in the French tradition, an effort that would accelerate over the next few years with his reading of Joris-Karl Huysmans's great novel *À rebours* in 1884, his composition of *The Picture of Dorian Gray* in late 1889/early 1890 and his composition (in French) of his decadent drama *Salome* in late 1891.

This effort to remake himself as a *décadent* had important personal ramifications too. Sherard primly records seeing Wilde talking 'under a sexual impulse' to Marie Aguétant, a well-known demi-mondaine, at the Eden Palace ('a sort of music hall, which *cocottes* used to frequent') and then inferring from a remark made by Wilde the next morning ('Robert, what animals we are') that Wilde had 'succumbed to her allurements'.[8] Sherard's anecdote suggests a link between Wilde himself and the subject-matter of 'The Harlot's House', in which a young man and his 'love' hear seductive music emanating from a brothel at night. Many years later Wilde would remark that sex with a female prostitute was like 'chewing cold mutton', and within a few years of writing 'The Harlot's House', he willingly engaged in sexual relations only with a series of young men. Perhaps for this reason, a very personal sexual confusion lies at

John Vassos, lithographic illustration to 'The Harlot's House', 1929.

the heart of 'The Harlot's House', in which female sexuality is at once the object of fascination and revulsion. In the closing stanzas, the male speaker watches aghast as his female 'Love', lured by the brothel's seductive music, passes 'into the house of lust', leaving him standing forlorn in the street where the dawn 'creeps like a frightened girl'.

A similar sexual confusion lies at the heart of 'The Sphinx', Wilde's decadent masterpiece and one of the greatest poems of imaginative and verbal excess written in English. A young male student studying late into the night whips himself into a frenzy of sexual excitement by imagining the progressively more bizarre and perverse erotic dalliances of the decidedly feminine sphinx ('half-woman and half-animal') whom he addresses and imagines to be present in his study. In his increasingly feverish imagination, she passes from mythical lover to lover, her insatiable quest for sexual gratification eventually culminating in her frenzied coupling with the great god Ammon:

> Great Ammon was your bedfellow! He lay with you beside
> the Nile!
>
> The river-horses in the slime trumpeted when they saw
> him come
> Odorous with Syrian galbanum and smeared with spikenard
> and with thyme.
>
> He came along the river-bank like some tall galley
> argent-sailed,
> He strode across the waters, mailed in beauty, and the
> waters sank.

He strode across the desert sand: he reached the valley
where you lay:
He waited till the dawn of day: then touched your black
breasts with his hand.

You kissed his mouth with mouths of flame: you made
the hornèd god your own:
You stood behind him on his throne: you called him
by his secret name.

You whispered monstrous oracles into the caverns
of his ears:
With blood of goats and blood of steers you taught
him monstrous miracles.

White Ammon was your bedfellow! Your chamber was
the steaming Nile!
And with your curved archaic smile you watched his passion
come and go.

With Syrian oils his brows were bright: and widespread
as a tent at noon
His marble limbs made pale the moon and lent the day
a larger light.

His long hair was nine cubits' span and coloured like that
yellow gem
Which hidden in their garment's hem the merchants bring
from Kurdistan.

His face was as the must that lies upon a vat of new-made
wine:
The seas could not insapphirine the perfect azure of his eyes.

His thick soft throat was white as milk and threaded with
thin veins of blue:
And curious pearls like frozen dew were broidered on his
flowing silk.

But the student's excited fantasy of how passionately the sphinx 'kissed [Ammon's] mouth', 'watched his passion come and go' and 'made the hornèd god your own' recoils upon him as he gradually realizes how completely he has identified himself with her and projected his own hidden desires onto her. His vicarious enjoyment of her conquests then is ultimately tempered by a newfound revulsion at unrestrained female sexuality, which, as in 'The Harlot's House', is here both the object of fascination and abhorrence. In his 1883 draft, Wilde even refers to the sphinx's 'harlotries', allying her directly with the grotesque female prostitutes of 'The Harlot's House', as he imagines her 'crouching down' between Ammon's knees, and waking 'wild passions' in her 'bruised bedfellow'. Both terror and excitement colour his speech as he imagines with relish the bodies of her lovers come alive in his room:

But these, thy lovers, are not dead. Still by the hundred-
cubit gate
Dog-faced Anubis sits in state with lotus-lilies for thy head.

Still from his chair of porphyry gaunt Memnon strains
his lidless eyes

Across the empty land, and cries each yellow morning
unto thee.

And Nilus with his broken horn lies in his black and oozy bed
And till thy coming will not spread his waters on the
withering corn.

Your lovers are not dead, I know. They will rise up and
hear your voice
And clash their cymbals and rejoice and run to kiss
your mouth! And so,

Set wings upon your argosies! Set horses to your ebon car!
Back to your Nile! Or if you are grown sick of dead
divinities

Follow some roving lion's spoor across the copper-coloured
plain,
Reach out and hale him by the mane and bid him be
your paramour!

Couch by his side upon the grass and set your white teeth
in his throat
And when you hear his dying note lash your long flanks
of polished brass

And take a tiger for your mate, whose amber sides are
flecked with black,
And ride upon his gilded back in triumph through the
Theban gate,

And toy with him in amorous jests, and when he turns,
and snarls, and gnaws,
O smite him with your jasper claws! And bruise him with
your agate breasts!

Desire turns to sadism and revulsion as the speaker urges the sphinx to bite, bruise and 'lash' the objects of her desire. But a sense of sexual panic drives these lines, and it comes as no surprise shortly afterwards that the student, terrified by the implications of what he has summoned up, wishes to banish all further thought of the sphinx herself:

. . . Get hence! I weary of your sullen ways,
I weary of your steadfast gaze, your somnolent
magnificence.

Your horrible and heavy breath makes the light flicker
in the lamp,
And on my brow I feel the damp and dreadful dews of night
and death.

Your eyes are like fantastic moons that shiver in some
stagnant lake,
Your tongue is like a scarlet snake that dances to fantastic
tunes,

Your pulse makes poisonous melodies, and your black throat
is like the hole
Left by some torch or burning coal on saracenic tapestries.

Away! The sulphur-coloured stars are hurrying through
    the western gate!
Away! Or it may be too late to climb their silent silver cars!

See, the dawn shivers round the grey gilt-dialled towers,
    and the rain
Streams down each diamonded pane and blurs with tears
    the wannish day.

What snake-tressed fury fresh from hell, with uncouth
    gestures and unclean,
Stole from the poppy-drowsy queen and led you to
    a student's cell?

What songless tongueless ghost of sin crept through the
    curtains of the night,
And saw my taper burning bright, and knocked, and bade
    you enter in?

. . .

Get hence, you loathsome mystery! Hideous animal,
    get hence!
You wake in me each bestial sense, you make me what
    I would not be.

You make my creed a barren sham, you wake foul dreams
    of sensual life,
And Atys with his blood-stained knife were better than
    the thing I am.

As he rejects everything he has excitedly summoned up moments previously, the speaker's dramatic recoil only highlights all the more sharply the perverse imaginings and fiery-coloured language that have driven the poem hitherto. The poem closes with Wilde's sexual ingénue attempting to exorcize this 'ghost of sin', clutching his crucifix desperately as he intones 'only one god has ever died./ Only one god has let his side be wounded by a soldier's spear.' 'Leave me to my crucifix,' he insists, 'Whose pallid burden, sick with pain, watches the world with wearied eyes,/ And weeps for every soul that dies, and weeps for every soul in vain.'

On one level, by closing the poem with the language of creed, crucifix and sin, Wilde is trying to reconcile 'The Sphinx' to Victorian notions of propriety. But on another level, the clash between sexual paganism/homoeroticism and a severely chaste Catholicism represents the unresolved clash between elements warring within Wilde himself. Given his ambivalent sexuality at this time, as well as his earlier fascination with the rituals of Catholicism, it would seem that a dormant religiosity had briefly returned to check him in his excess and provide an acceptable, conventional outlet for a confusion that has threatened to reveal itself too openly in the poem.

Although Wilde had gone to Paris ostensibly to compose *The Duchess of Padua*, 'The Sphinx' is the richest and ripest fruit born of his three months there, and he always spoke of this visit as one during which he had worked productively. He continued working sporadically on 'The Sphinx' over the ensuing years, occasionally reciting it out loud to friends, so that by the time the poem was eventually published in 1894, it was already widely known by repute. Only half-jokingly Wilde ascribed this delay

THE SPHINX BY OSCAR WILDE

WITH DECORATIONS BY CHARLES RICKETTS
LONDON MDCCCXCIV
ELKIN MATHEWS AND JOHN LANE . AT THE SIGN OF THE BODLEY HEAD.

THE SPHINX

N A DIM CORNER OF MY ROOM FOR LONGER THAN MY FANCY THINKS
A BEAUTIFUL AND SILENT SPHINX HAS WATCHED ME THROUGH THE SHIFTING GLOOM.

INVIOLATE AND IMMOBILE SHE DOES NOT RISE SHE DOES NOT STIR
FOR SILVER MOONS ARE NAUGHT TO HER AND NAUGHT TO HER THE SUNS THAT REEL.

RED FOLLOWS GREY ACROSS THE AIR THE WAVES OF MOONLIGHT EBB AND FLOW
BUT WITH THE DAWN SHE DOES NOT GO AND IN THE NIGHT-TIME SHE IS THERE.

DAWN FOLLOWS DAWN AND NIGHTS GROW OLD AND ALL THE WHILE THIS CURIOUS CAT
LIES COUCHING ON THE CHINESE MAT WITH EYES OF SATIN RIMMED WITH GOLD.

UPON THE MAT SHE LIES AND LEERS AND ON THE TAWNY THROAT OF HER
FLUTTERS THE SOFT AND SILKY FUR OR RIPPLES TO HER POINTED EARS.

COME FORTH MY LOVELY SENESCHAL! SO SOMNOLENT, SO STATUESQUE!
COME FORTH YOU EXQUISITE GROTESQUE! HALF WOMAN AND HALF ANIMAL!

COME FORTH MY LOVELY LANGUOROUS SPHINX! AND PUT YOUR HEAD UPON MY KNEE!
AND LET ME STROKE YOUR THROAT AND SEE YOUR BODY SPOTTED LIKE THE LYNX!

AND LET ME TOUCH THOSE CURVING CLAWS OF YELLOW IVORY AND GRASP
THE TAIL THAT LIKE A MONSTROUS ASP COILS ROUND YOUR HEAVY VELVET PAWS!

A THOUSAND

The Sphinx (Elkin Mathews & John Lane, 1894), decorative title page and text opening, originally printed in three colours.

in completing and publishing the poem to his fear that it 'would destroy domesticity in England', but he was simply awaiting the proper moment and format. When it eventually appeared, with illustrations and hand-drawn illuminated capitals by Charles Ricketts, Wilde's literary fame and success went before him and the poem was immediately proclaimed by one critic to be 'about as fin-de-siècle a business as you ever saw'.[9] Finely printed in three colours and bound in gorgeous, rare materials, in its published form it was the supreme example of Art Nouveau bookmaking in England, as well as one of the most beautiful and expensive trade books ever published.[10] Using only capital letters and exquisite hand-drawn decorations, the poem in its form as a printed book perfectly embodied the rare, exquisite artefact at its core, resulting in a perfect marriage of form and content. But sexual panic and gender-bending run rampant in the poem, and it is an important precursor to later works such as *The Picture of Dorian Gray*, *Salome* and *The Importance of Being Earnest*, in all of which Wilde tackles the sexual puritanism of the Victorian age more openly and aggressively.

When he returned to London at the end of April 1883, Wilde had drafted a five-act play and two of his finest poems while simultaneously forging connections in the French literary and artistic world that would bear fruit years later. But he had also burned through his lecture-tour earnings along with the advances paid by Anderson and Prescott. Although he had expectations of having a hit with *Vera* later in the year, it was an impecunious and uncertain Oscar Wilde who showed up in mid-May at the door of his mother's fashionable Mayfair flat, on Park Street, where he resided for the next few days. Here he called in a debt of $200, borrowed £1,200 from an obliging moneylender, and within days had set himself up in his own elegant apartment nearby on Charles Street.

He would continue to be bedevilled by money problems for the rest of his life, even at the height of his success in the early 1890s. In June 1883, realizing that there was money to be had by lecturing in Britain, he sought the assistance of Colonel W. F. Morse, who had managed his North American tour, in arranging a lecture tour of Britain. In July he lectured at Prince's Hall, in Piccadilly, on his 'Personal Impressions of America'. Well-reviewed in *The World* and *Queen*, this lecture spawned further engagements throughout Britain, including an invitation to lecture students of the Royal Academy on 'Modern Art Training', and by the end of December he had spoken upwards of 66 times.[11] When he embarked for New York on 2 August to supervise Prescott's premiere of *Vera*, he must have held hopes that his lecturing career would be short-lived. But *Vera* received decidedly mixed reviews when it opened on 21 August, and it closed after only a week. The event marks the beginning of an eight-year hiatus in Wilde's career as a dramatist, and it only brought home the urgency of finding a steady income stream.

Shortly after returning from America in mid-September, he embarked again on the lecture circuit, delivering a series of lectures, on 'The House Beautiful', his 'Personal Impressions of America' and (from mid-February 1884 onwards) 'The Value of Art in Modern Life', that was to continue unabated until his marriage in May 1884. By the end of April 1884, he had delivered as many as 148 lectures throughout the British Isles, sometimes giving two lectures a day and as many as eight or nine in the course of a week. In January 1884 he told Lillie Langtry that he was 'getting quite rich', and Sherard says that on more than one occasion, after briefly returning to London, Wilde 'pulled out of the pocket of his fur coat a handful of notes and gold which he had earned so distastefully in the provinces'. While the level of remuneration was not up to the American standard, writes Morse drily, 'the amount that Mr. Wilde received was sufficient to provide for his immediate future and to enable him to carry out certain plans that he had formed.'

Money was not the only thing on his mind. The 'plans that he had formed' at this time included marriage. Perhaps because he had no reliable income, and as a way of quelling such gossip as Goncourt's about his dubious (*douteux*) sexuality, Wilde's mother had been keen for years to see him married to an independently wealthy wife. For his part, Oscar wished to support his impoverished, widowed mother and would do anything to please her, so he was very willing to oblige. He had proposed unsuccessfully to the wealthy Charlotte Montefiore as early as 1880 or 1881, replying to her rejection of him that 'with your money and my brain we could have gone far.'[12] Montefiore's rejection did not rankle, however, because as early as June 1881 he was already paying court to the 23-year-old Constance Lloyd, who three years later would become his wife. He discussed his prospects of marrying Constance with his mother both before and during his year-long residency in the United States in 1882; and during Wilde's long absence, Lady Wilde played an active role in courting Constance by inviting her to her weekly salons and keeping up friendly relations with Constance's family. Wilde seems not to have seen his future wife immediately on returning from America, but no sooner did he return from Paris in April 1883 than he invited her to his mother's apartment. He saw much of her over the summer of 1883, before his departure for New York in August; and when

Constance Wilde, early 1880s, photographer unknown. Born Constance Lloyd, she altered her name to Constance Holland after Wilde was imprisoned. She is identified as 'Constance Mary, daughter of Horace Lloyd QC' on her tombstone, although in 1963 the phrase 'Wife of Oscar Wilde' was added.

he came back from New York, he resumed seeing Constance whenever his lecturing commitments allowed. Within weeks he was being received as her suitor, and it can have come as no surprise to either family when, at the end of November 1883, during a five-day visit to Dublin where Constance was staying with her grandmother and Wilde saw her almost daily in between his lecturing commitments, he proposed to and was unhesitatingly accepted by the ecstatic Constance.

In light of Wilde's later sexual affairs with men and the distaste for female sexuality already hinted at dimly in his poetry, the courtship and marriage of Wilde and Constance Lloyd has excited a great deal of comment. Some believe that the couple were genuinely in love, while others believe it was a marriage of convenience in which Constance's wealth played a significant role. Constance brought a not-inconsiderable income to the marriage, estimated by Wilde himself to be as much as £1,000 a year, and set to rise significantly on the death of her mother.[13] The truth probably lies somewhere between the two poles. From one perspective, the couple was well matched: Constance was an intelligent, spirited woman with artistic and intellectual interests of her own. In the early years of their marriage at least, Wilde freely entered into these interests. In a letter written from Edinburgh six months after their wedding, Wilde told his wife: 'I feel incomplete without you,'[14] and his poem 'To My Wife', handwritten by Wilde into Constance's autograph book in June 1886 and published seven years later, seems to bear this out. A surviving manuscript of Wilde's children's story 'The Selfish Giant', written in Constance's hand in the mid-1880s, suggests the overlapping of their intellectual and artistic interests, if not Constance's role in the story's composition. For Constance too was a children's author: her story collection *There Was Once* appeared in the same year (1888) as Oscar's *The Happy Prince and Other Tales.* From another perspective, however, there is evidence to suggest that Wilde felt dissatisfied with his wife within days of his marriage. Richard Ellmann says that Wilde felt 'summoned . . . towards an underground life totally at variance with his aboveboard role as Constance's husband', partly as a result of reading Joris-Karl Huysmans's recently published decadent novel *À rebours* (Against the Grain) during the course of his honeymoon.[15] Moreover, if Robert Sherard's recollections are correct, in the course of his honeymoon Wilde would enjoy 'slumming' visits, accompanied by Sherard and a few other male friends, to 'the haunts of the lowest criminals and poorest outcasts of the city, the show-pieces of the Paris Inferno'.[16]

Wilde's sexual and intellectual distaste for his wife is evident in letters written shortly before or after he came out of jail in 1897: 'Whether I am married or not is a matter that does not concern me,' he writes in April 1897, when Constance was considering divorcing him; 'for years I disregarded the tie. But I really think it is hard on my wife to be tied to me. I always thought so.' 'Women are so petty, and Constance has no imagination,' he writes harshly six months later, when living in Naples with Lord Alfred Douglas, at which point Constance was refusing to give him further monetary support.

While it is easy to read too much into letters written in the wake of Wilde's imprisonment and the breakdown of his marriage, strain had been palpable to close observers many years earlier. In 1888, on visiting the Wildes on Christmas Day, W. B. Yeats perceived that their home life 'suggested some deliberate artistic composition'. Alfred Douglas observed at the commencement of his friendship with Wilde, in 1891, that Wilde 'was not very kind to his wife . . . [H]e was often impatient with her, and sometimes snubbed her, and he resented, and showed that he resented, the attitude of slight disapproval that she always adopted towards him.'[17] The biographer Neil McKenna writes that the marriage was 'passionless' and premised on 'emotional and sexual indifference', at least on Wilde's part. 'Men marry because they are tired; women, because they are curious; both are disappointed,' Lord Henry Wotton quips cynically in *The Picture of Dorian Gray*. Wotton's precarious marriage to Victoria in Wilde's only novel is often said to be based on Wilde's own marriage.

Certainly there is something artificial and mannered about Oscar's and Constance's recorded announcements of their marriage to relatives and friends: 'I am engaged to Oscar Wilde and perfectly and insanely happy,' wrote Constance to her brother Otho on the day of their engagement. Otho had been privately 'baffled by Wilde's interest in his sister', says Ellmann; he doubted Wilde's love for her, and tellingly he did not attend their wedding.[18] 'We are, of course, desperately in love . . . we telegraph to each other twice a day, and the telegraph clerks have become quite romantic in consequence,' Wilde told Waldo Story. Constance is 'a grave, slight, violet-eyed little Artemis', he told Lillie Langtry, 'with great coils of heavy brown hair, which make her flower-like head droop like a blossom, and wonderful ivory hands which draw music from the piano so sweet that the birds stop singing to listen to her'. One wonders what Constance thought about not merely her husband's poem 'The New Helen', written and published in homage to Langtry five years earlier, but also the overwrought and strangely passionless love poem to

Langtry that Wilde published under the title 'Roses and Rue' in the bi-weekly magazine *Society* in 1885.[19]

Whatever potential strain existed in private, in public the couple presented a loving and devoted front, and the marriage was a matter of national interest. The engagement was announced in the gossipy magazines *Society* and *Truth* as well as in a number of regional papers: 'Bunthorne is to get his bride,' announced the *Liverpool Daily Post*.[20] The wedding took place on 29 May 1884, at St James's Church, Paddington. It was a widely publicized, 'Aesthetic' affair. Legend has it that Wilde himself designed the dresses of his wife-to-be and her bridesmaids;[21] and while modern scholars follow Wilde's own son, Vyvyan Holland, in disputing this,[22] Wilde certainly designed Constance's engagement ring: a heart formed of diamonds, enclosing two pearls, surmounted with another bow of diamonds, which remains in the possession of the couple's descendants today.[23] They honeymooned in Dieppe and Paris, where Constance's wedding dress made a sensation. In Paris they dined with Bourget, Sargent and the wealthy American hostess Henrietta Ruebell, and from Paris, as the *New York Times* reported, Wilde assured a friend that he 'has not been disappointed in married life'.[24]

On returning to Britain, the couple rented and set about furnishing a home on Tite Street in artistic Chelsea, closely adjacent to their friends the painters Sargent and Whistler. It was to be a living embodiment and symbol of 'The House Beautiful'. The Aesthetic architect and stage designer E. W. Godwin, who had already designed homes for Whistler and Frank Miles, planned the decor, while the explorer and Orientalist Walter Harris helped design 'the most awe-inspiring room in the house' – Wilde's smoking room.[25]

But the costs of setting up 'The House Beautiful' were large, and before his wedding Wilde had announced that he would resume lecturing in the autumn. He began his new lecture series at Ealing on 1 October 1884 with a new lecture titled 'Dress'. Possibly written with help from his wife, who would herself soon become a popular spokesperson for 'rational dress', the new lecture was an expansion and finer articulation of the ideas that Wilde had already expressed in 'The House Beautiful' about the deficiencies in both Victorian men's and women's fashion. The lecture tapped into the new mood for so-called dress reform and overlapped conspicuously with the interests of the recently formed and popular Rational Dress Society, of which Constance was a member (she edited its monthly *Gazette* for the entirety of its brief six-month run in 1888–9). The lecture also overlapped closely with the interests of the couple's friend and neighbour Godwin, whose recent book *Dress, and Its Relation to Health and Culture*, published to accompany the International Health Exhibition of 1884, influenced Wilde. Wilde's new lecture was immediately popular and widely reported in the press. It elicited a lengthy correspondence in London's *Pall Mall Gazette*, and in 1885 the lecture was abridged and published as an article titled (after Poe) 'The Philosophy of Dress' in the *New York Daily Tribune*.

While the new lecture on 'Dress' possesses intrinsic interest in its own right, it is important too for indirectly precipitating a career in journalism that was to assume tremendous importance over the next five years. The lively correspondence about the lecture in the *Pall Mall Gazette* in turn elicited a lengthy reply by Wilde, published on 14 October 1884 under the title 'Mr. Oscar Wilde on Woman's Dress' (although Wilde's reply also concerned men's dress). Often reprinted in its own right, Wilde's reply was the beginning of an association with the *Pall Mall Gazette* that was to play an important role in his career. In the wake of further letters to the editor taking issue with Wilde, the *Gazette* invited him to write an article, with accompanying illustrations, setting out his ideas about dress in further detail. Published under the title 'More Radical Ideas on Dress Reform' on 11 November, this article was reprinted some days later in the *Gazette*'s sister paper, the weekly *Pall Mall Budget*. Over the next few years, Wilde would write dozens of reviews and articles for the *Pall Mall Gazette* (many of them similarly reprinted days later in the *Budget*), as well as for other papers and magazines; and while he would not earn anything like a reasonable living from journalism until October 1887, when he assumed the editorship of *The Lady's World* (which he promptly retitled *Woman's World*), the articles and reviews that Wilde wrote for press publication from 1884 onwards are of great significance to his career as a prose writer. In them he honed the witty, epigrammatic prose style for which he is renowned, sharpening his sense of himself as an author while developing an instinctive feel for his audience. Moreover, in longer, more cerebral pieces written for the prestigious monthlies *The Nineteenth Century* and *The Fortnightly Review* (the latter now a monthly magazine), he would develop positions and create minor masterpieces that are now central components of his literary and intellectual oeuvre.

Of the journalism written in the immediate wake of Wilde's lecture on 'Dress', two pieces are especially significant. In May 1885 he published a lengthy, important essay titled 'Shakespeare and Stage Costume' in *The Nineteenth Century*. This essay, possibly commissioned by the magazine's editor, was ostensibly a disquisition on the importance of costume to Shakespeare.[26] But in it Wilde outlined theoretical positions that were to become central to his thinking about aesthetics in subsequent years. 'The point . . . I wish to emphasise is,' Wilde maintained, 'not that Shakespeare appreciated the value of lovely costumes in adding picturesqueness to poetry, but that he saw how important costume is as a means of producing certain dramatic effects.'[27] Even 'small details of dress', Wilde explained, 'become in Shakespeare's hands points of actual dramatic importance, and by some of them the action of the play is conditioned absolutely.' Other dramatists have 'availed themselves of costume as a method of expressing directly to the audience the character of a person', Wilde went on, 'but nobody from the mere details of apparel and adornment has ever drawn such irony of situation, such immediate and tragic effect, such pity and pathos, as Shakespeare himself'. Far from being a peripheral matter, costume was vital to the drama because it underscored the play's essentially illusory and theatrical character: 'it has the illusion of truth for its method, and the illusion of beauty for its result.' With only small variations, including a new final paragraph in which he wittily underscores that his essay merely 'represents an artistic standpoint, and in aesthetic criticism attitude is everything', Wilde reprinted the essay under the deliberately paradoxical title 'The Truth of Masks' in his 1891 intellectual manifesto *Intentions*, alongside such vital later theoretical statements as 'The Decay of Lying' and 'The Critic as Artist'.

The other important journalistic upshot of the 'Dress' lecture was a review of Whistler's 'Ten O'Clock' lecture that appeared in the *Pall Mall Gazette* on 21 February 1885, one day after Whistler had delivered his important lecture on the nature of art and artistry. The piece is vital because it marks the beginning of Wilde's falling-out with Whistler, who had done so much to influence Wilde and advance Aestheticism over the years immediately preceding. The review contained plenty of praise for Whistler and ended by remarking not only that he was 'one of the very greatest masters of painting' but that his lecture itself was 'a masterpiece' that would be remembered years hence. But the review was also laced with acerbic barbs. Whistler was, according to Wilde, 'a miniature Mephistopheles, mocking the majority!' who made 'a holocaust of humanity'. Wilde clearly realized that he had himself been the target of Whistler's attacks in the lecture upon 'the unattached writer' or 'Aesthete' who made himself 'the middleman' in matters of Art, and unsurprisingly Wilde's review contained serious intellectual disagreements. An artist 'is not an isolated fact', Wilde maintained; 'he is the result of a certain milieu and a certain entourage, and can no more be born of a nation that is devoid of any sense of beauty than a fig can grow from a thorn.' Nor could Wilde accept Whistler's dictum that only a painter can be a judge of painting:

> I say that only an artist is a judge of art; there is a wide difference. As long as a painter is a painter merely, he should not be allowed to talk of anything but mediums and megilp, and on those subjects should be compelled to hold his tongue; it is only when he becomes an artist that the secret laws of artistic creation are revealed to him. For there are not many arts, but one art merely – poem, picture and Parthenon, sonnet and statue – all are in their essence the same, and he who knows one knows all. But the poet is the

> supreme artist, for he is the master of colour and of form, and the real musician besides, and is lord over all life and all arts.

Wilde's critique of Whistler, which he elaborated in a further review titled provocatively 'The Relation of Dress to Art: A Note in Black and White on Mr. Whistler's Lecture', published in the *Gazette* a week later, marks an important phase in what Whistler had once termed 'the war between the brush and the pen'. Whistler had spent nearly a decade elevating the claims of the painter over those of the writer (he had bankrupted himself in 1878 when pursuing a foolhardy libel suit against the critic John Ruskin), and Wilde must have known it would rankle.[28] As importantly, the review marks an important event in Wilde's evolving theory of art, which he would develop and articulate more fully in such later pieces as 'The Decay of Lying', 'The Critic as Artist' and his 1891 Preface to *The Picture of Dorian Gray.*

Although Wilde writes around this time that 'by journalism a man may make an income' and that 'you must carve your way to fame,' at first he made little money from journalism, and the early years of his marriage were marked by financial strain. At one point, Constance was obliged to borrow small sums from a neighbour; and the illustrator Sir Bernard Partridge, who became a good friend, says that Wilde was 'rather hard-up' when he first met him around this time.[29] (It was Partridge who induced Wilde in 1887 to write for *The Lady's Pictorial*, where Partridge was employed as an illustrator.) Wilde continued lecturing well into 1885, although his audiences and income were now starting to dwindle. In the summer of 1885 he enlisted his friend George Curzon's help in trying to obtain a position as an Inspector of

Schools, and some months later he unsuccessfully applied for the Secretaryship of the Beaumont Trust. These applications were doubtless prompted by the birth of his first son, Cyril, in June 1885, and made doubly urgent by the birth of a second son, Vyvyan, in November 1886. In 1887 the couple's financial problems were serious enough that they contemplated sub-letting their house; and in the process of obtaining a loan of £500 from her brother Otho, Constance confessed that they lived 'rather too expensively as we neither of us have a notion how to live non extravagantly'.[30] The couple's dire financial situation following the birth of their children doubtless goes some way to explain Wilde's decision to accept the editorship of *Woman's World* in May 1887, a position that brought in over £400 for 1887 alone and which he occupied for two years.

But the early years of Wilde's marriage to Constance are notable for far more than the creation of a 'house beautiful' or the financial strain that accompanied the birth of their children. The couple evidently ceased having sexual relations shortly after Vyvyan was conceived; and according to Wilde's friend Frank Harris, within a year or so of his marriage Wilde found Constance physically 'loathsome' and 'disgusting' on account of her pregnancies. 'Desire is killed by maternity' and 'passion buried in conception', Wilde purportedly told Harris. It was not necessarily changes in Constance's appearance that were to blame. It is far more likely that Wilde was increasingly willing to act on his desires for other men. He had been haunted by crude taunts of 'unmanliness' and 'effeminacy' for years, and as Neil McKenna has argued, there is likely to have been a sexual component to some of his male friendships at school and college, even if Wilde never acted on his desires for other boys or, as is more likely, considered them a normal part of emergent male sexuality.[31] In 1875 Wilde had befriended the young homosexual portrait painter Frank Miles, two years his senior, with whom he later cohabited in London for over two years. (This close friendship ended abruptly in 1881, when Miles's father, fearing that Wilde was a corruptive influence, insisted that his son should have nothing further to do with him.) In 1876 Miles had introduced Wilde to his mentor and patron Lord Ronald Gower, the most abandoned and notorious homosexual of his day, widely believed to be a real-life model for Lord Henry Wotton in *The Picture of Dorian Gray*. In her study of the triangular relationship between Wilde, Miles and Gower, Molly Whittington-Egan calls Gower 'a mature, seasoned, practising lover of boys', 'a grossly reckless frequenter of "rough trade"' and 'an extreme corrupting influence on Oscar and Frank'.[32] While there is no clear evidence that Wilde was sexually involved with or even sexually interested in either Gower or Miles, scholars agree that there is an atmosphere of homosexuality about what Whittington-Egan calls this 'great trinity' and also that Gower, who was some years older than both Wilde and Miles, exerted a 'corrupting' influence upon the younger men. As Joseph Bristow puts it, 'Gower's sexual career . . . opened Wilde's eyes to the homosexual subculture with which he became closely acquainted in the early 1890s,' and 'the same is true of Miles.'[33] Certainly Wilde would have known of Gower's scandalous reputation and exploits; and he relished Gower's friendship and company long after he was forced by Miles's father to break off his intimate friendship with Miles.

A similar uncertainty surrounds Wilde's friendship with a young man named Harry Marillier, whom Wilde had first known when Marillier was still a schoolboy, in 1880 or 1881, and lodged in the same building in the Strand where Wilde and Miles lodged. But the friendship, which McKenna sees as unequivocally sexual, intensified in 1885 when Marillier, by now an undergraduate at Cambridge University, invited Wilde to attend an undergraduate production of Aeschylus' *Eumenides*. The letters that Wilde wrote in the wake of Marillier's invitation certainly seem suggestive of intense affection and desire: 'You must certainly come and see me when you are in town', Wilde told Marillier when accepting the invitation, 'and tell me . . . what moods and modulations of art affect you most.' (McKenna interprets this innocent-sounding counter-invitation as 'a cautious and subtle interrogation of Harry's sexual preferences.') 'Why did you let me catch my train?' Wilde asked three days later, after they had met hastily in London, just prior to Wilde's departure for northern England to lecture; 'It was an hour intensely dramatic and intensely psychological.' 'You have the power of making others love you,' he told Marillier six days later still, when advising him to consider schoolteaching as a profession. 'Does it all seem a dream, Harry?' he again wrote after returning from visiting Marillier in Cambridge some days *before* the *Eumenides* production (during this visit to Cambridge, as McKenna observes, Wilde almost certainly introduced Marillier to his friend, the pederastic don Oscar Browning). He had felt 'one evil omen' during the visit, he told Marillier: 'your fire! You are careless about playing with fire.' 'You too have the love of things impossible,' he wrote to Marillier fifteen days later in an important letter that scholars today understand as being a coded confession of Wilde's homosexuality, as well as a clarification of the sexual basis of his relationship with Marillier:

> *l'amour de l'impossible* (how do men name it?). Some day you will find, even as I have found, that there is no such thing as a romantic experience: there are romantic memories, and there is the desire of romance – that is all. Our most fiery moments of ecstasy are merely shadows of what somewhere else we have felt, or of what we long some day to feel . . . I myself would sacrifice everything for a new experience . . . I would go to the stake for a sensation and be a sceptic to the last.

Whatever the exact nature of his friendships with Miles, Gower and Marillier, scholars agree that in 1886, some months after his passion for Marillier had burned out, Wilde entered into a sexual relationship with another smart, well-educated and precocious young man, soon also to be a Cambridge undergraduate: the seventeen-year-old Robert Ross. The exact date and nature of their first meeting are unrecorded, but despite his young age Ross was an experienced, confident and unashamed lover of men, and both men later spoke of the friendship as the first in which Wilde was sexually involved with another man. The sexual element in their relationship is generally understood as lasting until late 1888, when Ross left London for Cambridge and when other young men supplanted him in Wilde's affections. But the intellectual and emotional friendship between the two endured until Wilde's very last breath. It was one of the two or three most important personal relationships of Wilde's life. Ross would prove the most loyal and devoted of Wilde's friends both during and after his two years of imprisonment, from 1895 to 1897; and following Wilde's death in 1900, as we shall see, Ross would, in his formal capacity as Wilde's literary executor and administrator of his estate, dedicate the final eighteen years of his own life to the editing of Wilde's collected works, to the restoration of Wilde's estate, and to the recuperation of Wilde's personal and literary reputation.

Wilde's long and close relationship with Ross drove home what Wilde had probably already begun to feel in late 1885 as his epistolary seduction of Marillier had unfolded – that, as Lord Henry Wotton puts it in *The Picture of Dorian Gray*, the 'one charm of marriage is that it makes a life of deception necessary for both parties'. By late 1886 Wilde understood that his marriage was predicated on self-division and spousal deception. 'If I ever get married, I'll certainly try to forget the fact,' proclaims Algernon Moncrieff, a character based closely on Wilde himself, in *The Importance of Being Earnest*. Algernon's announcement – like that of his manservant, Lane, in the same play, that marriage is the 'consequence of a misunderstanding' between young people – is a tacit expression of what Wilde himself had come to feel years earlier. The heterosexual basis of Victorian marriage was a crippling confinement; and if it led Wilde to pursue his love for men surreptitiously and in secret, he could nonetheless pursue such love confidently, without any sense of shame or guilt. Both recognitions were to drive his most supreme imaginative works, as they emerged from his pen over the next few years.

FIVE

The Rhythmical Value of Prose: Wilde's Career in Fiction

The rhythmical value of prose has never yet been fully tested. I hope to do some more work in that genre.

WILDE, letter to Robert H. Sherard, April 1883

It was not just the fact of marriage that obliged Wilde to pursue his desires for young men in secret. About one year before Wilde's affair with Ross began, Britain's Parliament, in a panic at the explosive growth in the white slave trade, passed the Criminal Law Amendment Act (1885). The Act was designed originally 'for the Protection of Women and Girls, the suppression of brothels, and other purposes', but at the eleventh hour and after hurried Parliamentary debate, the so-called Labouchere Amendment was added (named after Henry Labouchere, the radical MP and journalist who proposed it), outlawing 'gross indecency' between men. The amendment ran as follows:

> any male person who, in public or private, commits, or is a party to the commission of, or procures, or attempts to procure the commission by any male person of, any act of gross indecency with another male person, shall be guilty of a misdemeanour, and being convicted thereof, shall be liable

> at the discretion of the Court to be imprisoned for any term not exceeding two years, with or without hard labour.[1]

Upon becoming law, Labouchere's rushed and vaguely worded amendment was to have the most pernicious and long-standing ramifications. By outlawing 'gross indecency' rather than any specified sex act, the Act made even the most innocent actions and forms of behaviour among men liable to criminal prosecution. The criminal standard was loosely defined and subjective, and the burden of proof dangerously low. It has been said that the Act brought the modern male homosexual into being, for it created panic, paranoia and a new sense of sexual identity among both men with same-sex desires and those most desirous of policing them. The Act quickly became known as the 'Blackmailer's Charter'; 'gross indecency' was a catch-all phrase, and two years before he fell foul of the Act in 1895, Wilde himself was subjected to blackmail by virtue of letters he had recently written to Alfred Douglas and that Douglas had incautiously let fall into the hands of the blackmailer Alfred Wood.

The Act cast a long shadow over Wilde's life and writing career, and ten years after its passage into law he would be arrested, convicted and imprisoned under Labouchere's amendment. In the short term, however, in combination with Wilde's apparently new willingness to act on his desires for other men, the Act's passage brought about an important change in his consciousness. 'After 1886 he was able to think of himself as a criminal, moving guiltily among the innocent,' writes Richard Ellmann; 'he was now in league with the underworld of people who pretended to be what they were not.'[2] His public persona had always been a fabrication, created partly to mask his Irish roots and accelerate his advancement as a self-created Apostle of Aestheticism. Now it masked his sexual dissidence and criminality from family members and strangers alike.

Together with this change in consciousness, the Act gave a vital spark to Wilde's imagination, catalysing his career as a fiction writer. Within a year of the commencement of his affair with Robert Ross, Wilde had published three short stories – 'Lord Arthur Savile's Crime', 'Lady Alroy' (republished in 1891 under the title 'The Sphinx without a Secret') and 'The Model Millionaire' – in which aristocratic Londoners live a double life and harbour grave personal secrets. 'Lord Arthur Savile's Crime', a serio-comic dress rehearsal for *The Picture of Dorian Gray*, has perhaps the most direct bearing on Wilde's life at this time. Lord Arthur Savile is a much-liked young man-about-town, 'a young man of birth and fortune [who had lived] a life exquisite in its freedom from sordid care [and] its beautiful boyish insouciance'. When the story begins, he is on the threshold of marrying and starting a family. But when a palm-reader predicts a future in which he will commit a serious crime, a darker and more dangerous side is revealed to Lord Arthur. Henceforth he must reconcile himself to this secret criminal element in his make-up while concealing it from the world and preserving his persona of incorruptibility.

The relevance of the story to Wilde's life is hinted at by the centrality of palmistry to the story. When the story was written, palmistry, known as 'cheiromancy' to the Victorians, was a fashionable fad among the elite. If he did not believe in palmistry wholeheartedly, Wilde seems at least to have succumbed to its faddishness. He was good friends with the fashionable cheiromantist and polymath Edward Heron-Allen: in 1885, shortly after the birth of his first child, Wilde asked Heron-Allen to cast the child's horoscope, and some months later Heron-Allen published a diagram of Wilde's hand in *The Daily Graphic*.[3] After 'Lord Arthur Savile's Crime' appeared in Britain, Wilde asked Heron-Allen to help sell the story in America and also to write a short preface on its cheiromancy (both requests came to nothing), and later still, in 1893, Wilde visited another palm-reader, 'Cheiro', who told him that 'his left hand promised brilliant success while the right showed impending ruin.'[4] A measure of Wilde's personal fascination with cheiromancy may be implicit in the story's original subtitle, 'A Study of Cheiromancy', although on republishing the story in 1891 he substituted a new subtitle, 'A Study of Duty'. The later subtitle squarely makes Lord Arthur's conduct the focus of critical attention even as it mocks the Victorian notion ('duty') that life must be conducted according to strict social and moral values external to ourselves. The highest of all duties is 'the duty that one owes to oneself', Wilde writes in *The Picture of Dorian Gray*: 'the aim of life is self-development. To realise one's nature perfectly – that is what each of us is here for.'

'Lord Arthur Savile's Crime' is notable for how deeply its protagonist is haunted by the notion of his own criminality. Tellingly, the story's comedy dissipates at the moment when Lord Arthur learns that his destiny is to commit murder, leading him to fly hastily from Lady Windermere's reception, his face 'blanched with terror, and his eyes wild with grief'. But the story returns to farce as we follow the failure of Lord Arthur's pathetic and hilarious attempts to commit the murder in order that he might rid himself of the burden of his foreknowledge and so be free to marry his fiancée, Sybil Merton.

Wilde's comedy at once suggests and obscures serious matters. In seeking to fulfil his destiny and realize his own nature, Lord Arthur is forced to wear a mask, to obscure his private identity from friends and family. Moreover, his crime – which he eventually commits impulsively, in the most unexpected of circumstances and with the most unexpected of victims – is treated by Wilde as a matter of comedy and personal self-realization, drained of any larger moral seriousness. It is not the crime itself that disturbs the reader. If the story ends disturbingly, this is because it ends with Lord Arthur happily married and untroubled, having committed the murder undetected, his wife and two children blissfully unaware of the truth on which their domestic idyll is predicated. As Lady Windermere quips early in the story, 'the proper basis for marriage is a mutual misunderstanding.' A more savage and comical indictment of the Victorian paterfamilias is hard to imagine.

If 'Lord Arthur Savile's Crime' strips away the veneer of the Victorian domestic idyll, 'Lady Alroy' and 'The Model Millionaire' suggest that taboo sexual desires lurk just beneath the surface of Victorian English social rituals and practices. Like Lord Arthur Savile, Lady Alroy pursues a secret double life at odds with her public aura as a respectable, wealthy young widow. Unknown to anybody in her elite social circle, she rents rooms in a shabby little street far from London's West End, where she periodically goes undetected and 'deeply veiled'. But the story deliberately leaves us uncertain about what motivates her clandestine behaviour. Her besotted would-be lover Lord Murcheson, on accidentally discovering her secret, suspects her of sexual assignations and of being 'in the power of some man'. After confronting her with his suspicions, he breaks off their relationship, though he continues to be tortured by his love for her. But the unnamed friend in whom he confides and from whose standpoint the story is narrated reassures Murcheson that 'she took these rooms for the pleasure of going there with her veil down . . . She had a passion for secrecy, but she herself was merely a sphinx without a secret.'

By adopting this last phrase as the story's revised title in 1891, Wilde appears to be endorsing the viewpoint of Murcheson's unnamed friend, a *flâneur* who enjoys 'watching the splendour and shabbiness of Parisian life' from a café terrace. Probably for this reason the story has sometimes been understood as representing the Victorian woman's craving for a 'room of her own' as well as an affirmation of the Victorian man's profound ignorance of her emotional and imaginative needs. In this reading, Lady Alroy is an exemplary, ground-breaking figure, who remains inscrutable to the male gaze in death as much as in life.

But this is to ignore the possibility that Lord Murcheson's suspicions are well founded and that in asserting his conviction that Lady Alroy is merely a sphinx without a secret, Wilde's narrator is telling a deliberate lie, perhaps in order to spare Lord Murcheson further pain and embarrassment. He has already privately conceded to the reader that Lady Alroy's face was that of 'someone who had a secret', and he has also privately shown his contempt for absolute honesty with his remark that Murcheson 'would be the best of fellows if he did not always speak the truth'. As importantly, there is a hint of unspoken homoeroticism about the narrator's feelings for the brainless and unsophisticated Murcheson, whom he declares privately to be 'so handsome, so high-spirited, and so honourable'. Wilde's narrator is evidently also someone with 'a passion for secrecy'. When he asserts that

Lady Alroy is a sphinx without a secret, then, the narrator is not merely contradicting earlier private reflections. He is concealing his personal affinities with Lady Alroy, since he too is subject to thoughts and feelings that he cannot reveal to the straightlaced Murcheson. When we attend to these subtle details in the narrator's account of his interactions with Murcheson, the story's focus shifts from Lady Alroy to the decidedly edgy dynamic between two Victorian gentlemen, one of whom conceals the homoerotic basis of his friendship from the other.

'Lord Arthur Savile's Crime' and 'Lady Alroy' can both be read as subtle interrogations of the Victorian gentlemanly ideal in the wake of the Criminal Law Amendment Act, and to some extent this is true of 'The Model Millionaire' as well. The title character is a wealthy cosmopolitan bachelor, Baron Hausberg, who secretly wishes to reinvent himself and make his customary self illegible by posing for his portrait dressed as a beggar. But the ostensible narrative is again part of a larger, more obscurely told story that unfolds in the form of a conversation between two close gentleman friends. As with 'Lady Alroy', one of these men, Hughie Erskine, is a handsome but brainless young bachelor of conservative tendencies ('a delightful ineffectual young man with a perfect profile'), while the other, Alan Trevor, is more sophisticated and worldly. Trevor is an artist, 'a real master [whose] pictures were eagerly sought after', and as with 'Lady Alroy', there exists an air of unspoken homoeroticism about his friendship with the other. Trevor 'had been very much attracted by Hughie at first', says Wilde's unnamed narrator, 'entirely on account of his good looks' (Wilde altered this telling confession, on republishing the story in his 1891 collection *Lord Arthur Savile's Crime and Other Stories*, to the less incriminating 'on account of his personal charm'). Like Wilde himself in the years when he took London by storm, Trevor believes that 'the only people a painter should know . . . are people who are *bête* and beautiful . . . men who are dandies and women who are beautiful.'

Hughie, however, is devoted to a young woman named Laura Merton, whom he hopes to marry, and he remains unaware of the basis on which his friendship with Trevor is grounded. Once again the story ends with an uneasy affirmation of the Victorian heterosexual marriage idyll when Baron Hausberg, initially mistaken by Hughie for a real beggar and subsequently revealed by Trevor to be 'one of the richest men in Europe', gives the impecunious Hughie the money to enable him to marry Laura. But if Hughie is blissfully happy when he gets the girl, he is also blissfully ignorant about the secret motivations of the two confirmed bachelors, Trevor and Hausberg, who serve as best man and chief toast-giver respectively at his wedding celebration. As with 'Lady Alroy', the secret lives of the unmarriageable constitute the fulcrum on which the marriage plot turns.

The ostensibly happy endings to the marriage plots of 'Lord Arthur Savile's Crime' and 'The Model Millionaire' contrast sharply with a second batch of stories that appeared in print one year later, in which happy endings are resolutely resisted. The five stories in Wilde's first published story collection, *The Happy Prince and Other Tales*, published in May 1888, are often described as children's stories or fairy tales, and according to his younger son there were tears in Wilde's eyes when he read 'The Selfish Giant' to his own children. 'A child would delight in the tales without being worried or troubled by their application,' declared the *Athenaeum* in a brief notice, adding that although Wilde's stories have a character all their own, they are

The Happy Prince and Other Tales (David Nutt, 1888), cover design featuring pictorial device by George Jacomb-Hood.

'not unworthy to compare with Hans Andersen'. However, as one reviewer pointed out at the time of their publication, the dominant spirit of these stories is one that children are unlikely to appreciate, a spirit of 'a bitter satire differing widely from that of Hans Andersen'.[5] In fact it is not the repeated note of bitter social satire alone that disturbs the childlike air. Where Andersen's stories affirm the triumph of the human spirit and of romantic love, the stories in Wilde's *Happy Prince* collection generally end in death and with an air of personal tragedy. For these are stories about the impossibility or failure of love in a cold, unreceptive world.

These traits are vividly on display in 'The Nightingale and the Rose', which Wilde felt to be 'the most elaborate' of the stories. The titular nightingale – the only 'true lover, if there is one' in the story, Wilde said – sacrifices her life in order that the besotted young student might present a red rose to the daughter of the professor. But the student neither knows nor cares about the nightingale's sacrifice, and when the girl petulantly rejects the rose, saying that it will not go with her dress and she vastly prefers jewels, he throws it in the gutter to be crushed by cartwheels, declaring that love is 'silly' and 'not half as useful as Logic'.

In the title story, the impossibility of love has a decidedly more homoerotic cast. 'The Happy Prince' centres on the statue of a once-happy prince who secretly weeps for the state of mankind. When a migrating swallow rests briefly on his pedestal and asks why he is weeping, he replies that when he was alive he was oblivious to human suffering and 'did not know what tears were'. But now that he is dead and set on a pedestal, he can 'see all the ugliness and . . . misery of my city, and . . . cannot choose but weep'. Accordingly he instructs the swallow to strip away all his jewels and finery and distribute them to the poor and needy.

On one level, the title story dramatizes the failure of sentimental altruism or philanthropy, since the Prince's generous acts do nothing to ameliorate the terrible social and political conditions that make him weep. But the love that grows between him and the swallow over the course of the story is equally important. The swallow does the Prince's bidding reluctantly at first, since he is 'in love with the most beautiful Reed' and longs to join his fellow swallows in Egypt for the winter. But when the Prince instructs him to remove the rubies from his eyes and give them to a young student and a poor match-girl respectively, the swallow, who had begun 'to tire of his lady-love' before the story begins, announces that he will henceforth stay with the Prince forever.

It is a suicidal decision on the part of the swallow, for he becomes weaker and weaker as winter sets in. But he refuses to leave the Prince, Wilde tells us, because 'he loved him too well.' His love for the Prince is eventually reciprocated in the most tragic of circumstances. For when the swallow realizes that he is dying and wishes to say a final farewell, the Prince asks him to kiss him on the lips, saying 'I love you.' This moment of open love is the story's climax: on kissing the Prince's lips, the swallow falls down dead, whereupon the Prince's metal heart breaks and he dies as well. The tragedy is compounded when the townsfolk throw the broken heart and the swallow's corpse onto a rubbish-heap after first melting down the rest of the Prince's statue in a furnace (the broken heart refuses to melt) so that the metal might be used to create a statue of the Mayor.

To be sure, Wilde half-heartedly attempts to ameliorate this tragedy by appending a two-sentence coda in which God, after asking his angels to bring him the two most precious things in the city (they bring him the Prince's broken heart and the dead bird), announces that 'in my garden of Paradise this little bird shall sing for evermore, and in my city of gold the Happy Prince shall praise me.' But many readers find this coda perfunctory and lacking in conviction, especially after the biting social satire of the frame narrative, in which the townsfolk argue narrow-mindedly about the value and fate of the Prince's statue. As Perry Nodelman writes,

> Wilde often seems to be teasingly insistent on undermining the apparent moral thrust of his stories, to suggest that

> only fools could believe that goodness is rewarded . . . The heavenly conclusions of stories like 'The Happy Prince' are undermined by the wry and possibly mocking tone with which Wilde describes the events that precede them.[6]

And given his evident distrust of gold's false allure ('the living always think that gold will make them happy,' the Prince tells the swallow), how happy will the Prince be in God's 'city of gold', especially if the swallow remains confined to the garden of paradise?

Wilde told one correspondent that 'The Happy Prince' represents 'an attempt to treat a tragic modern problem in a form that aims at delicacy and imaginative treatment'.[7] That Wilde had serious political intentions for the story is implicit in the fact that he sent copies to Gladstone, Ruskin and the librarian of Toynbee Hall, the East End settlement, among others. *The Happy Prince* was written 'not for children, but for childlike people from eighteen to eighty', he told the American writer Amélie Rives Chanler. But Wilde's intentions for *The Happy Prince* were more complex than this makes it sound. The collection was 'meant partly for children', he confided to his friend George Kersley, and it contains a series of 'studies in prose', he informed another correspondent, 'put for Romance's sake into a fanciful form'. It constitutes 'a reaction against the purely imitative character of modern art', he told Leonard Smithers, a lawyer who, ten years later, would become Wilde's publisher. 'I did not start with an idea and clothe it in form,' he told the schoolteacher Thomas Hutchinson, 'but began with a form and strove to make it beautiful enough to have many secrets.' It was an experiment in form and style – the redemption of his promise of 1883 to test the 'rhythmical value of prose'. Wilde must have been gratified by the praise he received from Walter Pater, England's leading prose stylist, who complimented him on writing 'genuine "little poems in prose"' and remarked that 'the whole . . . book abounds with delicate touches and pure English.'

This desire to explore the imaginative form and style of the fairy tale characterizes Wilde's final story collection, *A House of Pomegranates*, as well. The later collection contains some of Wilde's most spellbinding narrative and descriptive prose. Once again a note of bitter social criticism is present throughout, particularly in 'The Birthday of the Infanta' and 'The Young King', where the pomp, cruelty and exploitativeness of the Court come in for sharp criticism. The priesthood too becomes a focus of Wilde's critique: in 'The Fisherman and His Soul' a priest heartlessly condemns the love of the fisherman for the mermaid and orders their corpses to be buried in unconsecrated ground with 'no mark above them, nor sign of any kind'. In 'The Young King' a bishop cares nothing for the poverty and injustice that the Young King sees prior to his coronation, telling him to have nothing to do with beggars and lepers, and that 'He who made misery [is] wiser than thou,' before instructing him to 'put on the raiment that beseemeth a king'.

But the longest and most important stories in *A House of Pomegranates* are concerned with forbidden love and its tragic defeat. The sensitive young dwarf in 'The Birthday of the Infanta' harbours an impossible love for his young mistress, despite her haughty mockery and disdain for him, and he eventually dies of a broken heart, crushed by a sense that he is monstrous in the eyes of others. Similarly, the young fisherman in 'The Fisherman and His Soul' harbours an impossible love for the young mermaid

A House of Pomegranates (Osgood McIlvaine & Co., 1891), title page, designed by Charles Ricketts.

whom he catches in his net; and although he is willing to lose his soul and transgress every social edict to be with his beloved, declaring at one point that 'love is better than wisdom, and more precious than riches, and . . . fires cannot destroy it, nor can the waters quench it,' both he and the mermaid are destroyed by their love. Their burial in unconsecrated ground in the 'Field of the Fullers' anticipates Wilde's own burial in a pauper's grave beyond the city limits of Paris.[8]

Much of the latter story centres on the fisherman's battle with his own soul: he must relinquish his soul in order to claim the mermaid as his lover, and his efforts to rid himself of it foreshadow Dorian Gray's uneasy efforts to quieten conscience

Alastair [Hans Henning von Voigt], 'The Dancing Dwarf', frontispiece to *The Birthday of the Infanta* (Black Sun Press/Editions Narcisse, 1928).

and live according to a 'new Hedonism'. 'The Fisherman' was in fact a dress rehearsal for Wilde's only novel; he began composing it in late 1889 to satisfy a commission to write a story for *Lippincott's Monthly Magazine*, and he turned to the composition of *The Picture of Dorian Gray* only when he reached an impasse in composing the story he had originally intended to submit.

By the beginning of the 1890s Wilde's fiction was becoming increasingly provocative. That male same-sex desire was the real subject behind his stories of forbidden love would become clear from the panicky critical reaction to his final fiction, *The Picture of Dorian Gray*, condemned by British reviewers as 'unclean', 'leprous' and of 'medico-legal' interest on its publication in the summer of 1890. Five years later the novel was used in court, during Wilde's abortive libel suit against the Marquess of Queensberry, to prove that Wilde both promoted and practised 'sodomy'. But Wilde had already laid the groundwork for this reaction by writing 'The Portrait of Mr W. H.', his most candid and direct fictional representation of male same-sex love to date, published in *Blackwood's Magazine* in 1889 and begun as early as 1887. Wilde revised this story heavily following its publication and made repeated efforts to secure book publication for it, but it was never published in book format in his lifetime and is often overlooked today.

The reasons for the story's neglect today are not difficult to see. 'The Portrait of Mr W. H.' contains multiple narrative layers. The frame narrative – another conversation set in Wilde's own day between two Victorian bachelors, one of whom, at forty, is significantly older than the other – outwardly concerns the genesis and significance of the 'portrait' of the story's title, purportedly a portrait of the mysterious 'Mr W. H.' to whom the first edition of Shakespeare's sonnets was dedicated in 1609. As the older of the two bachelors, named Erskine, tells the younger (who is the unnamed narrator of the story), this 'portrait' had been deliberately faked years earlier by a third young man, Cyril Graham, now deceased, but a close friend of Erskine when he was alive, who had become convinced that 'Mr W. H.' was a young actor in Shakespeare's own theatre company named William

Hughes. Through close analysis of the sonnets themselves, Graham had inferred that Shakespeare had been in love with Hughes and had cryptically encoded Hughes's identity into the sonnets in the process of addressing them to him. But after rigorous searches in the historical archives, Graham had found no independent corroborating evidence of Hughes's existence, and as a result he had failed to convince his friend Erskine, who had insisted on the production of such evidence. As a result he had forged the portrait, pretending that it was a genuine Elizabethan article which he had fortuitously discovered in an old chest, in an effort to persuade his friend.

Both the present-day frame narrative and the story Erskine tells of his dead friend Graham's reasons for faking the portrait possess considerable interest in their own right, particularly once we perceive the unspoken relations of desire between the men who mediate the story of Shakespeare's love for Willie Hughes, as well as the fluctuations in belief to which two of them are subject. Considered as a fiction, the story suggests the unknowability of sexual orientation and identity at the same time as it represents the power of homosocial and homosexual desire. But at its core 'The Portrait of Mr W. H.' contains an argument about the obscure textual traces of love for another man that Shakespeare left and deliberately concealed in perhaps the greatest sonnet sequence ever written, and much of Wilde's story consists of a close textual exegesis and contextualization of Shakespeare's sonnets. Perhaps for this reason, the story – termed 'an essay in imaginative scholarship' by the *Publishers' Weekly* in 1895 – was for many years classed as an essay rather than a fiction. Indeed Wilde himself described the story as 'put[ting] forward an entirely new theory as to the identity of the mysterious Mr.

W. H. of the famous preface [to Shakespeare's sonnets]',[9] and at one point he suggested that it was 'too literary' for a collection of stories and belonged instead in a volume of 'essays and studies'.

'Mr W. H.' was widely noticed notwithstanding its publication in the pages of a magazine. Ignoring the fictional framework, many critics of Wilde's day understood it as a serious contribution to Shakespeare scholarship. In his 'witty and ingenious article . . . Mr. Oscar Wilde . . . is prepared to startle literature by a new explanation of Shakespere's [*sic*] Sonnets', declared the reviewer for *The Tablet*; 'omitting the surroundings in which the theory is encased, his conclusion is briefly that these strange and passionate poems addressed to Mr. W. H. were not written to Lord Pembroke, but to the boy actor for whom the great female parts of the plays were written.' 'Mr. Oscar Wilde, a serious student, has [a new] theory of Mr. W. H.,' declared Andrew Lang in a leading article in *The Daily News*; 'he is too sagacious to bring it out in a big volume, or even in an earnest hypothesis. He places it before the world and the readers of *Blackwood's Magazine* in a kind of apologue.' But a more ominous note was sounded by an unsigned notice in the *Scots Observer*, which pronounced the story 'out of place in [*Blackwood's*] or, indeed, in any popular magazine'. This led Wilde to complain privately to the *Scots Observer*'s editor that 'the Philistines in their vilest forms have seized on you.' The story 'gave [Wilde's] enemies for the first time the very weapon they wanted', later declared Wilde's friend and editor Frank Harris, whose own magazine, *The Fortnightly Review*, had declined to publish Wilde's story.

According to the scholar Horst Schroeder, only one other paper, *The World*, took exception to 'Mr W. H.' on moral or sexual grounds, and 'all the other papers saw no harm in the story.'[10]

If Harris exaggerates where 'Mr W. H.' alone is concerned, however, his judgement is borne out by the critical reaction to *The Picture of Dorian Gray*, on its appearance in the July 1890 number of *Lippincott's Monthly Magazine*. Wilde's only novel is on one level a refiguring of the Faust myth: a once-innocent man makes an evil, supernatural compact whereby he receives seemingly unlimited power and worldly pleasure in exchange for his soul. On another level it refigures the Narcissus myth: on seeing his handsome face in the portrait lovingly painted by Basil Hallward, the young Dorian Gray, realizing the full measure of his personal beauty for the first time, says he would give anything if he could trade places with his painted image and remain forever young while the image grows old in his stead. The ensuing chapters describe the outcome of this narcissistic Faustian pact. Answering only to the dictates of his own desire, Gray learns to relish the power and opportunity that eternal youth provides, not least an air of innocence and incorruptibility that prevents any suspicion of him as the perpetrator of increasingly questionable and criminal deeds. But at the same time, he loses his moral compass, becomes the subject of scandalous rumours and commits increasingly outrageous acts. He lives according to a 'New Hedonism', committed only to pleasure and a new 'spirituality' of the senses, treating crime or evil 'simply as a mode through which he could realize his conception of the beautiful'.

Filled with repartee and written in a decorative prose that arrests the senses, Wilde's only novel is a remarkable depiction of the aesthete's unsettling descent into decadence. In many ways, it embodies a full-blown assault on the Victorianism that preceded it, and the British press was outraged. 'Why go grubbing in muck-heaps?' began the *Scots Observer*'s review, continuing:

> The world is fair, and the proportion of healthy-minded men and women to those that are foul, fallen, or unnatural is great. Mr. Oscar Wilde has again been writing stuff that were better unwritten; and while *The Picture of Dorian Gray*, which he contributes to *Lippincott's*, is ingenious, interesting, full of cleverness, plainly the work of a man of letters, it is false art – for its interest is medico-legal; it is false to human nature – for its hero is a devil; it is false to morality – for it is not made sufficiently clear that the writer does not prefer a course of unnatural iniquity to a life of cleanliness, health and sanity. The story – which deals with matters only fitted for the Criminal Investigation Department or a hearing *in camera* [out of public scrutiny] – is discreditable alike to author and editor. Mr. Wilde has brains, and art, and style; but if he can write for none but outlawed noblemen and perverted telegraph boys, the sooner he takes to tailoring (or some other decent trade) the better for his own reputation and the public morals.

It was not just the absence of any explicit narrative condemnation of Dorian Gray that reviewers found shocking, or the suggestion, palpable in the closing chapters of the *Lippincott's* version, that Wilde endorsed Gray's actions and the 'New Hedonism' that drove them. As the reviewer's cryptic allusions to 'outlawed noblemen', 'perverted telegraph boys' and 'a hearing *in camera*' suggest, the novel stirred sexual and legal anxieties that had reached fever pitch some months earlier, in the winter of 1889–90, during the so-called Cleveland Street Scandal, when police discovered that a group of messenger boys employed by the Central Post Office were simultaneously working as prostitutes at a male brothel in London's Cleveland Street. The brothel catered to the sexual needs of predominantly aristocratic and well-connected clients, and the scandal consolidated a popular view of male homosexuality as an aristocratic and 'establishment' vice. Crucially, none of the brothel's aristocratic clients was successfully prosecuted in the ensuing scandal, although an arrest warrant was issued for Lord Arthur Somerset, the Queen's Equerry, who fled into exile on the European mainland. The press, perhaps rightly, sensed a cover-up.

These anxieties carried over into critical reactions to Wilde's novel, four months after the Cleveland Street Scandal's end. Reviewers' descriptions of the novel as 'unclean', 'unnatural', unhealthy and of 'medico-legal interest' are now easily recognized as paranoid expressions of homophobia. But it was Gray's relationships with the novel's older male characters to which British reviewers took special exception. When one reviewer called Wilde's novel 'a gloating study of the mental and physical corruption of a fresh, fair, and golden youth', he was specifically likening Dorian Gray to the young men – widely viewed as innocent victims or 'boys', although most of them were in their late teens – caught up in the Cleveland Street Scandal.

By this token, the real villain of Wilde's story was not its hero, Dorian Gray, but rather Lord Henry Wotton, the aristocrat who purportedly corrupts him, often said to be modelled on the notorious real-life homosexual (and Wilde's friend) Lord Ronald Gower, or perhaps the novel's Society painter Basil Hallward, said by some to be modelled on Frank Miles, whose lovingly painted portrait of Dorian Gray awakens his narcissism. For once again Wilde's central narrative is framed by a conversation between Victorian bachelors whose relations are more complex than they appear. And if the direct speech of Wotton and Hallward, like that of Erskine, Trevor and the unnamed narrator of 'Lady Alroy' before them, reveals only occasional hints of the desire they feel for the younger man, Wilde's narrative obligingly fills in certain blanks.

This is especially the case with the version of the novel Wilde originally submitted in typescript to *Lippincott's* in the spring of 1890, which was censored by its editor before publication so as to 'make it acceptable to the most fastidious taste'.[11] In the original typescript, Wilde's narrator tells us 'there was love in every line' of Hallward's portrait of Gray, 'and in every touch there was passion'. Similarly, he tells us, using a language of 'sterility' widely understood by Victorians as code for male same-sex desire, that there was 'something infinitely tragic in a romance that was at once so passionate and so sterile'.

But despite the editor's removal of these and other controversial passages, the version of the novel published in *Lippincott's* still outraged reviewers, as we have seen, leading W. H. Smith's to ban it from its railway bookstalls. If Wilde harboured hopes of republishing the novel as a freestanding book in its own right, he must have been alarmed when Ward Lock & Co., the British distributor of *Lippincott's* as well as publisher of the first book edition, told him some days after Smith's ban that his story had 'been characterized by the press as a filthy one', 'this is a serious matter to us' and 'We should be glad if you would give us a call.' Undoubtedly Ward Lock made it clear to Wilde that they would publish the novel in book form only if he muted its most sexually suggestive elements.

It was in this climate of legal and sexual paranoia that Wilde further censored his own novel as he prepared it for book publication, almost certainly because he and Ward Lock feared prosecution. In the longer 1891 version, Wilde greatly diminished the eroticism in Basil Hallward's professions to Dorian Gray, eliminating for instance Hallward's confession that he 'worshipped' Gray 'with far more romance of feeling than a friend should ever give to a friend', and he altered Hallward's 'worship' into something more innocuous, the painter's quest for a Platonic ideal in art. Perhaps fearing that he might be personally identified with the novel's protagonist (an identification that Wilde actively encouraged in private, telling one admirer 'Dorian [is] what I would like to be – in other ages, perhaps'), Wilde also altered the age at which Gray commences a life of unprecedented criminality, from 'the eve of his own thirty-second birthday', the age at which Wilde's affair with Ross had begun, to 'the eve of his own thirty-eighth birthday'. He also added new material to 'counteract any damage' done by the novel's publication in *Lippincott's*, as he put it to his future publisher, partly by acceding to the latter's suggestion that he make the ending more moralistic.[12] Some of the new material is highly entertaining, particularly three new scenes in which Lord Henry gives full rein to his witty repartee. But much of it is mawkish, incongruous or too hastily written to be convincing. Like the *Lippincott's* version that preceded it, the 1891 version of *The Picture of Dorian Gray* is a censored text, and many readers now find more satisfying the uncensored version based on the typescript that Wilde submitted to *Lippincott's*, first published in 2011.

But if Wilde was in 1891 forced to censor his own work and in no position to restore the cuts made by the novel's editor before first publication, he did not go quietly.[13] The greatest single addition made to the 1891 version is its Preface, first published separately in its own right in February 1891, and often reprinted separately today as Wilde's artistic manifesto. Here Wilde gathered over his own signature 25 aphorisms about the independence of art and artists from the judgements of wrong-headed critics who, like the townspeople with no understanding of the Happy Prince, 'find ugly meanings in beautiful things and are corrupt without being charming'. It is one of the most brilliant things Wilde wrote, as well as one of the greatest ever manifestos for artistic freedom: 'The artist can express everything', Wilde declares, and 'when critics disagree the artist is in accord with himself.' 'There is no such thing as a moral book. Books are well written, or badly written. That is all.' Wilfully paradoxical and witty, the Wilde of the Preface sounds a great deal like Lord Henry and the dandies who would people his Society comedies over the next few years. Indeed, the Preface sounds a death knell for Wilde's career as a writer of fiction even as it marks the beginning of a new career as an artist of the paradox that would culminate in 'Phrases and Philosophies for the Use of the Young', 'A Few Maxims for the Instruction of the Over-educated' and the paradoxical wit of his greatest comedy.

SIX

Paradox and Perversity: Wilde as a Subversive Thinker

What the paradox was to me in the sphere of thought, perversity became to me in the sphere of passion.

WILDE, *De profundis*, composed 1896–7

Wilde had long been famous for his epigrammatic wit, but even so, the paradoxes of the Preface to *The Picture of Dorian Gray* are remarkable for their militancy. Taken on their own terms, and as Wilde's personal signature beneath them indicates, they constitute the written manifesto for a radical Aestheticism: far from subordinating creativity to the purposes of representation or morality, as Victorian critics hitherto would have it, 'the artist is the creator of beautiful things.' And rather than embodying a form of self-expression on the part of the artist, the aim of any creative work must be 'to reveal art and conceal the artist'. For the value of the artwork lies not in what it *says*, but rather in its power of *affect*, and it presupposes the existence of a reader or critic who will 'translate into another manner or a new material his impression of beautiful things'. As the terms 'manner', 'material' and 'thing' indicate, even a play or a poem has an objective existence, inseparable from the form(s) in which it engages our senses. But it is by no means sufficient unto itself, for it exists in dialectical tension with readers or critics whom it brings into full being,[1] and indeed 'diversity of opinion about a work of art shows that the work is new, complex, and vital.' In all other respects, the artwork is defiantly 'useless'. It bears no direct relation to, and serves no direct purpose in, the world we presently inhabit. Its 'only excuse' is that 'one admires it intensely', and if it possesses meaning, its meaning is 'only Beauty'.

Understood in this way, the aphorisms of the Preface to *The Picture of Dorian Gray* bear a direct relation to other critical, wilfully paradoxical pieces that Wilde published around this time. They crystallize the principles of the 'new aesthetics' espoused by Vivian, one of two interlocutors (both named after Wilde's children) who feature in Wilde's witty critical dialogue 'The Decay of Lying', first published in the *Nineteenth Century* in January 1889. Here too we find the notions that 'the only beautiful things . . . are the things that do not concern us,' that 'the object of Art is not simple truth but complex beauty' and that 'when Art surrenders her imaginative medium she surrenders everything.' For art 'is a veil, rather than a mirror', Vivian argues, and 'finds her own perfection within, and not outside of, herself. She is not to be judged by any external standard of resemblance.' Far from holding a mirror up to life, the 'proper aim of Art' is 'Lying, the telling of beautiful untrue things'. It follows that 'Life imitates Art far more than Art imitates life,' Vivian maintains, since art provides us with forms through which we come to realize ourselves and understand what seems real: 'Things are because we see them, and what we see, and how we see it, depends on the Arts that have influenced us.'

The Preface to *Dorian Gray* also bears a direct relation to Wilde's witty two-part dialogue 'The Critic as Artist', first published under the title 'The True Function and Value of Criticism' in the summer of 1890. At 28,000 words, this dialogue is more wide-ranging than 'The Decay of Lying', but at its core it elaborates the parallels between fine criticism and artistry implicit in Wilde's aphorisms, 'The critic is he who can translate into another manner or a new material his impression of beautiful things' and 'those who find beautiful meanings in beautiful things are the cultivated.' In fact the antithesis between creativity and criticism is 'entirely arbitrary', asserts Gilbert, the more thoughtful and prolix of the dialogue's two interlocutors, since 'all fine imaginative work is self-conscious and deliberate' and 'without the critical faculty, there is no artistic creation at all.' For a similar reason criticism can legitimately be called a 'creative art', he says, for 'it works with materials, and puts them into a form that is at once new and delightful':

> Indeed, I would call criticism a creation within a creation. For just as the great artists, from Homer and Aeschylus, down to Shakespeare and Keats, did not go directly to life for their subject-matter, but sought for it in myth, and legend and ancient tale, so the critic deals with materials that others have, as it were, purified for him, and to which imaginative form and colour have been already added. Nay, more, I would say that the highest Criticism, being the purest form of personal impression, is in its way more creative than creation, as it has least reference to any standard external to itself, and is, in fact, its own reason for existing . . . It is more delightful than philosophy, as its subject is concrete and not abstract, real and not vague. It is the only civilized form of autobiography, as it deals not

> with the events, but with the thoughts of one's life, not with life's physical accidents of deed or circumstance, but with the spiritual moods and imaginative passions of the mind . . . [T]he critic, with his fine sense of distinction and sure instinct of delicate refinement, will prefer to look into the silver mirror or through the woven veil, and will turn his eyes away from the chaos and clamour of actual existence, though the mirror be tarnished and the veil be torn. His sole aim is to chronicle his own impressions. It is for him that pictures are painted, books written, and marble hewn into form.

Yet as the note of excess here suggests, Wilde does not expect us to take Gilbert's protestations at face value. After all, it is his more conventional interlocutor who is named 'Ernest', while Gilbert often seems borne away on the wings of his own rhetoric, and Ernest more than once brings Gilbert up short. As in 'The Decay of Lying', the form of the dialogue is at least as important as the ideas it contains. Indeed, when we attend to its form, it is by no means clear that Wilde's dialogue 'contains' ideas at all, if by 'contain' we understand 'hold together; keep under control, restrain, restrict, confine' (*Oxford English Dictionary*), so much as that it sports with ideas, unleashing them like fireworks in order to let them sparkle, dazzle and self-combust.

Like many of his fictions, Wilde's dialogues unfold as tête-à-tête conversations between two Victorian gentlemen, a form that begs (but leaves unresolved) the question of what sort of relationship exists between these men, and as Wilde writes elsewhere, 'recreation, not instruction, is the aim of conversation.' If in places the wiser of Wilde's two interlocutors appears to be set on convincing the other of what he does not know or understand, in others he elaborates his ideas to the point of excess or absurdity, with his tongue firmly in his cheek. The effect is unsettling, draining his ideas of their apparent wisdom and implying other, more obscure and personal purposes behind his utterances. (Tellingly, Gilbert says plaintively in 'The Critic as Artist' that while 'it is easy to convert others', it is 'so difficult to convert oneself'.) In 'The Decay of Lying', for instance, Vivian tells Cyril that life imitates art so completely that 'Japanese people are the deliberate creation of certain artists,' 'the whole of Japan is a pure invention' and even 'those wonderful brown fogs that come creeping down our streets' were invented by the Impressionists. Like Vivian's attempt to prove art's power over life by relating how a friend of his named Hyde accidentally found himself living out the opening scene of Robert Louis Stevenson's novella *Dr Jekyll and Mr Hyde*, such moments of absurdity and wit only emphasize the seductiveness of ideas as such, underscoring that Vivian's real motive is to provoke a marked reaction in his interlocutor.

Any truth claims that the interlocutors of Wilde's dialogues advance, moreover, are self-conscious effects of language and verbal style. The test of good writing, Wilde writes, is 'the spoken word in its musical and metrical relations' and the presence of a good voice. With their spellbinding rhetoric and countless quotable aperçus, Wilde's dialogues return ideas to the cut and thrust of live conversation, underscoring his claims elsewhere that conversation is an art and that what makes a good conversationalist is not 'gravity of demeanour' but 'the possession of a musical voice' as well as a willingness to 'direct the conversation into other channels'.[2] In 'The Critic as Artist', the dialogue becomes utterly self-conscious when Gilbert reflects on its history as a 'wonderful literary form' in which the 'thinker', from Plato to Lucian to Carlyle,

> can both reveal and conceal himself, and give form to every fancy, and reality to every mood. By its means he can exhibit the object from each point of view, and show it to us in the round, as a sculptor shows us things, gaining in this manner all the richness and reality of effect that comes from those side issues that are suddenly suggested by the central idea in its progress.

The dialogue form, in other words, is an intellectual theatre or workshop in which Wilde is the director or puppetmaster. We see this clearly and amusingly too in Ernest's self-reflexive comment that by means of dialogue, the thinker can also 'invent an imaginary antagonist, and convert him when he chooses by some absurdly sophistical argument'.

Ernest's candour crystallizes that we should understand Wilde's dialogues not as manifestos, treatises or essays, but as wilfully paradoxical and conversational forms whose absurdities, excesses and contradictions are at least as important as what Wilde's interlocutors 'say'. 'There will be many who take him seriously,' wrote Wilde's friend Richard Le Gallienne when reviewing *Intentions*, the 1891 collection into which Wilde gathered 'The Decay of Lying' and 'The Critic as Artist', 'but let me assure them that Mr. Wilde is not of their number.' Le Gallienne proposed that Wilde was essentially a humorist who wrote at the expense of those who take his ideas 'with such open mouth'. But humour wasn't the only end Wilde had in mind, for as the teasing title of *Intentions* seems to acknowledge, by adopting paradox and dialogue as leading principles, Wilde placed his own intentions out of his reader's reach. In all the pieces gathered into *Intentions*, Wilde is the consummate liar, dedicating himself to unsettling sincerity and truth, even truths about art, in order to make space for their subversive opposites. Truth is simply an effect of a superb style, Wilde holds, and 'To know the truth one must imagine myriads of falsehoods.'

That Wilde had by early 1891 become not merely a paradoxical thinker but a deeply subversive one becomes especially clear from 'Pen, Pencil, and Poison', Wilde's biographical account of the artist, writer, forger and murderer Thomas Griffiths Wainewright, first published in January 1889, as well as from the apparently straight-faced essay 'The Soul of Man under Socialism' that Wilde published in the *Fortnightly Review* in February 1891. If paradox and dialogue represent strategies for unsettling truth and sincerity in the name of their subversive opposites, these two pieces each give a familiar name to that opposite: crime and socialism.

Written in the form of a mock-biography, 'Pen, Pencil, and Poison' discusses Wainewright's secret life of crime in relation to his public life as an artist and writer in a way that drains the former of its moral repugnance, making it appear inseparable from Wainewright's creative legacy in art and prose. With its haughty but well-reasoned disdain for passing moral judgement on its subject, the memoir still has the capacity to shock. A prominent man of taste in 1820s London and the 'pioneer of Asiatic prose', Wainewright possessed 'an extremely artistic temperament', Wilde begins; he followed 'many masters other than art, being not merely a poet and a painter, an art critic and antiquarian and a writer of prose, an amateur of beautiful things and a dilettante of things beautiful'. Not the least of Wainewright's 'achievements', Wilde tells us with tongue firmly in cheek, was his remarkable work as a criminal, for he was 'also a forger of no mean or ordinary capabilities' and 'a subtle and secret poisoner almost without rival in this or any age'.

Wilde spends nearly three-quarters of 'Pen, Pencil, and Poison' eulogizing Wainewright as an important forerunner of himself – an artistic critic, consummate prose stylist, Aesthete and dandy. For instance, Wainewright possessed 'that curious love of green which in individuals . . . is always the sign of a subtle artistic temperament' and a conviction 'that Art's first appeal is . . . purely to the artistic temperament', while he realized early in life that 'it was quite easy . . . to make the public interested in his own personality.' However, Wilde admits early on that 'if we set aside [Wainewright's] achievements in the sphere of poison, what he has actually left to us hardly justifies his reputation,' and the core of Wilde's mock-memoir is the partly tongue-in-cheek discussion of Wainewright's criminal life that occupies the final quarter.

This discussion still startles for the lightness of tone with which Wilde memorializes breathtaking acts of forgery and murder, as well as the moral and aesthetic equivalence he draws between murder and creative expression: 'we must not forget that the cultivated young man who . . . was so susceptible to Wordsworthian influences was . . . one of the most subtle and secret poisoners of this or any age.' As our shocked reaction to this sentence registers, Wilde is not condoning murder in 'Pen, Pencil, and Poison'. Despite Wilde's concluding reflection that Wainewright 'is far too close to our own time for us to be able to form any purely artistic judgement about him', Wainewright (who died in 1847, seven years before Wilde's birth) had long ago become a figure of art and myth – he stands behind criminal heroes in Dickens and Dostoevsky, as Wilde points out – and Wilde was perfectly happy to accept the legend of 'Wainewright the murderer' that had developed even in Wainewright's own lifetime notwithstanding the lack of firm evidence against him. (Wilde was fully aware that Wainewright was never formally accused or convicted of murder – in Wilde's own words, that 'his murders . . . were more than were ever made known judicially.') Wainewright was for Wilde an unreal, mythic figure like Nero or Caesar Borgia, 'and nobody with the true historical sense ever dreams of blaming . . . or censuring' them. Such figures long ago became 'like the puppets of a play', Wilde maintains: 'They may fill us with terror, or horror, or wonder, but they do not harm us.'

Part of the humour of 'Pen, Pencil, and Poison' derives from seeing with what a straight face Wilde morphs from discussing Wainewright's writings and personal style to discussing his crimes in the same implacable tone. From the evident joy with which he relates Wainewright's purported reply when a friend questioned why he had murdered Helen Abercrombie ('Yes, it was a dreadful thing to do, but she had very thick ankles'), we would be forgiven for thinking that even Wilde accidentally drops the mask of seriousness on occasion, amused by his own detached demeanour and secretly shocked more than he lets on at Wainewright's apparent callousness. In this respect, the memoir demonstrates perfectly that if 'art is the only serious thing in the world, the artist is the only person who is never serious'.

And yet we should remember that 'nothing succeeds like excess' and the memoir is finally far more paradoxical than it seems. It ends with Wilde's immortal axioms: 'the fact of a man being a poisoner is nothing against his prose,' 'there is no essential incongruity between crime and culture' and 'we cannot rewrite the whole of history for the purpose of gratifying our moral sense.' The strong personal tone and style of these axioms is significant. If Wainewright the murderer is merely a puppet in history's 'play', Wilde is nonetheless serious in his admiration for Wainewright as a man of strong individual personality and art. Indeed Wilde's own life experiences to date corroborated his conviction that 'one can fancy an intense personality being created out of sin.' If we are shocked that Wainewright's 'crimes seem to have had an important effect upon his art' and gave a 'strong personality' to his later style, this is nonetheless true too of Wilde himself in the years when he acted on his criminal desires for other men. As would also be the case years later in *The Ballad of Reading Gaol*, the murderer is, in one sense at least, a symbolic reflection of Wilde himself. To view the artist as criminal and tie his artistic success to his criminality is to take a proper measure of the artist as subversive.

Subversion is written clearly in 'The Soul of Man under Socialism' too. 'The chief advantage that would result from the establishment of Socialism', Wilde begins, is 'the fact that Socialism would relieve us from that sordid necessity of living for others which, in the present condition of things, presses so hardly upon almost everybody'. With this one paradoxical sentence, Wilde undermines the central tenets of both the capitalist class system and the various collectivist political ideologies that had descended from the late eighteenth century into the writings of the Communists, Democratic Socialists and Fabians of Wilde's own day. The route to equality and justice, he implies, lies in recognizing and meeting the fundamental needs of oneself. Or, as he would put it rather differently in 1894, 'to love oneself is the beginning of a life-long romance.'

Could there be a more socially subversive principle than this elevation of the individual self? It comes as little surprise that Wilde quickly pivots to a critique of charity, philanthropy and 'the use of private property . . . to alleviate the horrible evils that result from . . . private property', on the grounds that charity 'degrades' and 'demoralises' (by which Wilde means deprives or vacuates the recipient of all moral responsibility) and thereby 'creates a multitude of sins'. (Wilde's phrasing here is a deliberate inversion of the words of the apostle Peter, that 'charity covers a multitude of sins' (1 Peter 4:8).) In place of acts of charity, Wilde calls for the overthrow of private property, the reconstruction of society on such a basis that poverty will be impossible, the redistribution of private property into public wealth and the substitution of co-operation for competition in order to 'ensure the well-being of each member of the community'. If such revolutionary aims appalled and alienated many of Wilde's bourgeois readers, they probably ingratiated him briefly with the small but growing number of socialist intellectuals in Britain, such as Henry Hyndman, the translator of Karl Marx and founder of England's first socialist party, who had argued in *England for All* (1881) that 'The day for private charity and galling patronage is at an end; the time for combination and political action in redress of social wrongs is at hand.' Hyndman might well have been sympathetic too to Wilde's defence of the poor man's discontent and his insistence that stealing is finer than begging or than gratefully receiving 'the crumbs that fall from the rich man's table', as well as Wilde's revolutionary assertions that 'disobedience . . . is man's original virtue' and 'man should not be ready to show that he can live like a badly fed animal.' But what must Hyndman and other socialist intellectuals have made of Wilde's insistence that 'something more' than 'Socialism, Communism, or whatever one chooses to call it' was needed and that 'for the full development of Life to its highest mode of perfection . . . [w]hat is needed is Individualism'?

Authoritarian socialism would not do, Wilde argued, since 'if there are Governments armed with economic power as they are now with political power; if, in a word, we are to have Industrial Tyrannies, then the last state of man will be worse than the first.' 'I confess that many of the socialistic views that I have come across seem to me to be tainted with ideas of authority,' he explained, 'if not of actual compulsion. Of course, authority and compulsion are out of the question. All association must be quite voluntary. It is only in voluntary associations that man is fine.' The innate dignity and personality of the individual are paramount, and rather than the establishment of a centralized government, what is needed is conditions that will enable individualism to be 'far freer, far finer, and far more intensified than it is now' – conditions under which each citizen might 'freely develop what is wonderful, and fascinating, and delightful in him' and thereby experience 'the true pleasure and joy of living'.

In this undermining of socialist orthodoxy no less than in Wilde's resistance to the urgings of private property and the class system, the iconoclasm of 'The Soul of Man under Socialism' comes into view. By insisting that each citizen experience the pleasure and joy of living, Wilde subverts political orthodoxy on both the left and the right by making artistic, bodily and intellectual self-fulfillment the main aim of life. In fact Wilde's argument is foreshadowed in the writings of William Morris, as well as in Marx's theory of the worker alienated from the products of his own labour.[3] More to the point, he is insisting on aesthetic principles that he had formulated as early as 1882 in his American lectures, with the difference that he now articulates them in the language of political and human rights as well. Only with the abolition of private property will the 'perfect man' develop, 'one who is not wounded, or worried, or maimed, or in danger'. What Wilde terms the 'true personality' or 'soul' of man will then ripen and

> grow naturally and simply, flowerlike . . . It will never argue or dispute. It will not prove things, it will know everything. And yet it will not busy itself about knowledge. It will have wisdom. Its value will not be measured by material things. It will have nothing, and yet it will have everything, and whatever one takes from it, it will still have, so rich it will be . . . It will be as wonderful as the personality of a child.

It is not merely the child who is a symbol of the liberated 'soul' under socialism. Another important symbol is the figure of Christ, Wilde says, whose secret or 'message' was 'simply "Be Thyself"'. In Wilde's rendering of him, Christ is a saviour not because he redeemed humankind from its sins, but because he lifted his subjects out of servitude and subjection, insisting to each of them:

> You have a wonderful personality. Develop it. Be yourself. Don't imagine that your perfection lies in accumulating or possessing external things. Your perfection is inside of

> you . . . You should give up private property. It hinders you from realizing your perfection. It is a drag upon you. It is a burden. Your personality does not need it. It is within you, and not outside of you, that you will find what you really are, and what you really want.

Christ teaches that we must resist any form of authority beyond ourselves, Wilde argues, and

> he who would lead a Christ-like life is he who is perfectly and absolutely himself. He may be a great poet, or a great man of science; or a young student at a University, or one who watches sheep upon a moor; or a maker of dramas, like Shakespeare, or a thinker about God, like Spinoza; or a child who plays in a garden, or a fisherman who throws his net into the sea. It does not matter what he is, as long as he realizes the perfection of the soul that is within him.

Although Wilde here equates the perfection of the poet with others who are 'perfectly and absolutely themselves', he sees the artist as a special case.[4] Unlike other figures, the artist is in more or less constant conflict with public opinion, especially as expressed by reviewers and cultural commentators in the popular press. Partly for this reason, 'Art is the most intense mode of Individualism that the world has known.' The idea that a philosopher or scientist should forebear from disturbing popular opinion would in modern times elicit only smiles, Wilde insists (although he concedes that 'it is really a very few years since both philosophy and science were subjected to brutal popular control'). By contrast, 'the public try to exercise over [art] an authority that is as immoral as it is ridiculous,' especially where the novel and the drama are concerned. In these genres, public taste – asserted not merely in the press, but also by timorous editors, publishers, libraries, licensing bodies and other authorities who might claim to have the artist's interests at heart – impedes art's development, forcing the artist either to 'do violence to his temperament' and so compromise his work, or else to live in conflict with the world of which he is a part.

Wilde could not have foreseen how these ideas would be corroborated by the treatment afforded his play *Salome* in 1892, when it was banned from theatrical performance by the Examiner of Plays. The ban prompted him briefly to contemplate leaving England and taking up residence permanently in France henceforth; and a year after it came into effect, the *Times* newspaper, taking its cue from the Censor, greeted the play's publication as a book by calling it 'an arrangement in blood and ferocity, morbid, bizarre, repulsive, and very offensive'. But Wilde was not alone in decrying what he called 'the force of public opinion' when it came to the modern novel.[5] Indeed he need only have looked for corroboration to the treatment of *The Picture of Dorian Gray* in the British press and by the editor of the magazine in which it first appeared. The artist who remained true to his principles was an avant-garde figure, in permanent conflict with the public as well as with those institutions through which the public made its influence felt. Indeed 'an artist in England gains something by being attacked,' Wilde maintained, so much so that if he were to produce work that was understood publicly as 'quite intelligible and highly moral', he would 'begin seriously to question whether in its creation he had really been himself at all, and consequently whether the work was not quite unworthy of him'.

We would be misguided, however, to take Wilde's assertions of the artist's subversiveness and disinterestedness entirely at face value. Although built around the paradox that socialism would enable individualism to flourish, 'The Soul of Man' is in other respects among the least ironic of Wilde's prose writings, and it is hard to shake the suspicion that, like the Preface to *Dorian Gray*, those parts of it dealing with the artist's iconoclasm and the tyranny of public opinion were written with sincerity in the heat generated by the press attacks on Wilde and *The Picture of Dorian Gray* in the summer of 1890. Indeed, anticipating the line he would take in 'The Soul of Man' eight months later, Wilde had protested 'most strongly' as early as June 1890, to the editor of the *St James's Gazette*, against the suggestion that 'the Government of a country should suggest a censorship over imaginative literature.' Faced with the possibility of being prosecuted for writing the novel, Wilde possessed strategic and legal reasons for stressing the artist's dedication to his art and independence from public opinion. He might well insist publicly that the artist 'stands outside his subject' and 'expresses everything'. But as his censorious cuts for the 1891 version of *Dorian Gray* indicate, it had been necessary to concede ground to the 'tyranny' of the novel's earliest critics. Wilde's high-handed Preface to the 1891 version of the novel notwithstanding, it remains the case that the 1890 serial version (and still more the uncensored typescript on which it was based) represents same-sex desire between men more openly than the longer version – and more openly than any other popular novel of the nineteenth century.

We should be sceptical too about Wilde's public protestations against the 'unpardonable crime' of 'confus[ing] the artist with his subject-matter'.[6] Some years after writing *The Picture of*

Dorian Gray, Wilde confessed privately to a young male correspondent (whom he was conceivably wooing) that there was far more of himself in the work than he had let the public know:

> I am so glad you like that strange coloured book of mine: it contains much of me in it. Basil Hallward is what I think I am: Lord Henry what the world thinks me; Dorian what I would like to be – in other ages, perhaps.[7]

While the world at large might think Wilde to be a harmless, charming spinner of paradoxes, Hallward's desire for Dorian Gray was, for Wilde personally, an expression of his own desire for younger men; and in other ages Wilde would be free to forge a new spirit from a liberation of his own senses. If 'art's aim' is to 'reveal art', we must remember, it is simultaneously to 'conceal the artist'. And in Wilde's case, there was much to conceal.

This belated and private confession of a biographical motive behind *Dorian Gray* relates to remarks Wilde made later in life about how a personal note, as well as an equivocal recognition of pain and suffering, runs through many of his writings. Looking back on his career from his jail cell in 1897, he writes in *De profundis* that a 'note of Doom' runs 'like a purple thread . . . through the gold cloth of *Dorian Gray*', while 'in "The Critic as Artist" it is set forth in many colours' and 'in *The Soul of Man* it is written down simply and in letters too easy to read.' He is implying, of course, that there is far more to his past writings than meets the eye – some 'foreshadowing' and 'prefigurement' of the terrible situation in which he now found himself, as he puts it. Elsewhere in *De profundis* he links this personal note directly with his pursuit of homosexual pleasure, saying that 'what the paradox was to me in the sphere of thought, perversity became to me in the sphere of passion.' We would be going too far if we used this remark to see Wilde's cultivation of paradox as a simple 'expression' of his 'perversity', but Wilde's analogy between paradox and 'perversity . . . of passion' is nonetheless telling. As the scholar Jonathan Dollimore remarks, Wilde's paradoxes and dialogues on art express 'a transgressive desire which makes its opposition felt as a disruptive reaction upon, and inversion of, the categories of subjective depth which hold in place the dominant order which proscribes that desire'.[8] Or, as Wilde's contemporary Ernest Newman put it more simply, 'A paradox is simply a truth of the minority, just as a commonplace is the truth of the majority.'[9]

Perhaps the clearest articulations of Wilde's subversive aesthetics can be seen finally not in his paradoxes and dialogues about art, but in the oft-overlooked 'phrases and philosophies' and maxims that he published quietly in late 1894, around the time he was putting the finishing touches to *The Importance of Being Earnest*. The subversive and counter-cultural ambitions of these paradoxes are clear from their full titles: 'A Few Maxims for the Instruction of the Over-educated' and 'Phrases and Philosophies for the Use of the Young' – or at least they are clear once we have read Wilde's aphorisms themselves. In both cases, Wilde's aphorisms run counter to all conventional notions of education and 'use', openly flaunting that (as the first aphorism of 'A Few Maxims' puts it) 'nothing that is worth knowing can be taught.' Still, Wilde's attack on the dominant order is as clear as his attempt to inscribe a transgressive desire: 'public opinion exists only where there are no ideas'; 'the English are always degrading truths into facts'; 'the only link between Literature and the Drama left to us in England . . . is the bill of the play'; 'the only thing that can console one for being poor is extravagance' ('A Few Maxims'); 'wickedness is a myth invented by good people to account for the curious attractiveness of others'; 'if the poor only had profiles there would be no difficulty in solving the problem of poverty'; 'the condition of perfection is idleness: the aim of perfection is youth'; 'There is something tragic about the enormous number of young men . . . in England . . . who start life with perfect profiles and end by adopting some useful profession' ('Phrases and Philosophies'). While 'A Few Maxims' was published in the reputable *Saturday Review*, edited by the iconoclastic Frank Harris – who as editor of *Fortnightly Review* had previously published 'Pen, Pencil, and Poison', the Preface to *Dorian Gray* and 'The Soul of Man under Socialism' – 'Phrases and Philosophies' was published in the only issue of a little-known undergraduate periodical titled *The Chameleon* alongside subversive homosexual writings by John Gambril Nicholson, John Francis Bloxam and Lord Alfred Douglas. When pressed in court in 1895 on his association with this magazine, Wilde tried to distance himself from it. But it should come as no surprise to modern readers that 'Phrases and Philosophies' was associated in court with the militant homosexuality of Bloxam's and Douglas's contributions, or that Wilde's assertions under oath that he had written his paradoxes with no intention other than to 'produce literature' and 'stimulate thought' fell on deaf ears.[10] No less than 'Pen, Pencil, and Poison' or 'The Soul of Man under Socialism', 'Phrases and Philosophies' was a perfect encapsulation of Wilde as a subversive thinker.

SEVEN

Drama as a Mode of Personal Expression

I took the drama, the most objective form known to art, and made it as personal a mode of expression as the lyric or the sonnet.

WILDE, *De profundis*, composed 1896–7

The year 1891 has been called Wilde's *annus mirabilis* or 'amazing year'. In April *Dorian Gray* appeared in book form, followed in May by *Intentions*, the first of three books by Wilde to appear that year from Osgood, McIlvaine, & Co., a new publishing firm founded by two Americans keen to make a mark by repackaging in book form the best of what Wilde had recently published in the press. *Intentions* was followed in July and November respectively by *Lord Arthur Savile's Crime and Other Stories* and *A House of Pomegranates*, the latter containing revised versions of 'The Young King' and 'The Birthday of the Little Princess' (now retitled 'The Birthday of the Infanta') along with two new stories, 'The Fisherman and His Soul' and 'The Star-Child'.

Even as he was putting the finishing touches to these publications, Wilde was making plans to return to playwriting. The actor George Alexander had read *Dorian Gray* admiringly and, after leasing the St James's Theatre with a view to producing as well as acting in plays by English authors suited for Society audiences, he approached Wilde for a play. By the late summer of 1891 – having marvelled in April at the first English production of Ibsen's *Hedda Gabler*, a play which he likened to a Greek tragedy – Wilde had finished the commission. 'For the past twelve years, we have been entertaining a dramatist unawares,' remarked Alexander, 'when he ought, on the contrary, to have been entertaining us.'

Lady Windermere's Fan was the first of four hugely successful Society comedies that Wilde was to write for the London stage over the next three and a half years. As Peter Raby remarks, 'Wilde, with one eye on the dramatic genius of Ibsen and the other on the commercial competition in London's West End, targeted his audience with adroit precision.'[1] 'One of the most elegant audiences that ever gathered at a West End premiere received [Wilde's play] with enthusiasm', the theatre historian W. Macqueen-Pope tells us, and 'soon the first-night flutter filled the town, extended to the suburbs, and far beyond.'[2] Like its successors, *Lady Windermere's Fan* owes much of its plot and melodrama to the 'well-made' plays of France, as well as such now-forgotten English melodramas as Hadden Chambers's *The Idler*, and it is not insignificant that upon completing it Wilde immediately set about attempting to get the play translated and staged in Paris. At the same time, it transcends its formal limitations and is a distinctly Wildean production, filled with Wilde's trademark paradoxes and repartee. 'If we have had more sparkling dialogue on the stage in the present generation, I have not heard it,' declared the critic A. B. Walkley; the play 'carries you along' and 'the man or woman who does not chuckle with delight . . . should consult a physician.'[3]

If the play seems designed to entertain and flatter Society audiences, beneath its witty dialogue Wilde's contempt for the English aristocracy is writ large. The play relentlessly exposes the hypocrisy and vacuity at the heart of English Society in Wilde's day, especially in matters to do with gender and sexuality. Its emphasis on women as victims of a sexual double standard, by which male sexual behaviour outside marriage is granted a licence denied to women, as well as its critique of the ideology of sexual purity on which Victorian notions about femininity were built, marks a radical departure for Wilde. For the heroine of the play is a woman, Mrs Erlynne, the lineal descendent of Wilde's 'Lady Alroy', who finds through bitter experience that 'a heart doesn't suit' her, that 'what consoles one . . . is not repentance but pleasure' and that 'besides, if a woman really repents, she has to go to a bad dressmaker . . . And nothing in the world would induce me to do that.' Women were the gatekeepers of English Society in Wilde's day, the play shows, inviting only those whom they chose into the salons and ballrooms that constituted the precincts of respectability. But even women opposed to the sexual double standard could be ideologues for their sex's confinement to a narrow domesticity, he suggests: 'I will have no one in my house about whom there is any scandal,' innocently remarks Lady Windermere early on. As her own marriage demonstrates, even the angel in the house has a demon within her, and the play argues forcefully that

> there is the same world for all of us, and good and evil, sin and innocence, go through it hand in hand. To shut one's eyes to half of life that one may live securely is as though one blinded oneself that one might walk with more safety in a land of pit and precipice.

Originally titled *A Good Woman*, a title that applies equally to Lady Windermere and to Mrs Erlynne, the real heroine, *Lady Windermere's Fan* transvalues Victorian notions of femininity, good and bad in order to show that, as Lady Windermere puts it, 'what are called good women may have terrible things in them' while 'bad women, as they are termed, may have in them sorrow, repentance, pity, sacrifice.' More broadly, it shows that the unrealistic values of English society in Wilde's day were in conflict with the needs of the modern individual, especially women, with the result that society tolerated and protected male sexual predators such as Lord Darlington at the expense of women such as Mrs Erlynne, who is polyamorous, witty, accomplished, intelligent and abundantly kind. The latter is a woman with 'a character as yet untouched in literature', Wilde proudly proclaimed – 'perfectly and absolutely herself', as he might once have said – but she cannot be confined by the institution of marriage and she ends the play an exile.

Wilde sustained and enriched this biting assessment of the English ruling class in his next three Society comedies, culminating in the withering comic critique of *The Importance of Being Earnest*. *A Woman of No Importance* and *An Ideal Husband* again attack the sexual double standard and extend Wilde's criticism of marriage as a form of confinement for women, while simultaneously criticizing the puritanism that would deny women sexual agency. Both plays also deepen a critique of the Victorian patriarchy – the oligarchy of parliamentarians, government ministers, landed peers and Anglican Church officials who preside over a sexually unequal society – that Wilde had begun in *Lady Windermere's Fan*, and as in the earlier play it is women who take centre stage. Hester Worsley and Mrs Arbuthnot in *A Woman of*

No Importance are ground-breaking women morally and socially, while the powerful, cynical and predatory Lord Illingworth, for all his wit and repartee, is shown to be 'a man of no importance'. Into the mouth of the American Hester Worsley Wilde places his most direct and outspoken critique of the English ruling class – 'you rich people in England . . . don't know how you are living,' she says angrily, 'you shut out from society the gentle and the good. You laugh at the simple and the pure. Living, as you all do, on others and by them, you sneer at self-sacrifice, and if you throw bread to the poor, it is merely to keep them quiet for a season. With all your pomp and wealth and art you don't know how to live' – and it is not insignificant that *A Woman of No Importance* culminates with its most heroic characters on the point of leaving England in search of 'better, wiser, and less unjust lands'.

Yet for all the sharp moral critique contained in Wilde's social comedies, it was impossible for early audiences not to come away from them entertained and amused, as Walkley observed. Wilde seemed to 'turn the theater into a drawing room', the critic Regenia Gagnier remarks, putting his audience at ease by insisting on stage sets and costumes that directly reflected the latest fashions as well as the luxurious interiors of the theatres in which the plays were performed.[4] (The furniture on stage could be bought from Frank Giles & Co. of Kensington, the programme for *The Importance of Being Earnest* informed audiences.) Moreover, the plays are so brilliantly constructed and executed that, as with Wilde's dialogues, they inevitably raise questions about his intentions. Does their author seriously mean the social criticism they contain?, we feel compelled to ask. Or does he flatter his audience's intelligence and vanity in order to give his aspirations to write a popular and entertaining play the veneer of intellectual respectability? For plays so loaded with critique of the English moneyed classes, it is not irrelevant that Wilde and his producers made a small fortune from them and that they are now classics of the English theatrical repertoire. Wilde might well have said of them, as he writes at the end of 'The Truth of Masks':

> Not that I agree with everything that I have said . . . There is much with which I entirely disagree . . . For in art there is no such thing as a universal truth. A Truth in art is that whose contradictory is also true.

This doubleness is perhaps clearest in the case of Wilde's final and most brilliant social comedy, *The Importance of Being Earnest*, whose title alone highlights how impossible it is to take Wilde seriously. As with his previous plays, the fashionable first-night audience included highly placed aristocrats and politicians, many of whom Wilde had met socially. Yet none of his plays so sharply and relentlessly highlights the power and stupidity of both the English aristocracy and the Anglican Church, as well as the gross over-importance attached to money, respectability and material possessions, and the hollowness of aristocratic marriage rituals. The Swedish sociologist Thorstein Veblen, originator of the concepts 'conspicuous leisure' and 'conspicuous consumption',[5] might have found much to admire in Wilde's play – as might the early English feminist Mary Wollstonecraft – so relentless is Wilde's critique of the Victorian leisure class, the fetishism of expensive possessions and marriage as a kind of commodity market.

And yet, as the *New York Times* informed its readers, never had been 'heard such unrestrained incessant laughter from all parts of the theatre' on the opening night. As its subtitle proclaims, the play is a 'trivial comedy for serious people', and in our own time it is a byword for farcical comedy and wit. There is virtually no social value prized by the Victorian elite that the play doesn't expose, hilariously, to be hollow and meaningless. And where Wilde's earlier social comedies allow room for emotion and sentiment, this play's characters live entirely according to the dictates of art and convention, unmoored to reality, so much so that they themselves seem wholly artificial or fictive entities. Algernon and Jack in *The Importance of Being Earnest* may not be poets in the narrow sense, but no less than the writers and painters Vivian admires in 'The Decay of Lying', they dedicate themselves to the telling of 'beautiful untrue things' only to find that their fictions become the reality according to which they and others live. Along with its farcical plot, the play's witticisms are now legendary: 'If I am occasionally a little over-dressed, I make up for it by being always immensely over-educated'; 'I hate people who aren't serious about meals. It is so shallow of them'; 'the amount of women in London who flirt with their own husbands is simply scandalous'; 'modern culture . . . isn't the sort of thing one should talk of in private'; 'we have already missed five if not six trains – to miss any more might expose us to comment on the platform.'

The apparent contradictions within *The Importance of Being Earnest* between the elements of entertainment, wit and social and moral critique have fascinated audiences and scholars alike. Regenia Gagnier suggests that the play operates on three levels simultaneously: Wilde offers his opening-night audience an outwardly reassuring mirror-reflection of itself while subtly criticizing the governing rituals and values of that audience, and at the same time allowing that audience to feel superior to the action through laughter. By inviting his audience to see the play's action as 'trivial comedy', Wilde masks or makes palatable his all-too-accurate 'self-portrait of power' and offers up instead a 'spectacle' of the 'existing order's uninterrupted discourse about itself'.[6]

Wilde's social comedies, then, are finally as paradoxical as the essays and dialogues of *Intentions*; and in *The Importance of Being Earnest* he shows that daily life imitates art more wholly than we recognize when we limit art narrowly to what exists in a gallery or within the pages of a book. In these respects, Wilde's comedies well deserve their author's judgement, in *De profundis*, that they are 'as personal a mode of expression' as any sonnet or lyric poem. They are distinctly Wildean inventions. More than in the annals of drama, their true literary precedents are to be found within Wilde's own literary oeuvre, in 'Lord Arthur Savile's Crime', 'Pen, Pencil, and Poison', 'The Soul of Man under Socialism', 'The Decay of Lying' and *The Picture of Dorian Gray*.

In describing his plays as a 'personal mode of expression', however, Wilde meant more than that his plays manifest a paradoxical style or set of intellectual preoccupations similar to those found in his non-dramatic prose. One striking feature of Wilde's social comedies to which modern audiences are especially sensitive is his concern with the performance of gender, as well as his challenge to traditional concepts of sexuality. Wilde is no essentialist about such things. His plays approach gender as a matter of displaying and inhabiting conventional *signs* rather than one of biological essence. Thus Mrs Erlynne and Mrs Cheveley appear 'unwomanly' to more conventional women because they refuse to conform to accepted notions of femininity, just as Lord Goring appears 'damaged' in the eyes of his own father because he has no interest in acquiring a wife. In *The Importance of Being Earnest* the play's four young lovers are 'androgynes of manners', to employ the critic Camille Paglia's useful phrase, inhabitants of a world narrowly circumscribed by the drawing room, whose genders and sexuality are indeterminate and even sexless from conventional standpoints. The world of the androgyne of manners is effectively 'an abstract circle', writes Paglia, 'in which male and female, like mathematical ciphers, are equal and interchangeable' and 'personality becomes a sexually undifferentiated mask.'[7] Thus the male becomes 'feminine in his careless, lounging passivity, the female masculine in her brilliant, aggressive wit', each seeming to possess 'the profane sleekness of chic'. Paglia's observations help explain why in our own day *The Importance of Being Earnest* is so frequently performed in cross-dress. As Wilde himself had written shortly before the play's composition, 'of all the motives of dramatic curiosity used by our great playwrights, there is none more subtle or more fascinating than the ambiguity of the sexes.'[8]

Such ambiguity is especially marked in the case of Algernon Moncrieff, who embodies a fluid, unstable concept of masculinity. For much of Act One of *The Importance of Being Earnest*, he berates his friend Jack Worthing for his attention to women, and he is a man who 'neglects his domestic duties', to employ Gwendolen's phrase, and becomes 'attractive' and 'painfully effeminate' as a result. In his elaborate dandyism, sartorial elegance and verbatim echoes of Wilde's own bon mots, he incarnates elements of Wilde himself. Moncrieff is perhaps the ultimate expression of a figure who dominates the dramatic universe of Wilde's comedies: the droll, well-dressed, epicene commentator on the foibles of his age. As Terence Brown observes, in each of his comedies Wilde invests a good deal of authority in this figure, whose 'languid, sardonic worldly knowingness . . . implies an observational, superior status to the other characters . . . and to the social order in which they function'. In his earlier comedies, Wilde had seemed uncertain about the status or function of this figure in the world of which he is a part. In *The Importance of Being Earnest*, however, the dandy's self-possession 'becomes the wonderfully controlled, self-possessed artifice of the whole dramatic production', the expression of a world 'where paradox rules from an unassailable vantage point in the consistently epigrammatic scintillation of [the play's] dialogue'.[9]

The Importance of Being Earnest relates to Wilde personally in other ways too. The play is preoccupied with the dichotomy between public and personal identity – '[I am] Ernest in town and Jack in the country,' the seemingly upstanding Jack declares – and in the historical wake of Wilde's criminal trials, it is difficult not to read the play as an encoded representation of Wilde's reckless secret life as a lover of men. The business of 'Bunburying' – and indeed the very term 'Bunbury' – has excited a deal of critical comment. The term is a neologism coined by Wilde in the persona of Algernon to denote the deliberate creation of an elaborate fiction as a pretext for avoiding social or familial duties and pursuing a secret life of pleasure instead: Algernon tells Jack that 'I have invented an invaluable permanent invalid called Bunbury in order that I may go down into the country whenever I choose.' And when Jack tells Algernon that he is 'Ernest in town and Jack in the country', Algernon accurately tells him that he is 'one of the most advanced Bunburyists I know'. Whether scholars of our own day are correct in surmising that 'Bunbury' is Wilde's way of encoding a furtive meeting at Sunbury with a schoolboy who once entered his train at Banbury, or even 'a collection of signifiers that straightforwardly express their desire to *bury in the bun*', is matter for conjecture.[10] But without doubt Wilde's witty neologism means the pursuit of secret and surreptitious pleasures while simultaneously suggesting a form of behaviour or way of life undertaken with flagrant and self-conscious disregard for social rules and conventions.

Given the elaborate subterfuges forced upon Wilde and other homosexual men in the wake of the 1885 Criminal Law Amendment Act, it is difficult in hindsight not to see Bunburying as an encoded expression of Wilde's own secret homosexual life. As we shall see, Wilde went to considerable pains to disguise from his wife and family the real reasons for his long absences from home, absences often spent dining and bedding a series of male sexual partners in London's West End. One scholar even describes the 'farcical interludes' in the family's holiday in the summer of 1894, precisely when Wilde set about composing *The Importance of Being Earnest* – interludes in which Wilde briefly abandoned his family (and his new play's composition) in order to 'amuse himself' with a local boy – as 'Bunburying-in-earnest' and 'juggling his several lives'.[11] The play encodes its author's own life in other ways as well – for instance, in Algernon's numerous confessions of distaste for married life ('If ever I get married, I'll certainly try to forget the fact'), in its echoes of Wilde's own courtship of his wife, and in the precise location of Jack/Ernest's London flat, 'E4 The Albany' (altered to 'B4 The Albany' for the first edition, possibly for legal reasons). The latter was the real-life address of Wilde's friend the secretive homosexual activist George Ives, in whose rooms Wilde met John Francis Bloxam, the editor of *The Chameleon*, around the time he was composing the play. Like the term Bunbury, the reference to Ives's flat in the Albany, an apartment building for bachelors near Piccadilly with a racy reputation by Wilde's day, reinforces our sense that the play is a highly coded text whose insouciant public face masks private meanings to which the majority are denied access.

There is one further respect in which Wilde 'took the drama . . . and made it as personal a mode of expression as the lyric or the sonnet'. The plays I have been discussing so far, all comedies, were designed to be popular and thoroughly modern. Their opening stage directions specify that they are set in the present day in a location that is recognizably London's fashionable West End. As we have seen, they were written with an eye to conforming (or seeming to conform) to popular theatrical conventions, as well as appealing to well-heeled, fashionable West End audiences. But around the time he finished *Lady Windermere's Fan* in October 1891, Wilde commenced writing an entirely different kind of play, based on the biblical legend of Salome. The story of how Salome danced for Herod's pleasure and, at her mother's instigation, demanded the head of John the Baptist as payment had long fascinated French artists and writers. It features prominently in works by Stéphane Mallarmé, Joris-Karl Huysmans and Gustave Flaubert, as well as the painter Gustave Moreau, and by 1891 Salome had become an icon or ideal of avant-garde French art and literature. Wilde's play was to be written entirely in French, and it was to be first published and staged in Paris too. Far from being a 'performable' play for a popular audience, this was to be a highly 'artistic' Symbolist drama, possibly for production at Paul Fort's Théâtre d'Art, a small avant-garde theatre rapidly developing a reputation as the home of Symbolist drama.[12] Much of the play was written during a two-month sojourn at the end of 1891 in Paris, where Wilde was lionized as the author of *Dorian Gray* and fraternized with many leading French writers and theatre directors. Contemporary French writing 'is in the direction of a richer Romanticism,' he declared, 'with subtleties of new colour and strange music and extended subject-matter'.[13] He received assistance when writing the original French version of *Salome*, on points of language at least, from a number of young writers operating in Mallarmé's orbit, and it is hard to escape the conclusion that Wilde wrote the play partly with the intention of remaking himself into a French Symbolist writer.

Yet if *Salome* owes debts to works of French Symbolism and Decadence, it is no less a distinctly Wildean production than *The Importance of Being Earnest*. As mentioned previously, performances of the play were banned in England when the Censor, in 1892, refused a stage licence while rehearsals for the first production were already underway with Sarah Bernhardt in the leading role. Some copies of the first edition (in French) of 1893 were sold and distributed in London, but the English quickly came to know the play by reputation, especially after Wilde licensed the publication in 1894 of an English version translated by his lover Lord Alfred Douglas and 'pictured' by Aubrey Beardsley. (Douglas did not translate the play alone; dissatisfied with his lover's earliest efforts, Wilde almost certainly had a hand in the production of the English text as eventually published.[14]) The play is unapologetic and direct in its representation of taboo and perverse desire – of the lascivious Herod for his

SALOME

A TRAGEDY IN ONE ACT: TRANSLATED FROM THE FRENCH OF OSCAR WILDE: PICTURED BY AUBREY BEARDSLEY

LONDON: ELKIN MATHEWS & JOHN LANE
BOSTON: COPELAND & DAY
1894

Salome, A Tragedy in One Act . . . Pictured by Aubrey Beardsley (Elkin Mathews & John Lane, 1894), frontispiece and title page by Aubrey Beardsley.

young step-daughter, and still more of Salome for the body, voice and mouth of the prophet Iokanaan – and in this respect it is a lineal descendant of 'The Sphinx', 'The Birthday of the Infanta', 'The Fisherman and His Soul' and *The Picture of Dorian Gray.*

In its form as a printed book, moreover, the first English edition of the play became an object of desire itself, with Beardsley's wonderful, weirdly erotic and sensuous illustrations exerting a strong fascination on the reader even as they set out to shock and repulse. Wilde knew that Beardsley's involvement in the printed book, which extended to cover design and title page in addition to the 'pictures' interspersed with Wilde's and Douglas's text, would mean that the play could still be a sensual spectacle notwithstanding the stage ban. And if the resulting book did not conform exactly with the scheme that Wilde had personally mapped out with the designer Charles Ricketts for the first stage production, it nevertheless went beyond it in other respects.[15] Beardsley, Wilde said, was 'the only artist who, besides myself, knows what the Dance of the Seven Veils is, and can see that invisible dance'.[16]

Salome possesses important continuities with 'The Sphinx', *A House of Pomegranates* and *The Picture of Dorian Gray* – works whose published formats incorporated innovative elements of graphic design, thereby extending the printed word into the realm of the decorative arts. In every respect the 1894 book stirs our senses and fires our minds; by foregrounding elements of design, it insists on its own 'art', and embodies what Vivian in 'The Decay of Lying' calls a 'beautiful untrue thing'. The book is 'the very essence of the decadent *fin-de-siècle*', proclaimed *The Studio* on reviewing the first English edition, 'the typical volume of the period'.

The play possesses continuities with Wilde's previous works in other respects too, particularly in matters of language. Although it was banned from performance in Britain, and Wilde was never to see the play acted on stage, the fact that arguably the greatest actress of Wilde's day, Sarah Bernhardt, was scheduled to perform the title role in the first English production gives an indication of Wilde's high hopes for the play.[17] 'Mais c'est heraldique, on dirait une fresque' (It's heraldic, like a fresco), Bernhardt purportedly told Wilde, and according to Ricketts, 'for days both author and actress discussed the pitch of voice required.'[18] Bernhardt was drawn to Wilde's evocative, rich language as much as to the drama, *mise-en-scène* and characterization. Whatever its debts to contemporary French writing, the play is a masterpiece of Symbolist writing in its own right and it elicited high praise from Mallarmé and Maeterlinck, among others.

The play's Symbolism is evident in plans Wilde drew up with Ricketts for the highly evocative first staging. 'I proposed a black floor', Ricketts tells us,

> upon which Salome's white feet would show . . . The sky was to be a rich turquoise blue, cut across by the perpendicular fall of strips of gilt matting, which should not touch the ground, and so form a sort of aerial tent above the terrace. Did Wilde actually suggest the division of the actors into separate masses of colour? His was the scheme . . . that the Jews should be in yellow, the Romans were to be in purple, the soldiery in bronze green, and John in white . . . I desired that the moonlight should fall upon the ground, the source not being seen; Wilde himself hugged the idea of some 'strange dim pattern in the sky'.[19]

Still more is the play's Symbolism evident in its incantatory language, which Maeterlinck found 'mysterious and strange' and of which Mallarmé wrote: 'everything . . . is expressed in such constant, dazzling strokes' while 'on each page [arises] the Unutterable and the Dream'.[20] Literal-minded readers have sometimes disagreed with Mallarmé's and Maeterlinck's judgements, finding either Wilde's French or Douglas's English (or both) to be stilted and artificial. The 1894 English version is 'wooden and rarefied', 'moribund' and 'intentionally archaic', claims the scholar Joseph Donohue, for instance, and it adopts a 'false . . . pseudo-King Jamesian dialect [full of] high-flown verbiage and grammatical obtuseness . . . unsuited for performance in a public theatre'.[21] Similarly, the original French text is written as if alienated from itself, and 'has to be acted with an English accent', remarks the French critic Philippe Jullian. But Wilde aspires to a language that is incantatory, evocative and poetic rather than naturalistic and conversational. 'Le mot doit tomber comme une perle sur une disque de cristal, pas de mouvements rapides, des gestes stylisés' (Words must fall like pearls on a disc of crystal, with no rapid movements and with purely stylized gestures), Bernhardt suggested when planning her stage production.

The play owes much of its rich language, imagery and exalted tone to the sacred writings of Christianity, especially *Revelations* and the *Song of Songs*, no less than to Symbolist precepts. Indeed Wilde himself described *Salome* as a religious play, and he told his friend Coulson Kernahan that his greatest ambition was 'not to be remembered hereafter as an artist, poet, thinker or playwright, but as the man who reclothed the sublimest conception which the world has ever known . . . with new and burning words'.[22]

For years he had been trying to break prose from what he called 'the crude brutality of plain realism', and like the jewelled prose of his fairy tales, prose poems and parts of *Dorian Gray*, the language of *Salome* is fiercely remote from any 'spoken' or habitual idiom. With *Salome* no less than with his society comedies, Wilde indeed took the stage drama, an ostensibly objective and impersonal literary form, and made it as personal as a sonnet or a lyric poem.

EIGHT

'A Poet Who Loves Boys'

A patriot put in prison for loving his country loves his country, and a poet in prison for loving boys loves boys. To have altered my life would have been to have admitted that Uranian love was ignoble.

WILDE, letter to Robert Ross, February 1898

No period more clearly demonstrates the personal contradictions embraced by Wilde than the three or four years leading up to his criminal conviction in 1895. His fame and worldly success had allowed him to create the public persona of 'Oscar Wilde', in part so as to efface his Irish roots and ease his acceptance into the pantheon of English greatness. Of late, he had become the most brilliant of playwrights, writing repartee-filled plays that added lustre to the English stage and a new word, 'Wildean', to the English language. To his family and close friends he was a dutiful son, doting father and – at least at first – affectionate husband. But during the three years or so before his conviction, these identities were increasingly in conflict with a private, corporeal and sexual self that is less easily categorized.

Scholars have long disagreed about when Wilde first acted on desires that we would now perhaps too confidently term 'homosexual', as well as when he first became conscious of those desires.

The matter is doubly complicated, first of all because Wilde's marriage to Constance and his fatherhood of two boys entered strongly into his sense of himself. 'O execrable facts, that keep our lips from kissing, though our souls are one,' he had written from Scotland to his wife seven months after their wedding. In the early years of his marriage at least, Wilde was affectionate to his wife – as late as 1892 he was 'still on great terms of affection' with her and 'adored his wife', wrote Wilde's lover Lord Alfred Douglas late in his own turbulent life – and his love for his children is clearly discernible in his surviving correspondence.[1] The matter is complicated too because while homosexuality is nowadays a matter of identity, not merely of sexual preference and desire, this was hardly the case in Wilde's day. Sex was what one did in private, but it did not necessarily define one's identity. Indeed the term 'homosexual' – never used by Wilde, but employed here to mean same-sex desire or a person who acts on such desire – did not enter the English language until 1892, when it was used adjectivally in a translation of Richard von Krafft-Ebing's *Psychopathia Sexualis* (it was first used as a noun in 1912). Moreover, sex with another man sometimes existed on a continuum with behaviours we would now confidently term 'heterosexual'. A degree of homosexual behaviour was tolerated, even accepted, in English public schools, for instance, where it was understood to be consistent with a boy's development into adulthood organized around marriage and his fatherhood of children.

I have already suggested that long before his marriage to Constance, Wilde pursued intense and sometimes flirtatious friendships with a variety of young men. His friendship and cohabitation with Frank Miles had so shocked the latter's prudish father that it caused a permanent breach, and Wilde's letters to Harry Marillier, one year after his wedding, with their heartfelt allusions to 'playing with fire', 'the love of things impossible' and 'the desire of romance', have led some scholars to see this friendship as having a sexual basis. Rumours of Wilde's homosexual preferences had dogged him in America and Paris, as we have seen, although they might have derived from his perceived 'unmanliness' in the eyes of a Goncourt or a Higginson more than from any obvious expressions of same-sex desire on Wilde's part.

But Wilde's sense of himself changed drastically in 1885–6, as I have suggested, as a combined result of the criminalization of 'gross indecency' between men in 1885 and the commencement of Wilde's affair with the seventeen-year-old Robert Ross in late 1886. Few concrete details about the affair are known, although both men later spoke of it as the first important homosexual affair of Wilde's life, and there was undeniably a sexual basis to it at first. ('Who do you think seduced me?' Wilde years later asked his friend, a confused Reginald Turner, 'it was Little Robbie.') Wilde's attraction to Ross had other, longer-lasting dimensions as well. Ross was 'as clever as can be, with excellent taste and sound knowledge', Wilde told Oscar Browning in 1888. In 1889 he told Ross that 'The Portrait of Mr W. H.' 'is half yours, and but for you would not have been written', while in *De profundis* he writes that out of an inexpensive dinner in a Soho café with Ross ('one of the most delightful dinners I remember ever having') came 'the first and best of all my dialogues [that is, 'The Decay of Lying']'. Ross was as witty and entertaining as he was erudite, and he was to prove the most devoted of Wilde's friends when disaster struck in 1895. Wilde nearly always consulted him when drafting new work, and a measure of how much he treasured

Portrait of Robert Ross by William Rothenstein, 1895, oil on canvas.

Ross's judgement is implicit in the fact that, upon leaving prison in 1897, he appointed Ross his literary executor and entrusted him with the manuscript of *De profundis*.

Ross went up to Cambridge in late 1888, precipitating a cooling-off in their relations, although he remained thereafter a truly loyal friend. Wilde was greatly touched when Ross sent a kitten as a gift for his children, and some months later, after visiting Oxford with Ross, he told Ross that 'it was a great pleasure to see you again, though your not writing to me was wrong.' If Ross was now more interested in the company of other men, his place in Wilde's own affections had been somewhat eclipsed as well. For the past six or seven years, Wilde had sought out close emotional attachments with actors, undergraduates and cultivated young men such as Marillier, Douglas Ainslie and Norman Forbes-Robertson. Now he pursued ever-closer and more intense relationships with, among others, the actors Clyde Fitch and Harry Melvill, the stage designer and painter W. Graham Robertson, a young City office clerk named Fred Althaus and the poets Richard Le Gallienne, George Kersley, Marc-André Raffalovich and John Gray.

Evidence that there was a sexual basis to Wilde's intimacy with these men is speculative, although his surviving correspondence with some of them is certainly flirtatious and his sexual fascination can be easily inferred. '*Nobody* loves you as *I* do,' remarked Fitch in one letter; 'When you are here I dream. When you are away, I awake . . . Make me what you will, only keep me yours forever.'[2] 'We must have a couple of days by the sea,' wrote Althaus in one of several letters that the biographer Matthew Sturgis sees as 'emphatically sexual', imploring Wilde to go away with him and enclosing a 'simply splendid' photo of himself.[3] 'With Oscar Wilde, a summer day/ Passed like a yearning kiss away,' begins a sonnet by Le Gallienne, to whom Wilde in turn inscribed a copy of his *Poems*: 'To Richard Le Gallienne, poet and lover, from Oscar Wilde. A summer day in June '88.' In another sonnet, titled 'To Oscar Wilde', Le Gallienne likened himself to 'the secret lover of a queen', who 'smiles to think of what his eyes have seen;/ The little room where Love did "shut them in",/ The fragrant couch whereon they twin did lie,/ And rests his hand where on his heart doth lie/ A bruisèd daffodil of last night's sin.' 'There can be no doubt that Oscar seduced Richard Le Gallienne,' concludes Neil McKenna. 'Despite such heated exchanges . . . this was nothing more than poetical posturing by both parties,' concludes Sturgis more cautiously; 'Le Gallienne delighted in playing the role of the impassioned poet, and so did Wilde.'[4]

Wilde's most important love affairs were with young poets, as McKenna has observed, and the exchange of passionate poetry was an important element in these affairs. 'It is perhaps hard to comprehend the importance of poetry to men who loved men at the end of the nineteenth century,' McKenna explains, for 'homoerotic poetry was the lingua franca of many men who loved men.'[5] Another young poet with whom Wilde became fascinated around this time was the handsome and youthful-looking John Gray, a poet of no mean abilities, whose knowledge of trends in contemporary French writing made him especially interesting to Wilde. Gray's first book of poems, *Silverpoints*, was instrumental in bringing about a wider appreciation in Britain for currents in French poetry, and Wilde undertook to pay for its publication at his own expense. Although no evidence exists to suggest that Wilde and Gray were lovers, Gray was unquestionably Wilde's protégé for a while, and 'their constant companionship led some to suppose that there must be a sexual dimension to their relations,' writes Sturgis; 'rumours began to form.' Many of Wilde's contemporaries believed that Gray was the model for Wilde's Dorian Gray, and the biographer Richard Ellmann writes that 'to give the hero of his novel the name of "Gray" was [for Wilde] a form of courtship.'[6] The only extant letter from Gray to Wilde, an autograph draft of Gray's shockingly decadent poem 'Mishka' dating from 1891, is signed 'Yours ever, Dorian', and Gray for some time eagerly embraced the persona of 'Dorian' Gray, even using it to gain entrance into fashionable society. However, when *The Star* publicly reported in its gossip column in February 1892 that Gray was 'said to be the original Dorian of the same name', Gray threatened to sue for libel and the report was immediately recanted. The incident was the beginning of a permanent breach between Wilde and Gray.

Although scholars disagree about how actively sexual these friendships with young men were, Wilde was clearly fascinated by men younger than himself, especially those with an interest in poetry or the theatre. 'I like the society of young men,' Wilde declared during his criminal trials; 'I am a lover of youth . . . I like to study the young in everything. There is something fascinating in youthfulness.'[7] If he acted sexually on this fascination, he was discreet, and his partners – almost all of whom were ambitious professionals of one kind or another – could be relied on for their discretion too. In the summer of 1891, however, shortly after *Dorian Gray* was published in book form, Wilde was introduced to the twenty-year-old Lord Alfred Douglas, whose life would be inextricably bound up with his own henceforth. From this point onwards, Wilde's relations with young men became more reckless and clearly sexual.

The friendship, at first 'no different from the many other friendships that Wilde began with young, intelligent, literary admirers', was slow to form initially.[8] Douglas was obsessed with *The Picture of Dorian Gray*, and after reading it nine times over,

John Gray, lithograph by Charles Haslewood Shannon, 1896.

Lord Alfred Douglas, 1891 or 1892, around the time Wilde first met him.

he claimed, he asked to be introduced to its author. His cousin (and bedfellow) Lionel Johnson brought Douglas to Tite Street, and Wilde duly inscribed a deluxe copy of the novel for him at their second meeting in July 1891. Thereafter Douglas and Wilde played very little part in each other's lives until some months later, when Douglas wrote, as Wilde later put it, 'appealing to me in a very pathetic letter to help him in terrible trouble with people who were blackmailing him'.[9] Details of the case are vague, but Douglas was probably being blackmailed over his relations with a young man at Oxford, and Wilde, who was touched by Douglas's letter, almost certainly paid the ransom. In a letter written in 1897 from Reading Prison, Wilde dates this event to May 1892, adding that he hardly knew Douglas at the time. Wilde always dated his friendship with Douglas from this moment, and while his recall of the exact month and year has been questioned, May 1892 accords well with Douglas's comments that 'three years . . . elapsed between my first meeting with Oscar and his conviction in 1895' and that 'familiarities' between the two men 'began about nine months after I first met Oscar'.[10]

According to Douglas, Wilde

> 'made up to me' in every possible way. He was continually asking me to dine or lunch with him, and sending me letters, notes, and telegrams. He flattered me, gave me presents, and made much of me in every way.

Douglas claims that he resisted Wilde's advances for many months but eventually succumbed, whereupon the relationship became unabashedly sexual for a while at least. 'I did with him and allowed him to do just what was done among boys at Winchester and Oxford,' Douglas revealed candidly in 1925 in a letter to Frank Harris; 'sodomy never took place, [although Wilde] added what was new to me . . . he "sucked" me.'[11] Douglas, a confessed paedophile attracted to boys younger than himself, told Harris that 'I never really liked this part of the business. It was dead against my sexual instincts, which were all for youth and beauty and softness', and 'After a time [Wilde] tumbled to the fact . . . and he very soon "cut it out" altogether.'

Most commentators agree that 'sex was never the most important element' and that in its latter stages at least, their relationship was 'ideal and idealised'.[12] But there can be no doubt that the two men fell swiftly in love: 'Bosie . . . is quite like a narcissus – so white and gold . . . He lies like a hyacinth on the sofa, and I worship him,' wrote Wilde from Kensington's Royal Palace Hotel in the early summer of 1892. In July 1892 the two visited Bad Homburg together for several days. In September Douglas visited Wilde (twice) at Cromer, in Norfolk, where the latter had taken a holiday cottage with his family; and in a letter conjecturally dated November 1892 by Wilde's editors, Wilde told Douglas: 'I should awfully like to go away with you somewhere where it is hot and coloured.' Douglas's aristocratic title and lineage added to his attractiveness, as did the fact that he was an aspiring – and not inconsiderable – poet. In the early days of their affair Douglas composed his famous poem 'Two Loves', with its last line 'I am the Love that dare not speak its name,' as well as the short lyric 'De profundis', which begins: 'I love a love, but not as other men/ Who tell the world their love for very pride,/ For the cold world loves not my love; and when/ My voice would sing my love I needs must hide.' 'It is a marvel that those red rose-leaf lips of yours should have been made no less for music of song

Wilde and Douglas, 1893.

than for madness of kisses,' an infatuated Wilde told Douglas in a letter signed 'always, with undying love'; 'Your slim gilt soul walks between passion and poetry. I know Hyacinthus, whom Apollo loved so madly, was you in Greek days.'

From November 1892 onwards, Douglas was the editor of the Oxford literary magazine *The Spirit Lamp*, and at some point around this date Wilde gave him a handwritten copy of his poem 'The New Remorse', whose final lines run:

> . . . Who is this
> Who cometh in dyed garments from the South?

It is thy new-found Lord, and he shall kiss
The yet unravished roses of thy mouth,
And I shall weep and worship, as before.

The sonnet was actually a retitled version of Wilde's 1887 sonnet 'Un amant de nos jours' (A Lover of Our Times), but Douglas was unaware of the poem's earlier existence and believed that Wilde had written it for him. Douglas was striving to give *The Spirit Lamp* a more frankly homosexual tone, and in December 1892 he printed Wilde's sonnet in the magazine, where it was followed, in February and June 1893 respectively, by Wilde's prose poems 'The House of Judgement' and 'The Disciple'.

It was in reference to 'The New Remorse' that Wilde revealed in early 1893 that his affair with Douglas now involved sex with other young men for payment. 'I never got *The Spirit Lamp*, nor even a cheque,' he jokingly wrote to Douglas from Babbacombe Cliff, in Devon, where he was staying; 'My charge for the sonnet is £300. Who on earth is the editor? He must be rented.' In the 1890s, among men who sought sex with other men, 'renter' was slang for a man who participates in homosexual acts for a reward (usually payment). In *De profundis* Wilde charges Douglas with bringing an 'element of Philistinism into a life that had been a complete protest against it', a charge that has often since been construed as meaning that Douglas introduced Wilde to the secret world of the male brothel and rent-boys that would prove Wilde's undoing. But Wilde was willing to reward young men for sex even before his affair with Douglas. He gave money to the bookish young publisher's clerk Edward Shelley, with whom he conducted an affair from February 1892 onwards; and in October 1892 he gave an expensive cigarette case to Sidney Mavor, with whom he had recently spent a night (at Wilde's expense) at the Albemarle Hotel.

Nonetheless, Wilde's affair with Douglas led him to be more risqué and reckless. By late February 1893 Douglas had joined him at Babbacombe Cliff, where Wilde jokingly commemorated the anarchy and permissiveness of their existence in a letter describing the house as a 'school' of which he was the headmaster and Douglas the 'boys':

> Babbacombe School:
> Headmaster – Mr. Oscar Wilde
> Second Master – Mr. Campbell Dodgson [Douglas's tutor]
> Boys – Lord Alfred Douglas
>
> Rules:
> Tea for masters and boys at 9.30
> Breakfast at 10.30
> Work 11.30–12.30
> At 12.30 Sherry and biscuits for headmaster and boys
> 12.40–1.30 Work
> 1.30 Lunch
> 2.30–4.30 Compulsory hide-and-seek for headmaster
> 5. Tea for headmaster and . . . brandy and sodas (not to exceed seven) for boys
> 6–7. Work
> 7.30 Dinner, with compulsory champagne
> 8.30–12.00 Ecarté, limited to five-guinea points
> 12.00–1.30 Compulsory reading in bed. Any boy found disobeying this rule will be immediately woken up.

'I have succeeded in combining the advantages of a public school with those of a private lunatic asylum,' Wilde ends this letter. Upon leaving 'Babbacombe School', their lives became more reckless still. In early March Wilde took rooms at London's Savoy Hotel for 'about a month',[13] where he was visited by a number of male sex workers and where Douglas had an adjoining room. When the French poet Pierre Louÿs visited him there, he was appalled at Wilde's sleeping arrangements, prompting Wilde to tell him, 'I've made three marriages in my life, one with a woman and two with men,' presumably referring to Ross as the other man.[14] In *De profundis* Wilde suggests that this hotel stay was instigated by Douglas, but a passionate letter written by Wilde later that month, of interest for many different reasons, indicates that Douglas was absent for large parts of the visit:

> Dearest of all Boys – Your letter was delightful – red and yellow wine to me – but I am sad and out of sorts – Bosie – you must not make scenes with me – they kill me – they wreck the loveliness of life – I cannot see *you*, so Greek and gracious, distorted with passion; I cannot listen to *your* curved lips saying hideous things to me – don't do it – you break my heart – I'd sooner be rented all day, than have you bitter, unjust, and horrid – horrid –
>
> I must see you soon – you are the divine thing I want – the thing of grace and genius – but I don't know how to do it – Shall I come to Salisbury – ? There are many difficulties – my bill here is £49 for a week! I have also got a new sitting-room over the Thames – but you, why are you not here, my dear, my wonderful boy – ? I fear I must leave; no money, no credit, and a heart of lead – Ever your own Oscar

The emotional, sexual and financial extravagance of the two men's lives together is clear, as is Wilde's obvious love for Douglas. (This letter, soon afterwards stolen from Douglas, was later obtained by Wilde's prosecutors and used to convict Wilde of 'gross indecency' in 1895.) Wilde's comment 'I'd sooner be rented,' which he glossed as 'blackmailed by every renter in London' when recalling the letter from prison in 1897,[15] is a tacit admission of the two men's involvement with such sex workers as the prostitute Charles Parker and the procurer Alfred Taylor, the latter of whom Wilde had visited in his rooms at Little College Street the previous October. During his trials, Wilde was to be interrogated about his interaction with such men; and although Taylor to his credit refused to give evidence against Wilde, Parker's evidence as well as that of several Savoy Hotel employees was to prove damning.

They continued pursuing this reckless, passionate life long after the fateful Savoy visit had ended. In May Wilde paid an extended visit to Douglas in his rooms at Oxford, and around this time Wilde was blackmailed about some of his letters to Douglas, which the latter had foolishly let fall into the hands of the blackmailer Alfred Wood, who had been a sexual partner of both men. In May too, Louÿs broke off his friendship after remonstrating with Wilde about his affair with Douglas and his neglect of his wife. In June, Wilde took a cottage at Goring-on-Thames – to 'please you', he tells Douglas in *De profundis* – where he engaged Douglas's own servants, at Douglas's request, and probably slept with Douglas's servant Walter Granger. In October, Wilde rented rooms in St James's Street, in the heart of London's West End, ostensibly so that he might complete his play *An Ideal Husband* in peace, though here too he was visited frequently by Douglas as well as a number of sex workers who later testified at his trials. In *De profundis* Wilde writes of those men's testimony that 'The sins of another were being placed to my account. Had I so chosen, I could . . . have saved myself at his expense.'

Wilde clearly enjoyed the attentions of men such as Parker and Taylor. 'People thought it dreadful of me to have entertained at dinner the evil things of life,' he writes in *De profundis*,

> and to have found pleasure in their company. But they . . . were delightfully suggestive and stimulating. It was like feasting with panthers. The danger was half the excitement. I used to feel as the snake-charmer must feel when he lures the cobra to stir from the painted cloth or reed-basket that holds it, and makes it spread its hood at his bidding, and sway to and fro in the air as a plant sways restfully in a stream. They were to me the brightest of gilded snakes. Their poison was part of their perfection . . . I don't feel at all ashamed of having known them. They were intensely interesting.

Wilde saw himself as a sexual renegade and took pride in such unconventional relationships. Consorting with sex workers outside the law was necessary, and perhaps inevitable, because sexual relations with men within the law were impossible. As he was to write defiantly shortly after his release from prison in 1897, when pressed about the renewal of his relationship with Douglas:

> A patriot put in prison for loving his country loves his country, and a poet in prison for loving boys loves boys. To have altered my life would have been to have admitted that Uranian love was ignoble.[16]

It perhaps goes without saying that 'boys' should not be understood here as meaning pubescent or pre-pubescent boys. Wilde was attracted to young men who were in their late teens, or older men such as Douglas and Gray who appeared to be so, and he was not a paedophile. Although he repeatedly refers in his correspondence to Douglas as a 'boy', the *Oxford English Dictionary* reminds us that, 'in playful, affectionate, or slighting use', the word 'boy' often means 'a young man, a fellow', much as the term 'girl' is today used playfully, affectionately or slightingly for a young woman. By 'a poet in prison for loving boys', Wilde means defiantly that he was a poet put in prison for loving young men.

Still more defiant is Wilde's comment that altering his life 'would have been to have admitted that Uranian love was ignoble'. From the Greek *Uranos*, 'Uranian' means 'heavenly' or 'celestial'. 'Uranian love' had for some years been a code-term for male same-sex love, the suggestion being that it was a higher kind of love than heterosexual love. The term had first been used in the 1860s by the German sexologist Karl Heinrich Ulrichs and later popularized in English in the writings of Edward Carpenter and John Addington Symonds, while Raffalovich's book *Uranisme et unisexualité* (1896) devoted an entire chapter to Wilde. Wilde's use of the term shows that by 1897 – and probably much earlier – he was familiar with such writings, while his rejection of anything ignoble about Uranian love shows that his homosexuality was now no longer simply a matter of sexual preference. It was a matter of sexual politics and identity too.

NINE

Prisoner C.3.3.

In the great prison where I was . . . incarcerated, I was merely the figure and letter of a little cell in a long gallery, one of a thousand lifeless numbers, as of a thousand lifeless lives.

WILDE, *De profundis*, composed 1896–7

Wilde's life with Douglas grew increasingly tumultuous in the two years before his arrest and conviction. In June 1893, shortly after allowing Wilde's compromising letters to fall into the hands of the blackmailer Alfred Wood, Douglas left Oxford in disgrace, without a degree. He now quarrelled more frequently and violently with Wilde, perhaps never more so than when Wilde disapproved of his efforts at translating *Salome* into English in August. Wilde eventually revised the English text himself and then published it without Douglas's name on the title page, after persuading Douglas that dedicating the book to him was 'of infinitely greater artistic & literary value'.[1] (While the book's title page states only 'translated from the French of Oscar Wilde', a separate dedication page reads: 'To my friend Lord Alfred Bruce Douglas, the translator of my play.')

In August 1893 Wilde went alone for two weeks to Dinard, in Brittany, for 'rest and freedom from the terrible strain of your companionship', he later told Douglas.[2] In October Douglas narrowly avoided prosecution for a liaison with a sixteen-year-old boy that was quietly hushed up. In November Wilde wrote to Douglas's mother suggesting that she send her son abroad for a while. 'Bosie seems to me in a very bad state of health,' he explained. 'He is sleepless, nervous, and rather hysterical. He seems to me quite altered . . . He does absolutely nothing, and is quite astray in life . . . If he stays in London he will not come to any good, and may spoil his young life irretrievably.' Douglas was duly dispatched to stay with well-placed friends in Egypt – at that time a de facto British protectorate. Whether this was an effort to effect 'an irrevocable parting, a complete separation' from Douglas, as Wilde later claimed in *De profundis*, seems dubious. In December, not three weeks after Douglas left, Wilde wrote to him: 'our love has passed through the shadow and the night of estrangement and sorrow and come out rose-crowned as of old . . . I think of you daily and am always devotedly yours.'

In March 1894, Douglas returned from Egypt via Paris, where Wilde spent eight days with him and 'the old passion was renewed with all its old force – and . . . extravagance too.'[3] Days later, after the two had returned to London, they were lunching together at the Café Royal when Douglas's father, the Marquess of Queensbury, came in and they invited him to their table. Their belief that they had won him over by doing so was shortlived; the very next day the Marquess wrote his son a threatening letter that set in motion the disturbing events that were to follow. 'Your intimacy with this man Wilde . . . must either cease or I will disown you and stop all money supplied,' Queensberry thundered. 'With my own eyes I saw you both in the most loathsome and disgusting relationship . . . No wonder people are talking as they are. Also I now hear on good authority . . . that his wife is petitioning to divorce him for sodomy . . . If I thought the actual thing was true, and it became public property, I should be quite justified in shooting him at sight.' The letter was signed 'Your disgusted so-called father'.[4]

But Douglas was as hot-tempered as his father, and he only stoked Queensberry's anger more by replying by telegram: 'WHAT A FUNNY LITTLE MAN YOU ARE.' This prompted a still worse response from Queensberry:

> You impertinent young jackanapes . . . If you send any more such telegrams . . . I will give you the thrashing you deserve . . . If I catch you again with that man I will make a public scandal in a way you little dream of. It is already a suppressed one. I prefer an open one.[5]

Wilde and Douglas disregarded this warning, however. Two weeks later, after Douglas had gone to Florence at his mother's instigation, Wilde wrote: 'The gay, gilt, and gracious lad has gone away – and I hate everyone else,' signing his letter to Douglas 'always, with much love, yours'. Within a few days he had joined Douglas in Florence.

When the two returned to London they made no effort to hide their continued friendship and the Marquess stepped up his attacks. On 30 June 1894 he showed up unexpectedly with a friend at Wilde's home. The ensuing confrontation eerily foreshadowed what was to follow. Wilde asked facetiously if Queensberry had come 'to apologise for the statement you made about my wife and myself in your letter to your son' and threatened Queensberry with prosecution for criminal libel. Far from apologizing, however, Queensberry revealed a disturbing degree of knowledge about Wilde's movements and activities over the past months, including Wood's efforts to blackmail him over the letter written from the Savoy Hotel, and he threatened to 'thrash' Wilde if he ever caught him in public with his son again. 'I don't say that you are it,' he answered angrily when asked by Wilde 'do you seriously accuse your son and me of sodomy?', 'but you look it and you pose as it, which is just as bad.'[6] As worryingly, he taunted Wilde that he couldn't be pursued for criminal libel on the basis of what he'd written to his son since the letter had been a private communication. Queensberry had clearly employed detectives to dig up dirt, but more distressingly he had retained excellent legal counsel, as Wilde shortly found out to his cost. When Wilde approached his friend the prominent Society lawyer Sir George Lewis a few days later with a view to initiating legal proceedings against Queensberry, Lewis only replied: 'I am acting for Lord Queensberry . . . and under these circumstances you will see at once that it is impossible for me to offer any opinion about any proceedings you intend to take against him.'[7]

Far from realizing the nature of Queensberry's threat, Douglas only taunted his father further, informing him by postcard (legally speaking, a public form of communication) that 'I treat your absurd threats with absolute indifference' and 'ever since your exhibition at O. W.'s house, I have made a point of appearing with him at many public restaurants . . . If O. W. was to prosecute you . . . you would get seven years . . . for your outrageous libels.'[8] The mutual contempt of father and son is unmistakeable – 'if you try to assault me, I shall defend myself with a loaded revolver,' threatened Douglas – and Wilde was undoubtedly right when he wrote to Douglas later that 'Hate blinded you.'[9] But to suggest, as Wilde later did, that Douglas thoughtlessly and hatefully prompted Wilde to seek legal recourse against Queensberry is unfair to both Wilde and Douglas. In an age when homosexuality is legally sanctioned and protected, we can now see that the two were understandably defiant about defending their moral right to love one another and remain free from Queensberry's persecution whether in public or in private.

Wilde later maintained in *De profundis* that after Douglas's return from Egypt he resisted and resented Douglas's attentions. But his surviving letters to Douglas from 1894 clearly contradict this claim. 'I can't live without you. You are so dear, so wonderful. I think of you all day long, and miss your grace, your boyish beauty, the bright sword-play of your wit, the delicate fancy of your genius . . . and, above all, yourself,' he wrote to Douglas in July 1894. 'I have no words for how I love you,' he concluded his letter. In early August he invited Douglas to visit him at Worthing, in Sussex, where he had rented a house to take a holiday with his family and also to compose *The Importance of Being Earnest* without the distractions (including the importunings of creditors) of London. 'Your father has been on the rampage again – been to Café Royal to enquire for us with threats, etc. I think now it would have been better for me to have had him bound over to keep the peace,' he informed Douglas, ending his letter: 'Fortunately there is one person in the world to love.' Douglas duly paid three separate visits to Worthing, each time at the invitation of Wilde, staying for about a month in total, and on one occasion he accompanied Wilde to Dieppe, in France, for a few days. 'Dear, dear boy, you are more to me than any one of them has any idea,' Wilde wrote to Douglas shortly after the end of

Douglas's first visit; 'you are the atmosphere of beauty through which I see life . . . the incarnation of all lovely things . . . I think of you day and night . . . I am always devotedly yours.'

While at Worthing Wilde befriended a young man, Alphonse Conway, just turned sixteen, to whom he gave an inscribed cigarette case, a new suit of clothes and other gifts before taking him to stay overnight at Brighton's Albion Hotel. Queensberry's lawyers subsequently secured a deposition from the young man, and Wilde was later interrogated in court about his relations with him, suggesting that Douglas's father had posted detectives to spy on the activities of Wilde and his son.

Over the next six months or so, Wilde's relationship with Douglas hurtled towards its perhaps inevitable, destructive denouement. Rumours about their relationship were now widespread, as witnessed by the satirical novel *The Green Carnation*, published anonymously on 15 September 1894, in which the two are mercilessly and skilfully parodied. (The novel, withdrawn from publication at the time of Wilde's trials after the damage had been done, was later revealed to have been written by the journalist Robert Hichens). In early October the two spent several days together at Brighton's Grand Metropole Hotel, and when shortly after this Wilde secured new lodgings for himself for ten days in the nearby town of Hove, partly so as to finish *The Importance of Being Earnest*, Douglas accompanied him. In *De profundis* Wilde says that this cohabitation was forced on him by Douglas, that he resented it and that he resolved thereafter to part from Douglas irrevocably. But once again Wilde's surviving letters contradict this. Back in London in late October, he promised a mutual acquaintance that Douglas would dine with them both 'with pleasure'. In early November, when Douglas was in mourning for the unexpected death of his older brother Viscount Drumlanrig, Wilde wrote: 'My dearest Bosie, I suppose you won't come up now, it is so late. Perhaps I shall hear from you tomorrow? I can't bear your sadness and unhappiness . . . But you know what a joy it will be to see you again,' while a few days later he wrote: 'My dearest Boy, I have been very lonely without you . . . I hate England: it is only bearable to me because you are here.' He jokingly proposed co-writing with Douglas a book titled *How to Live above One's Income: For the Use of the Sons of the Rich*, and when *The Importance of Being Earnest* entered rehearsals in January 1895, two weeks after the opening of *An Ideal Husband*, the two journeyed to Algiers – where 'there is a great deal of beauty' and 'the Kabyle boys are quite lovely', Wilde told Ross in a letter – for a fortnight together as sex tourists.[10]

Events came to a head in February 1895. *The Importance of Being Earnest* opened to rapturous applause and critical praise on the 14th, but the triumph was marred when the Marquess of Queensberry was only narrowly prevented from entering the theatre and denouncing Wilde from the stage. 'I had all Scotland Yard – twenty police – to guard the theatre. He prowled about for three hours, then left chattering like a monstrous ape,' Wilde wrote to Douglas, who had not yet returned from Algiers and who now rushed back immediately to stand by his friend ('you will of course stay with me,' added Wilde, who was himself staying at London's Avondale Hotel). Undeterred, Queensberry four days later left with the hall porter of Wilde's club the incriminating visiting card that would prove the fulcrum on which Wilde's fate turned. On it he had scrawled 'for Oscar Wilde, posing somdomite'. Despite Queensberry's hasty scrawl and mis-spelling of sodomite, leaving the card – like the postcard,

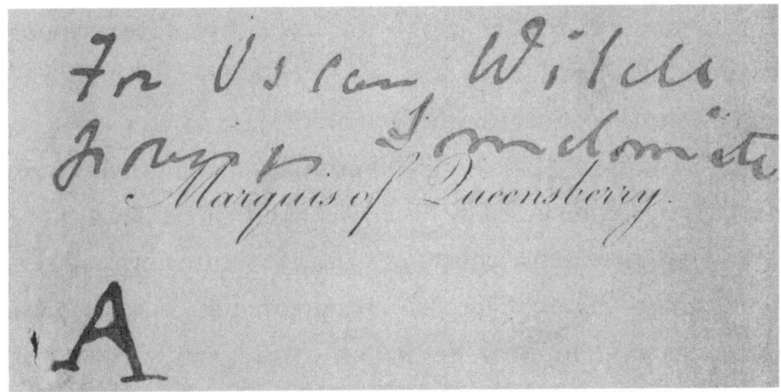

The offensive calling card that led Wilde to pursue an unsuccessful suit for criminal libel against the Marquess of Queensberry – and that ultimately led to Wilde's own conviction for gross indecency.

an 'unprivileged' and public mode of communication, legally speaking – was a carefully laid trap, designed to goad Wilde into prosecuting him for libel. Queensberry's employment of private detectives meant that he had all the evidence he needed. By accusing Wilde of *posing*, moreover, Queensberry absolved himself of needing to prove that Wilde had committed sodomy – although this would be precisely what Queensberry's courtroom lawyer would attempt to do – while simultaneously perpetuating and stoking public fears among Victorians that Wilde was an inauthentic and dangerous imposter. In a court of law, Queensberry needed only to prove that Wilde *represented* himself as a lover of men to defend his offensive accusation effectively.

Wilde did not receive Queensberry's card until 28 February, when he next visited his club, but upon reading it his decision to prosecute was immediate: 'I don't see anything now but a criminal prosecution. My whole life seems ruined by this man,' he wrote on this date. (In fact Wilde had already tried to instigate a criminal prosecution, for on the same date his lawyers wrote to him saying they were 'unable to carry out your instructions to prosecute the Marquis [*sic*] of Queensberry for his threats and insulting conduct towards you on the 14th instant at the St. James's Theatre'.) Wilde began his criminal action the very next day, when, accompanied by his lawyer and Douglas, he went to Marlborough Street Magistrates Court to secure a warrant for Queensberry's arrest. Queensberry appeared in court the next day and was committed for trial on 3 April. On 30 March he entered a Plea of Justification, specifying more than ten men – though not his son – whom Wilde had allegedly incited and solicited 'to commit sodomy and other acts of gross indecency and immorality'. But Wilde and his lawyers failed to heed this warning. A measure of how foolishly confident or simply careless Wilde was of success can be inferred from the facts that he took an expensive week-long holiday with Douglas, in Monte Carlo, in the weeks before Queensberry's trial, and that when the trial opened, Wilde arrived at court ostentatiously in a costly hired carriage and pair.

The contours of Wilde's failed libel action and subsequent criminal trials are now broadly known. By contrast, the malfeasance of Queensberry's lawyers and the judicial authorities remains poorly understood, and we still await a complete and well-edited transcription of the criminal trials to match that of the libel trial published by Wilde's grandson Merlin Holland in 2003.[11] At what price, financial or legal, Wilde's one-time lovers and associates were made or compelled to testify against him remains unknown. The high cost is suggested by how quickly several witnesses or potential witnesses subsequently left Britain and disappeared from the historical record. Some of them presumably feared prosecution themselves, and possibly this fear was used to secure their co-operation. At the libel trial, Wilde was confronted with his associations with a string of young men from 1892 onwards, as well as the damning constructions that could be put upon those associations, although Queensberry's lawyers did their best to keep Douglas largely out of the picture. Wilde and his lawyers had disastrously underestimated the depth of Queensberry's knowledge. Within two days, Wilde's action collapsed and he withdrew from the case, although he could do nothing to avert the jury's verdict that Queensberry's malicious libel was 'true in fact' and 'published for the public good'. More importantly, the evidence amassed by Queensberry's lawyers in his defence was passed on to the Director of Public Prosecutions.

The fact that Wilde was convicted on seven counts of gross indecency at the second of the two criminal trials that ensued is perhaps less surprising than that he was prosecuted so relentlessly in the first place and that, by initiating his libel action against Queensberry, Wilde willingly exposed his life and work to the law's scrutiny. As he later wrote, although 'there are many things of which I was convicted that I had not done, . . . there are many . . . that I had done, and a still greater number of things . . . for which I was never indicted at all.'[12] Practically speaking, Wilde's pursuit of the libel action was a disastrous decision, and so was his refusal to leave England for France when, within moments of his action's collapse, his arrest became imminent. But important points of freedom and principle were at stake, and from a twenty-first-century standpoint Wilde's actions were unquestionably heroic.

It has been suggested by many commentators that the government intentionally dragged its feet in issuing an arrest warrant, to afford Wilde adequate time to flee the country. Certainly, when the libel trial collapsed on 5 April 1895 at 11.15 a.m., Wilde must have anticipated his arrest as he hurriedly left the building. When advising his client to withdraw his suit, Wilde's attorney Sir Edward Clarke told him not only that he risked arrest but that his presence in court was not legally required. 'I hoped and expected that he would take the opportunity of escaping from the country,' Clarke later wrote, 'and I believe he would have found no difficulty in doing so.'[13] The arrest warrant was not issued till 4.55 p.m., and there was a lag of nearly ninety minutes before Wilde was arrested at London's Cadogan Hotel at 6.20 p.m.,[14] an event immortalized many years later in John Betjeman's poem 'The Arrest of Oscar Wilde at the Cadogan Hotel'.

But Wilde was not a man to flee: as he put it to the *Evening News*, explaining his decision not to call Lord Alfred Douglas as a witness against his own father, he was 'determined to bear on my own shoulders whatever ignominy and shame might result from prosecuting Lord Queensberry'. 'I decided that it was nobler and more beautiful to stay,' he told Douglas directly, adding, 'I did not want to be called a coward or a deserter.'[15] If imprisonment and personal ruin beckoned, they were worth enduring, or were at least endurable, by virtue of his love for Douglas. 'If prison and dishonour be my destiny,' he was to write to Douglas three weeks later, 'my love for you and [the] . . . divine belief that you love me in return will sustain me in my unhappiness and will make me capable . . . of bearing my grief most patiently.' 'In my solitude you will be with me,' he told Douglas five days before his conviction on 25 May 1895.

According to Wilde's own account, Douglas visited Wilde daily while he was on remand awaiting trial, in London's

Holloway Prison. One day before the first criminal trial opened, however, Wilde and his counsel persuaded Douglas, who risked prosecution himself, that it would be best if he went abroad. This was a telling decision. Although Wilde would be tried and convicted on his involvements with Wood, Parker, the noble Taylor and a series of other unfortunate young men, the motivating events had all concerned his relations with Lord Alfred Douglas, and Douglas remained a shadowy presence during the criminal trials notwithstanding his absence from England. ('In view of the intimacy between Lord Alfred Douglas and Mr. Wilde, was a warrant ever issued for the apprehension of Lord Alfred Douglas?' asked the foreman of the jury during the judge's summing up, moments before Wilde's conviction.) Following the collapse of Wilde's libel suit, Queensberry was feted in the press as a noble and conscientious parent doing his utmost to protect his son from an older corruptive 'sodomitic' influence. It is likely that public fears and disappointments about the legal miscarriages of the Cleveland Street Scandal played a role in the ferocity with which the authorities pursued Wilde and twice denied him bail, particularly after his first criminal trial ended in a hung jury.

Perhaps the most indelible moment was not when Wilde was presented with the testimony of a Parker or a Wood, but when he was pressed, during the first criminal trial, about his association with Lord Alfred Douglas and asked to explain 'the Love that dare not speak its name', as Douglas had described male same-sex love in the last line of his poem 'Two Loves'. Wilde's answer constitutes one of the most indelible, impassioned defences of such love in all of history:

"HOMOCEA"
INSTANTLY TOUCHES THE SPOT.

THE ILLUSTRATED
POLICE NEWS
LAW COURTS AND WEEKLY RECORD
ESTABLISHED 1864.

THE EARL OF CARRICK

No. 1628. [REGISTERED FOR CIRCULATION IN THE UNITED KINGDOM AND ABROAD.] SATURDAY, MAY 4, 1895. Price One Penny.

CLOSING SCENE AT THE OLD BAILEY.
TRIAL OF OSCAR WILDE

OSCAR WILDE AS A LECTURER 1882 AMERICA.

OSCAR WILDE AS A PRISONER 1895 BOW STREET

JURY

SALE OF OSCAR WILDE'S EFFECTS

OSCAR WILDE'S HOUSE 16 TITE STREET.

IMPROVED AND ENLARGED.

'Closing Scene at the Old Bailey', *Illustrated Police News*, 4 May 1895.

> 'The Love that dare not speak its name' in this century is such a great affection of an elder for a younger man as there was between David and Jonathan, such as Plato made the very basis of his philosophy, and such as you find in the sonnets of Michelangelo and Shakespeare. It is that deep, spiritual affection that is as pure as it is perfect. It dictates and pervades great works of art like those of Shakespeare and Michelangelo . . . It is in this century misunderstood, so much misunderstood that it may be described as the 'Love that dare not speak its name,' and on account of it I am placed where I am now. It is beautiful, it is fine, it is the noblest form of affection. There is nothing unnatural about it. It is intellectual, and it repeatedly exists between an elder and a younger man, when the elder man has intellect, and the younger man has all the joy, hope and glamour of life before him. That it should be so, the world does not understand. The world mocks at it and sometimes puts one in the pillory for it.[16]

The speech drew loud applause from the gallery. Appealing to an ancient Platonic idea of love, Wilde here counteracts an older notion of male homosexuality as 'sodomy', grounded in proscribed sex acts, with a powerful new conception of male same-sex love based on personal identity, mind, sensibility and emotion, as well as intellectual and social relationships. While he doesn't *name* the modern concept of homosexuality, at a stroke he brought into the public sphere, as the scholar Linda Dowling has argued, 'a modern discourse of male love . . . a new language of moral legitimacy pointing forward to Anglo-American decriminalization and, ultimately, a fully developed assertion of homosexual rights'.[17]

After the first criminal trial ended in a hung jury, Wilde was tried again and convicted on seven counts of gross indecency on 25 May 1895. His sentence, two years with hard labour, was the maximum permissible by law, although the presiding judge announced it 'totally inadequate for such a case as this'. It was effectively a death sentence to a man of Wilde's nature. Under the punitive late Victorian prison regime of 'hard labour, hard fare and hard board', Wilde would be kept isolated in a single small cell, forbidden to communicate or associate with other prisoners. Identified only by his cell number, he would be deprived of reading and writing materials, his diet and living conditions calibrated at the minimum necessary to maintain life. 'Hard labour' meant that, for an initial period at least, he would spend six hours per day climbing the prison treadwheel (an ascent of 2,630 m/8,640 ft, equivalent to six ascents of Chicago's Sears Tower) or longer still mindlessly turning a mechanical crank or picking oakum in his cell. This prison regime – which was to be made more humane by Act of Parliament shortly after Wilde completed his sentence, partly as a result of his own imprisonment – has been called 'the most severe system of secondary punishment in English history', and one which amounted to 'scarcely veiled torture'.[18] It was designed to break the spirit of even the toughest offenders, and mental breakdowns were a requent occurrence.

On being imprisoned in London's Pentonville Prison, Wilde entered a long downward spiral that would have far-reaching effects not just on him personally, but also on the administration of British prisons. Within days of his arrival, the press reported that his mental and physical condition was rapidly deteriorating and that prison officials were becoming anxious on his account.

In early June Wilde was released from the treadwheel, taken to the prison infirmary and then assigned less onerous hard labour (oakum-picking). But his condition worsened and the bad press reports alarmed government officials already politically nervous about the inhumane and controversial prison system. Just days before Wilde's conviction, the long-serving head of British prisons had been forced to resign when the Gladstone Committee, set up the previous year following a series of disturbing press exposés, submitted its formal report recommending a raft of prison reforms. Probably for political reasons, Wilde was visited in his cell in June by the Liberal statesman Richard Haldane QC, a member of the Gladstone Committee, who promised to obtain books for Wilde to read, and later in June he was transferred to Wandsworth Prison in south London.

At Wandsworth, Wilde only fared worse. He continued losing weight, spent long periods in the infirmary and contemplated taking his own life. In November 1895 he was transferred again, this time to the more secluded regional prison at Reading, in Berkshire, where he would spend the final eighteen months of his sentence in cell C.3.3. (cell 3 on landing 3 of cellblock 3) and where authorities probably hoped he would be largely invisible to the outside world. But his deterioration continued unabated – the prison's governor, Lt Col. Henry Isaacson, ruthlessly punished him for even minor infractions – and by the first anniversary of his conviction his friends were growing alarmed for his life and sanity. In June 1896 Frank Harris, one of the most influential journalists in London as well as one of Wilde's closest friends (Harris had tried to dissuade Wilde from pursuing his libel action against Queensberry), approached the new chairman of the Prison Commission with these concerns, and

Reading Prison, *c.* 1900.

to his surprise he was immediately dispatched to Reading to see for himself how Wilde was being treated and report back to the Commission upon his return.

Harris's visit on 16 June 1896 represents a critical turning point. Wilde wrote towards the end of his sentence that had he been released around the time of Harris's visit, he would have 'left this place loathing it and every official in it with a bitterness of hatred that would have poisoned my life'.[19] But the changes that ensued in the wake of Harris's visit ensured that Wilde completed his sentence and was eventually released in a very different spirit. The immediate upshot was that, probably at Harris's prompting, Wilde drafted the first and lengthiest of several petitions he was to compose to the Home Secretary seeking an early release. In it Wilde listed the many privations under which he suffered – none worse, he said, than the absence of books and 'the entire deprivation of literature to one to whom Literature was once the first thing of life' – and expressed his very real fears of losing both his mental and bodily health.[20]

An eloquent indictment of the late Victorian prison system as well as a forerunner to the detailed letters about prison conditions that Wilde would write to the press upon his release, this petition failed in its immediate objective of securing an early release. But Harris's intervention ensured that Wilde's complaints about the privations under which he suffered met with a sympathetic response from the new chairman of the Prison Commission. The latter duly set up a formal investigation into Wilde's health, reassigned the dictatorial Isaacson and replaced him with a new, more empathetic governor, and, perhaps most importantly of all, instructed Isaacson's replacement, Major James O. Nelson, to provide Wilde with adequate reading material as well as paper, pen and ink 'for use in his leisure moments'.[21] Wilde would later call Nelson 'the most Christ-like man I ever met' and would send him an inscribed copy of the first edition of *The Ballad of Reading Gaol*. One of Nelson's first acts as governor was to issue Wilde with a bound notebook and to approve the vast bulk of a long list of books requested by Wilde. This list included the works of Tennyson, Marlowe, Spencer, Keats and Chaucer, as well as a Greek Testament, a prose translation of Dante's *Divina Commedia*, Renan's *Vie de Jésus* (Life of Jesus) and *Les Apôtres* (The Apostles) in the original French, and essays by Carlyle, Newman and Emerson.

It is hard to overstate the importance of these reading and writing materials, as well as the regime change that accompanied them, for Wilde's sanity and imagination during the remainder of his sentence. He immediately set about reading and taking notes. Governor Nelson also encouraged Wilde to confide in him daily and relaxed the punitive regime enforced by his predecessor, allowing Wilde time to write late into the evening; and he stretched or simply ignored prison regulations so that Wilde might write frequently to his friends outside, sometimes with instructions for them to write back under cover to Nelson. By November 1896 Wilde had begun one of the most important and influential works of his life, a long letter to Lord Alfred Douglas in which he not only takes stock of his past life, including his relationship with Douglas, but constructs a meaningful future for himself by reflecting on the significance of all that had happened to him. Wilde would add to this letter incrementally over the next six months, by which time it would grow into something far more capacious and self-expressive than is usually understood by a 'letter'. But he would never send it to Douglas. By April 1897, one month before his release, Wilde had realized that the letter possessed lasting historical and literary importance. In a letter to Robert Ross written at this date, in which he laid out plans for disseminating the letter, he even playfully suggested treating it like a Papal Bull and giving it the Latin title *Epistola: In Carcere et Vinculis* (Letter: In Prison and in Chains). On leaving prison in May 1897, Wilde handed the manuscript to Ross, having the previous month given Ross 'complete control over my plays, books and papers' and named him his literary executor in the event of his death. In 1905, five years after Wilde's death, as we shall see, Ross published carefully selected excerpts from the letter to widespread acclaim under the title *De profundis* (meaning 'from the depths', after Psalm 130).

While large parts of Wilde's letter concern his relations with Alfred Douglas and are full of vituperation, Ross would publish only those parts of it that Wilde had identified as 'good and nice in intention' and of likely interest to readers concerned 'to know something of what is happening to my soul'.[22] Critics have long questioned the sincerity and depth of these parts, with their professions of newfound humility, penitence and Christianity, as well as the implicit egotism driving Wilde's connections between himself and Jesus Christ. Certainly Wilde's understanding of Christianity was unorthodox and deeply personal. The basis of Christ's nature, he argues, 'was the same as that of the nature of the artist', while in his relations with living people Christ 'realised . . . that imaginative sympathy which in the sphere of Art is the sole secret of creation'. So far as Wilde's reflections on Christ are concerned, the essay reflects his recent readings of Renan's historical *Vie de Jésus*, as well as recent incursions into the writings of Newman, Emerson and Carlyle, among others, although his assertions that 'Christ's place is . . . with the poets' and 'Christ is the most supreme of Individualists' extend the idea that 'he who would lead a Christ-like life is he who is perfectly and absolutely himself', which Wilde had first developed in 'The Soul of Man under Socialism'. With some justice, the letter has been called 'an act of auto-hagiography' and Wilde's attempt to write 'a gospel of his own'.

But judgements about the sincerity and depth of *De profundis* miss the point, for it is first and foremost a feat of writing. Its rhetoric is majestic, and even its invectives against Lord Alfred Douglas, heavily revised and sharpened over many weeks, have great emotional and verbal force. As Wilde's friend and sometime disciple Max Beerbohm explained about the 1905 text, 'the book [is] essentially the artistic essay of an artist.' Beerbohm was responding to a heavily redacted text, from which Wilde's embittered references to Douglas and Queensberry had been entirely cut. Nonetheless he reminds us that *De profundis* is fundamentally an imaginative and verbal document, not a truth-telling and historical record, and it is no less a 'beautiful thing' than the artworks Wilde had theorized about in 'The Decay of Lying' and the Preface to *Dorian Gray.* In the act of writing it, Wilde rediscovered and reclaimed himself, putting himself on a higher ethical footing than the society that had imprisoned him. He saved his sanity and his artistry in the process. The justice system had ruthlessly tried to silence him, stripping away his humanity until he became 'merely the figure and letter of a little cell in a long gallery, one of a thousand lifeless numbers, as of a thousand lifeless lives'.[23] But Wilde used the letter to reclaim and reassert his identity as both man and writer. 'Once a lord of language, [I] have no words in which to express my anguish and my shame . . . or to move with sufficient stateliness of music through the purple pageant of my incommunicable woe,' he had written bitterly, early in 1896, with regard to his mother's death.[24] With *De profundis*, Wilde became a 'lord of language' once again.

TEN

Sebastian Melmoth

Monsieur Sebastian Melmoth is my name now to the world

WILDE, letter to Mrs Bernard Beere, *c.* 22 May 1897

When Wilde left prison on 19 May 1897, his continued residence in Great Britain was out of the question. So too was any identification in public as 'Oscar Wilde'. His name was now permanently associated with disgrace and scandal in the eyes of the Victorians, and he never again employed it on the cover or title page of a book. His wife and children, now legally and permanently separated from him, resided in Italy, where they had adopted the last name 'Holland' in an effort to shield themselves from Wilde's disgrace. Upon release, Wilde exiled himself on the European mainland too, where he adopted 'Sebastian Melmoth' as a pseudonym.

Ostensibly this 'fantastic name' was a practical measure 'to avoid the prying eye and the foolish tongue' and 'prevent postmen having fits'.[1] But the name was carefully selected, and Wilde relished its symbolism: St Sebastian was an early Christian martyr, persecuted and savagely killed at the hands of the Romans. St Sebastian has been called the patron saint of homosexuals, and according to Thomas Mann he symbolizes 'an intellectual and

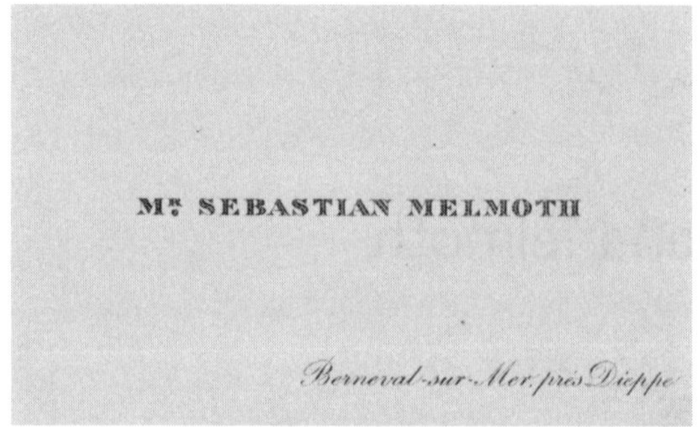

Calling card for 'Sebastian Melmoth', Wilde's pseudonym in exile in France.

virginal manliness, which clenches its teeth and stands in modest defiance of the swords and spears that pierce its side'.[2] Mann was probably thinking of the painted depiction of the martyred saint by Guido Reni that Wilde too had admired ever since first seeing it in Genoa's Palazzo Rosso in 1877 (see Chapter Two). It is easy to see the reasons for such admiration. With its evocations of gender-bending sensuality, visceral pain, eroticism and otherworldly transcendence, Reni's painting – one of seven he painted of St Sebastian – is a paean to youthful male beauty.[3] 'Melmoth' alludes to the Gothic novel *Melmoth the Wanderer*, by Wilde's Irish great-uncle Charles Maturin, whose Faust-like protagonist, half-hero and half-villain, having sold his soul to the Devil in exchange for an extended life, wanders the earth as the appointed day of his death draws near, haunting the dreams of men while hoping that one of them will absolve him of his pact.

Wilde immediately set about having visiting cards made up with his new name. He kept them in a silver card case, a gift from his old friend Ada Leverson, on which the name was also engraved, and he owned at least one shirt monogrammed with his new initials. These initials were also engraved on an expensive silver toiletry set given to him by his close friend Reggie Turner.

Guido Reni, *St Sebastian*, *c*. 1615, oil on canvas.

For the first few days after his release Wilde resided at Dieppe, on the Normandy coast, but his pseudonym failed to provide the privacy he craved. Dieppe was a fashionable destination for English and French tourists alike, roughly equidistant from both London and Paris, and also something of an artists' and writers' colony. But his presence there became well known and reported in the papers, and within a few days he decamped for the obscure coastal village of Berneval-sur-Mer, about 8 kilometres (5 mi.) away, where the name Sebastian Melmoth had a better chance of working.

Before leaving Dieppe, Wilde attended to two important pieces of unfinished business, both of which speak to his renewed sense of himself as a writer. A year earlier, on 11 February 1896, the French actor-manager Aurélien-Marie Lugné-Poe had given Wilde's play *Salome* its theatrical debut at the Théâtre de l'Oeuvre in Paris – the event had been widely reported in the papers – while other French intellectuals had exerted themselves before this by writing newspaper articles in support of Wilde. Wilde had been greatly affected by these tributes to his artistry on hearing about them in jail, and he felt that Lugné-Poe's *Salome* production had done much to bring about his better treatment by the English authorities. Five days after his release, therefore, he invited Lugné-Poe to do him the honour of dining with him. When Lugné-Poe took up Wilde's invitation the very next day, Wilde impressed on him 'the importance of writing no interview, and giving no details of my strange name, my place of sojourn, my altered appearance, and the like'.[4] Nevertheless he knew that Lugné-Poe was an important conduit to the French intelligentsia and he wanted him to publicize broadly 'how grateful I was and am to France for their recognition of me as an artist in the day of my humiliation, and how my better treatment in an English prison was due to the French men of letters'. At the same time, he discussed with Lugné-Poe the possibility of staging a new, as yet unwritten, play, based like *Salome* on a biblical incident. 'Being religious in surroundings and treatment of subject', he said, this would be 'not a play for a run, at all. Three performances are the most I think I could expect. All I want is to have my artistic reappearance, and my own rehabilitation through art, in Paris, not in London.'[5]

The other piece of unfinished business concerned prison conditions. 'The prison-system is absolutely and entirely wrong,' Wilde writes in *De profundis*; 'I would give anything to be able to alter it when I go out. I intend to try.' Within days of his release he had written to the *Daily Chronicle*, a champion of the cause of prison reform, detailing the daily abuses inflicted on prisoners and protesting at 'the cruelty inseparable from a stupid system'.[6] Prompted by a prison warder's recent dismissal for giving biscuits to a group of poor children imprisoned on remand for snaring rabbits, Wilde's letter highlighted the abusive treatment of children in prison, as well as the deleterious effects on prisoners' mental health of their permanent, silent, solitary confinement. As Jack London later wrote, 'Oscar Wilde, God rest his soul, voices the cry of the prison child, which, in varying degree, is the cry of the prison man and woman.'[7] Wilde's letter, subsequently published as a penny pamphlet titled *Children in Prison, and Other Cruelties of Prison Life*, is a masterpiece of unadorned rhetoric, and within days it was the subject of leading articles and questions on the floor of Parliament. Wilde signed his protest 'Oscar Wilde', determined to harness his name and fame to the cause of prison reform. But it was a rare public use of his birth name post-release, and the last time in his life that he signed a publication of any kind with this name.[8]

At first Wilde enjoyed the peaceful environs of Berneval, where he befriended the village priest, bathed regularly in the sea, attended Mass and briefly renewed his youthful flirtation with Roman Catholicism. He also set about composing *The Ballad of Reading Gaol*, another powerful protest against the late Victorian prison system, as we shall shortly see. But by the end of August he was becoming discontented and restless. The local villagers had eventually seen through his persona of Sebastian Melmoth and now steered clear of him ('If Sebastian Melmoth honoured Berneval by his presence . . . Oscar Wilde shamed us,' declared one resident many years later). There were other reasons for his restlessness too. Days after arriving in Berneval, he had sought a reconciliation with his wife and children, but Constance had rebuffed him (he was never to see his wife or children again), making him feel 'disgraced and evil', and he was dispirited at the thought of not seeing his children again.[9] 'Is there on earth a crime so terrible that, in punishment of it, a father can be prevented from seeing his children?' he was to ask a year or two later.[10]

At the same time, he was now engaged in a clandestine correspondence with Lord Alfred Douglas, who longed to see him and vice versa. Wilde had told Robert Ross that he had 'a real terror' of Douglas and 'I hope never to see him again.' He was aware that Ross thoroughly disapproved of his relationship with Douglas, however, and his surviving letters to Douglas tell a different story. By 6 June he was writing to Douglas every day, experiencing 'the strange new joy of talking to [Douglas] daily', and within a few more days he was exploring conditions for a possible reunion. In the middle of the month he invited his 'dear honey-sweet boy' to visit.[11] However, Ross got wind of the intended meeting and informed Wilde's family solicitor, Arthur Hansell, who promptly resigned as Wilde's personal lawyer while sternly reminding Wilde that, under the terms of his separation agreement with his wife (whereby Constance provided him with a small monthly stipend), a reunion between Wilde and Douglas was out of the question.

In Douglas's absence, Wilde entertained many old friends at Berneval in the weeks following his release, and he also periodically went in to Dieppe to carouse with the poet Ernest Dowson and the decadent publisher Leonard Smithers. Smithers, who would later publish *The Ballad of Reading Gaol* and the first editions of *The Importance of Being Earnest* and *An Ideal Husband*, would prove himself to be an especially firm friend. Wilde also made progress on *The Ballad of Reading Gaol*, which at this point he hoped to publish in the *Daily Chronicle* or the *New York World* when finished. But the legal obstacle placed in the way of any reunion with Douglas, as well as his wife's sustained obduracy over a visit, continued to rankle, and by the end of August Wilde was secretly making fresh plans to meet Douglas.

The two finally met in Rouen, nearly 80 kilometres (50 mi.) south of Berneval, on 28 or 29 August, where they stayed overnight at the Hôtel de la Poste under their own names. It was one of the most momentous events of Wilde's life. Douglas later recounted that after a tearful meeting at the railway station, the two 'walked about all day, arm in arm, or hand in hand, and were perfectly happy'.[12] Although it only lasted 24 hours, their clandestine reunion was to have grave consequences for the rest of their lives. They agreed that they would soon reunite for longer in Naples, where Douglas intended spending the winter.

After returning downcast and alone to Berneval, Wilde duly decamped for Naples in mid-September, Douglas joining him by arrangement on the journey there. They had told nobody of their plans to elope together, and when after a few days they took a house, the Villa Giudice, in Posillipo, even their closest friends were shocked. But the reunion, which Wilde had anticipated in *De profundis*, was predictable: 'My going back to Bosie was psychologically inevitable,' Wilde wrote to a reproachful Ross; 'setting aside the interior life of the soul with its passion for self-realisation at all costs, the world forced it on me . . . The world shuts its gateway against me, and the door of Love lies open.'[13] 'You leave out of consideration the great love I have for Bosie,' he remarked to a shocked Reggie Turner. 'I love him, and have always loved him.'[14] 'I must remake my maimed life on my own lines,' he insisted.[15]

It was a reunion based on mutual love – Douglas 'loves me very dearly, more than he loves or can love anyone else', Wilde wrote – as well as on mutual literary respect and aspirations. 'It is to a poet that I am going back,' Wilde told Turner, while telling Douglas that 'my only hope of again doing beautiful work in art is being with you.' The two were unquestionably productive at first: Douglas wrote a number of the lyrics and sonnets that were to open his acclaimed 1899 collection *The City of the Soul*, while Wilde added over one hundred lines to *The Ballad of Reading Gaol* and carefully revised the poem for publication. But the two men also enjoyed themselves in the 'evil and luxurious' atmosphere of Naples.[16] It was a city where homosexuality was openly tolerated and to which northern European homosexuals, fleeing from strict homophobic laws in their home countries, naturally gravitated. Their cohabitation caused an international scandal when it was reported in the papers, and when this scandal reached the ears of Wilde's wife and Douglas's mother, they each threatened to break off the allowances on which Wilde and Douglas lived unless the two pledged immediately to cease living together.

Consequently, Douglas was forced to depart Naples in early December 1897, though not without first getting his mother to bestow £200 on Wilde in addition to settling all their unpaid bills. He was followed by Wilde in February. Both men headed for Paris, perhaps the most permissive city in Europe, where doubtless they hoped to see one another without exciting

Wilde and Douglas in Naples, 1897.

comment, and it was on or around the day of Wilde's arrival there that *The Ballad of Reading Gaol* was published, by Leonard Smithers, in an attractive cinnamon-coloured cloth binding at Wilde's own suggestion. The coincidence of the poem's publication and Wilde's arrival in Paris was no accident. Wilde had long wanted to achieve a 'rehabilitation through art' in Paris ('the artistic capital of the world' and 'the abode of artists . . . *la ville artiste*'), and he hoped that *The Ballad* would facilitate such a rehabilitation in both Paris and London.[17] He had spent longer composing and revising the poem than just about any other of his works, and while he clearly hoped that *The Ballad* – which hauntingly dramatizes how 'the fetid breath of living Death/ Chokes up' each prison cell, and 'all, but Lust, is turned to dust/ In Humanity's machine' – would do much to advance the cause of prison reform, he hoped too that the poem would be his artistic swansong.

The
Ballad of Reading Gaol
By
C. 3. 3.

Leonard Smithers
Royal Arcade London W
Mdcccxcviii

The Ballad of Reading Gaol (Leonard Smithers, 1898), title page. Wilde's authorship is identified by his prison cell number ('C. 3. 3.'), not by his personal name.

The Ballad succeeds magnificently in both respects. Its dramatization of the regime of enforced silence, solitary confinement and 'hard labour, hard fare and hard board' under which Wilde had himself suffered is powerful, and within days of its appearance the poem was twice mentioned or quoted on the floor of Parliament, where reforms of the prison system were being debated in the run-up to passage of the 1898 Prisons Act.

'Everybody in this House has read the startling and striking poem, written by a prisoner recently liberated,' declared the Irish MP T. P. O'Connor.[18] To lend force to the poem as both a protest and a cry from the heart, Wilde signed it not with his own name but with his prison cell number, C.3.3., emphasizing his centrality as a witness to the cruel regime dramatized in the poem. Nonetheless he knew that he would be recognized as the poem's author – indeed, he was counting on it as the source of the poem's appeal to readers. Unsurprisingly, his authorship was alluded to indirectly in several of the laudatory reviews and notices that appeared in the press, although he was not explicitly named in any of them, with Arthur Symons going so far as to suggest that it was the finest work produced to date by an 'extraordinary talent' that had hitherto shown little concern with 'matters of common experience'.[19] The poem is 'good literature', another reviewer remarked, because 'the document is authentic' and the poem is 'the faithful record of experiences through which the writer . . . has passed'.[20] It was 'wrung out of me, a cry of pain', Wilde himself memorably remarked, like the 'cry of Marsyas, not the song of Apollo'.[21]

Nonetheless the poem is far more than propaganda in the cause of prison reform. Wilde carefully considered how to reconcile his artistic principles with the poem's urgent politics and realism. It is 'a sort of denial of my own philosophy of art in many ways', he told the illustrator and writer Laurence Housman, 'terribly realistic for me, and drawn from actual experience'. But Wilde skilfully employs the ballad form for both political and poetic purposes, lending the poem an imaginative and verbal power that is unusual among works that strive to achieve a political effect. In the years since its publication, it has elicited high praise from, among others, André Maurois, Albert Camus, W. B. Yeats, John Cowper Powys and Jorge Luis Borges. '*The Ballad* is true poetry,' observed Borges, 'a judgment which every reader's emotion confesses and repeats'; it is 'the best tragic ballad since "The Ancient Mariner"', said Cowper Powys.[22]

Moreover, *The Ballad* is as paradoxical as many of the works that Wilde had authored at the height of his success. It turns on its narrator's empathy with a convicted murderer, whom Wilde represents as the victim of a system that 'straws the wheat and saves the chaff/ With a most evil fan'. The convicted murderer, identified in the poem's dedication as the real-life Charles Thomas Wooldridge, executed at Reading Prison on 7 July 1896, is a symbolic reflection of Wilde himself; and Wilde's identification with him transvalues traditional notions of good and bad no less than his dramatizations of the sexual outcasts Mrs Erlynne, Mrs Arbuthnot and Mrs Cheveley had done years before. As importantly, the poem's central refrain, that 'each man kills the thing he loves,' while doubtless reflecting the misery Wilde had occasioned or been subject to in his own life, is an invitation to attend to the cruelty and violence that lurk just beneath the surface of every humane action. Implicitly it is also a plea for greater charity and empathy towards those who transgress, although it is conspicuous that only the murderer's fellow inmates show themselves capable of such empathy within the poem itself. For, as Wilde had written to the *Daily Chronicle*, 'suffering and the community of suffering makes people kind,' and prisoners exert a 'humanising influence' of which the prison system itself is incapable. The poem underscores the argument in his letter to the *Daily Chronicle* that 'it is not the prisoners who need reformation. It is the prisons.'[23]

For a brief while it appeared as if the poem would indeed bring about Wilde's artistic rehabilitation. The first edition sold out within days and, as already mentioned, the poem was well reviewed in Britain. Its appearance was timely: the movement for prison reform was coming to a head, interest in Wilde's incarceration was widespread, and one month after the poem's publication, as Parliament was debating the bill that would result in the 1898 Prisons Act, Wilde wrote a second lengthy letter to the *Daily Chronicle*, detailing some of the practical reforms that were needed in the bill. That he signed this letter 'The Author of *The Ballad of Reading Gaol*' is an indication of how confident and proud he now was of his poem's success. According to Wilde's bibliographer Christopher Millard, 'the Commissioners appointed to inquire in the question of Prison Reform . . . spent three days considering the suggestions' Wilde made in his letter.[24] Within four months the poem had entered its sixth edition, representing 5,000 copies, and Wilde's name was eventually added to the title page of the seventh edition (another 2,000 copies), one year after the first, in brackets after 'c.3.3.', confirming an authorship that everybody already knew.

The poem briefly promised to bring about Wilde's artistic redemption in France, too, where Wilde was for a while feted by the literary avant-garde. In April 1898 the poem was warmly reviewed in the *Mercure de France*, and the following month the same journal published a translation by Henry-D. Davray, followed some months later by a freestanding book edition, with Wilde's English and Davray's French on facing pages. But Wilde's rehabilitation in the eyes of France's literary class was short-lived, and just two months after his arrival in Paris he complained that he rarely met 'literary people' and his companions and friends were 'such as I can get and . . . have to pay for'. Respectable people now 'shut their doors to him', André Gide later remarked, while according to Vincent O'Sullivan 'even among those who had remained faithful the longest, some were now saying that Wilde was no longer fit to be seen.'[25]

This ostracism was almost certainly because in Paris Wilde, for the first time in his life, lived openly as a homosexual. He made the most of the city's numerous venues for meeting attractive and sexually available young men, he took several boyfriends, and he was particularly enamoured of the companionship of a young half-English ex-marine named Maurice Gilbert, whom he met two weeks after his arrival in Paris and who was later to prove one of the most loyal and considerate of Wilde's friends. By April 1898 Gilbert may even have been sharing Wilde's hotel rooms with him. 'The curves of his mouth are a source of endless fascination and wonder to me,' Wilde was to remark in July 1898. 'He grows dearer to me daily,' he had remarked of Gilbert four months earlier. Wilde introduced Gilbert to some of his closest remaining homosexual friends, including Ross, Turner and Douglas. (Douglas arrived in Paris in April following a long spell on the French Riviera with his mother, and he swiftly became enamoured of Gilbert too.) When Wilde's old friend the journalist Jacques Daurelle witnessed Wilde embracing Gilbert in public, he accused Wilde of having 'retourné à son vomissement' (returned to his vomit), and Wilde's unashamed, open homosexuality would also cause fallings-out with other old friends who feared for their own respectability.

Freed from the need to live hypocritically, Wilde was now determined to live on his own terms, and before long he was admitting to the absurdity of maintaining a pseudonym since he was 'as well known [in Paris] as in London'.[26] 'In the mortal sphere I have fallen in and out of love,' he observed to Robert Ross a few months before his death in 1900; 'I have fluttered hawks and doves alike . . . My mouth is twisted with kissing, and I feed on fevers.' He embraced his new bohemian existence with passion, spirit, recklessness and often with good humour. 'The Cloister or the Café – there is my future. I tried the Hearth, but it was a failure,' he wittily remarked to the often censorious Ross.

He paid a heavy price for being himself, however, and outwardly at least the final two-and-a-half years of Wilde's life make for a depressing summary. The return to Douglas put paid to all chances of respectability and social redemption, cementing Wilde's alienation from his wife and children. And when his wife died suddenly and unexpectedly not two months after his arrival in Paris, Wilde knew that any chance of once more seeing his beloved children was now gone. Ostracism and condemnation such as Daurelle's were frequent, although they did not prevent Wilde from enjoying the company and sexual favours of young men such as Gilbert, and as we have seen Wilde was defiant in admitting to being a 'Uranian'. If he made little concealment in London 'he made none at all in Paris,' remarked O' Sullivan; 'he made no secret of the fact that he had once more given himself over to his old habits,' confirms Douglas.[27]

Moreover, Wilde was constantly penniless and in debt – not for any lack of income, it must be added, but rather for his inability to retain the not inconsiderable sums that friends provided him with as support. Constance had renewed his allowance following his separation from Douglas in Naples, and this allowance continued after her death in April 1898 with Ross acting as agent. In Paris Wilde also received regular stipends from, among others,

Frank Harris, Leonard Smithers and (later) Alfred Douglas. But he spent money recklessly as he had always done. He loathed cheap restaurants and cheap lodgings, and he spent freely on others, especially drinking companions and attractive young men. He often cadged from friends who willingly turned a blind eye to his excesses, and while he never went to such extremes in obtaining money as his much-admired Thomas Griffiths Wainewright in 'Pen, Pencil, and Poison', he nevertheless entered into dubious financial schemes with several different individuals, assigning them the production rights for a new, as yet unwritten, play while knowing full well that he would never compose it and, still worse, knowing also that he had previously sold the rights to other brave prospectors. As he had once written, 'The only thing that can console one for being poor is extravagance.'[28]

Perhaps the most depressing aspect of Wilde's final two-and-a-half years was his inability to undertake new literary work. For all his determination to enjoy the company of the demi-monde, he knew that something vital had died in him: 'Poverty with its degrading preoccupation with money, the loss of many friends, the deprivation of my children . . . [and] the terrible effects of two years of silence, solitude, and ill-treatment – all these have . . . to a large extent, killed if not entirely that great joy in living that I once had,' he mournfully told his friend Georgina Weldon in May 1898. 'His will had been broken,' André Gide was later to write, somewhat exaggeratedly; 'the first months he could still delude himself, but he very soon gave way. It was like an abdication.' To be sure, in the summer of 1898 Wilde made extensive revisions to *The Importance of Being Earnest* after Smithers courageously offered to publish it in a format uniform with the exquisite editions of *Lady Windermere's Fan* and *A Woman of*

No Importance published in 1893 and 1894 respectively. Wilde worked hard at these revisions, sharpening the play's wit and adding many of its most memorable lines. But when the play eventually appeared in February 1899, bound in lilac cloth with a gilt cover design by Charles Shannon, readers and critics alike boycotted it much as audiences had done in the fateful days following Wilde's arrest. His revisions for the first edition of *An Ideal Husband*, published by Smithers in July 1899, were more perfunctory. The most important were the addition of witty, printed characterizations of the play's dramatis personae in the stage directions that are now among its most notable elements. After critics and readers boycotted this book too, Wilde never wrote another word for publication.

Nonetheless Wilde found loyal friends among the French demi-monde, such as the painter Henri de Toulouse-Lautrec and the young poets Jehan Rictus, Michael Robas and Ernest La Jeunesse. The last was one of many bohemians who regularly accompanied Wilde to the Calasaya Bar, a plush American-style bar near the Credit Lyonnais, next door to the offices of *La Revue blanche.* Wilde also fitfully sought solace on the French and Italian Riviera, in Switzerland, Rome or Sicily, as the guest of wealthy friends such as Frank Harris or Harold Mellor. But he quickly tired of his hosts' company and vice versa, and Paris, although expensive, operated on him like a magnet. To Paris he always returned, and it would be in Paris that he died and was buried in the winter of 1900 as the nineteenth century blended into the twentieth.

In addition to his desperation for money and for lively company, Wilde's final months were plagued by ill health, notably a recurrence of an inner-ear infection that had troubled him in prison and from which he would eventually die. But he was always skilled at seizing pleasure where it was least expected, at least for a moment, and over the final months of his life he went two or three evenings a week to the Paris World's Fair, which ran from April to November 1900. There he 'amused himself like a big child', admiring the exhibits, walking among the pavilions, in which 'he built again his own palace of fame, riches, and immortality,' and making himself at home in the Café d'Egypte, in the spectacular Egyptian pavilion, where he was served drinks by 'a slim brown Egyptian, rather like a handsome bamboo walking-stick', and dreamed of a 'wanton sylvan boy of Italy' who had recently visited him from Naples.[29]

By the late summer of 1900, Wilde's inner-ear infection had extended into the mastoid and was becoming life-threatening. From September onwards he was more or less permanently bedridden, and in October expensive, radical ear surgery was performed – only to prove futile. From mid-October onwards, an increasingly pain-ridden Wilde was attended by Turner and Ross, who came specially from England for this purpose, as well as by Gilbert and by Jean Dupoirier, the selfless owner of Wilde's cheap hotel, who had long stopped worrying about how Wilde would pay his bills and who instead concerned himself only with his tenant's well-being. Dupoirier would later attend Wilde's funeral, providing a cheap wreath of funerary beads inscribed simply 'À mon locataire' (For my tenant). The pain was now excruciating, largely untouched by the chloral and opium that his doctors prescribed as panaceas. There were a few moments in which Wilde was sufficiently restored to his old self to remark that he was 'dying beyond his means', that he was 'fighting a duel to the death' with his room's bilious wallpaper, featuring chocolate-coloured flowers on a blue background, and that 'one of us has to go.' In early November, Wilde told Ross and Turner that 'he did not care if he had only a short time to live' and wanted only 'to be out of pain'.

Wilde was still conscious and lucid on 12 November when Ross, obliged to leave Paris to attend to his mother, took a tearful final farewell. A few days later Wilde was delirious and it was evident to his doctors and nurses that he was dying. At Turner's insistence, Ross returned breathlessly on 29 November only to be told by Wilde's doctors that he could live for two more days at most.

Ross immediately set about searching for a priest who could administer Communion and the Last Rites, and effectively receive Wilde into his beloved Catholic Church. But the great wit and playwright was now unconscious, unable to take the Communion wafer, and although the attendant priest, Father Cuthbert Dunne, later swore that Wilde was 'inwardly conscious' of his ministrations, there has been considerable debate about whether Wilde was truly admitted into the Church at all. Possibly Dunne's ministrations owed more to Ross's own devout Catholicism or to his concern that Wilde's corpse would, if unconsecrated, be transported to the Paris Morgue (where it might be left unclaimed indefinitely under the name Sebastian Melmoth, under which Wilde was registered at his hotel) than to any sudden deathbed conversion on Wilde's part. As Richard Ellmann aptly puts it, nobody can be sure whether the application of sacred oils to Wilde's hands and feet in his final moments was truly 'a ritualized pardon for his omissions and commissions', on the one hand, or 'like putting a green carnation in his buttonhole' on the other.[30]

Wilde laid out shortly after his death, 30 November 1900.

Wilde died painfully on 30 November with the ever-loyal Ross and Turner ministering to him up until his last breath. Ross later gave a moving account of Wilde's deathbed agony that has often been reprinted or quoted, although, according to Turner, this account was an 'invention' and 'Oscar's end was as quiet and peaceful as that of an innocent child.'[31] Wilde was just 46 years old. A few days later, after a depressing, sparsely attended funeral in Paris, he was buried in a temporary plot at Bagneux Cemetery outside the city limits, about 6 kilometres (4 mi.) away. The burial was even more sparsely attended than the funeral service: only Douglas, Ross, Turner and Dupoirier accompanied the coffin to the interment, along with five or six loyal French intellectuals, including Paul Fort, Henry-D. Davray (later Wilde's first French biographer) and La Jeunesse, the last of whom would days later compose the most moving eulogy to his dead friend. The principal mourner was Douglas, who, according to Fort's later account, threw himself into Wilde's grave as the coffin was lowered, screaming 'Oscar! Oscar!', and had to be forcibly removed.

Wilde's grave was marked with a simple stone on which was inscribed 'Verbis meis addere nihil audebant et super illos stillebat eloquium meum, Job xxix, 22. R.I.P.' (To my words they durst add nothing, and my speech dropped upon them).

EPILOGUE

'A Man Who Stood in Symbolic Relations to . . . My Age'

I was a man who stood in symbolic relations to the art and culture of my age . . . Few men hold such a position in their own lifetime . . . It is usually discerned, if discerned at all, by the historian or the critic long after both the man and his age have passed away.

WILDE, *De profundis*, composed 1896–7

Buried in a pauper's grave beyond the city limits of his beloved Paris, with just a handful of loyal friends and acolytes in attendance, Wilde died a pariah, bankrupt and bereft. 'If he had begun a decent life people would have forgiven him,' privately remarked his one-time friend the writer Wilfrid Scawen Blunt, 'but he returned to Paris and his dog's vomit and this is the end.' He 'died as he should have died, in foul obscurity', fulminated the *North American Review* in one of many brief, unsympathetic press notices that appeared in the immediate wake of Wilde's death; 'that he should have been able to outlive exposure proves how utterly the manhood had been rotted out of him.'[1]

The venom and homophobia of these responses to Wilde's death appear shocking today. But we should remember that although homosexuality was partially decriminalized in England and Wales in 1967 (sex between men over 21 remained a crime in

Scotland and Northern Ireland until 1980 and 1982 respectively, while throughout Britain the age of consent for homosexual sex was not equalized with that for heterosexual sex until 2000), the crime of gross indecency remained on British statute books until 2003 and Wilde was not formally pardoned of the crimes for which he was convicted until 2017.

For much of the twentieth century, Wilde remained unmentionable even where his literary genius was acknowledged. His Society comedies retained their popularity on stage and on screen, notwithstanding audiences' ignorance of how much of their author himself they contained, but not until the 1960s would works such as *The Picture of Dorian Gray*, *Salome* and 'Pen, Pencil, and Poison' be widely read, much less taught in the classroom. The publication of Wilde's correspondence in 1962, coupled with the partial lifting of legal sanctions against homosexuality in 1967, sparked a public redemption of sorts. But the study and teaching of Wilde and his works only acquired academic legitimacy with the publication of Richard Ellmann's magisterial biography of 1987. And only in the twenty-first century have scholarly editors and university presses committed themselves to producing authoritative, well-edited, reliable texts of Wilde's writings, including the previously unpublished uncensored text of *The Picture of Dorian Gray*, first published in 2011.

If it was late in coming, Wilde's rehabilitation had begun promisingly and quietly more than a century before, in large part through the actions of his devoted friend and former lover Robert Ross. As we have seen, Ross cared for Wilde in his final illness, arranged his funeral, and had been appointed by Wilde as his literary executor. In fact Ross far exceeded the role of *literary* executor. His first acts in the wake of Wilde's death were dedicated to clearing Wilde's debts and lifting his estate from bankruptcy so that Wilde's orphaned children might be provided for. He shrewdly acquired Wilde's copyrights from the Bankruptcy Receiver, sometimes with his own money, and he was aggressive and successful in his legal pursuit of unauthorized republications. By 1906 he had removed the estate from bankruptcy and generated a small, steady income for Wilde's children. He had also begun making plans for relocating Wilde's remains to a more permanent and fitting resting place.

As importantly, Ross quickly set about publishing a redacted version of the long autobiographical letter to Alfred Douglas that Wilde had entrusted to him upon his release from prison. Wilde had told Ross, on the point of sending him the manuscript, that 'some day the truth will have to be known,' and that he was 'not prepared to sit in the grotesque pillory they put me into, for all time'. He had inherited a name of high literary distinction from his parents, he told Ross, and he could not 'for eternity, allow that name to be the shield and catspaw of the Queensberrys'.[2] Wilde knew, perhaps even in the act of composing it, that his letter to Douglas would redeem him in the eyes of posterity long after the event of his death. 'If you are my literary executor,' he told Ross, 'you must be in possession of the only document that really gives any explanation of . . . a course of conduct that from the outside seems a combination of absolute idiocy with vulgar bravado.' Wilde spoke to Ross of the letter as one of the works whose sale might one day produce income for Cyril and Vyvyan, his children. The implication was that Ross might one day see fit to publish at least those parts of the letter that reflected to his credit.

It is hard today to overstate the importance of Ross's partial publication of the letter for the restoration of Wilde's literary reputation. Using Wilde's own instructions to him identifying passages that might freely be disseminated 'welded together with anything else you may extract that is good and nice in intention', Ross carefully excised all references to Douglas and his father, as well as anything indicative of the text's original character as a letter. These moves, together with Ross's decision to publish the work under the title *De profundis*, ensured that when the unredacted portions came out in February 1905, with a gilt-stamped cover design by Charles Ricketts, the critical and popular reaction was profound and immediate. 'The charitable man . . . must take [Wilde's] book for expiation and in it find his martyrdom,' remarked the *Saturday Review*.[3] 'The publication of so extraordinary a document is an event in English literature,' observed the critic Edmund Gosse.[4] Wilde once again proved himself 'a lord of language', remarked Max Beerbohm in *Vanity Fair*:

> no modern writer has achieved through prose the limpid and lyrical effects . . . achieved by Oscar Wilde. The words sing. There is nothing of that formality, that hard and cunning precision, which marks so much of the prose that we admire . . . [T]he expression is always magically natural and beautiful.[5]

'It is the right sort of book to come now in order to touch the hearts of men made cruel by ignorance,' observed Laurence Housman; 'Its reception . . . [was] unprophesiable five or six years ago.'[6] The first edition's print run of 10,000 copies sold out

Wilde's tomb today in Paris's Père Lachaise Cemetery. Erected in 1912, the monument by Jacob Epstein proved controversial and was not unveiled until 1914.

within days, and within six months the work went into five more editions in England alone. Authorized editions were also published in America and Germany, where the reception was similar.

From the publication of *De profundis* in 1905 dates the still widespread perception that Wilde died a tragic martyr to an unjust Victorian age. *De profundis* created new demand for his works and laid the groundwork for further acts of importance to the restoration of his reputation. In 1908 Methuen published a widely reviewed multi-volume collected edition of Wilde's works, carefully edited by Ross, bound in white buckram covers of Ricketts's design. (An authorized version of this edition appeared two years later in North America, although by this date, a flood of unauthorized piracies had already appeared there.) The volume containing *De profundis* was the thirteenth edition of that work to date and it considerably expanded the extracts previously published in 1905, accompanied now by the two important letters that Wilde had written to the *Daily Chronicle* about prison conditions.

In 1909 Ross succeeded in having Wilde's corpse reinterred permanently in Paris's landscaped Père Lachaise Cemetery, where the last remains of Frédéric Chopin, Gertrude Stein, Max Ernst, Marcel Proust, Honoré de Balzac and Jim Morrison (among many other notables) now reside too. On this occasion Ross was the chief mourner, Douglas having by this date violently repudiated his love for Wilde as well as his own youthful homosexual tendencies. The spot, now a site of secular pilgrimage, is today marked by a splendid Sphinx monolith by the sculptor Jacob Epstein, erected by subscription in 1912, on which Ross had inscribed the following lines from *The Ballad of Reading Gaol*:

And alien tears will fill for him
Pity's long-broken urn,
For his mourners will be outcast men,
And outcasts always mourn.

Thereafter the redemption of Oscar Wilde largely ceased for another forty years or so, halted in part by a stream of self-serving memoirs of Wilde by Douglas, who often painted Wilde, falsely and hypocritically, as the corrupter of his youth. Douglas's death in 1945 sparked a significant change, however, as well as a fresh seriousness of enquiry. Wilde's younger son, Vyvyan Holland, was in the forefront of this change, determined to correct the misconceptions propagated by Douglas and others. In 1948 Holland wrote the Introduction to a compendious single-volume *Complete Works of Oscar Wilde* that is still in print to this day (today introduced and curated by Wilde's grandson Merlin Holland); in 1949 he published what purported to be 'the first complete and accurate' edition of *De profundis*; and then, in 1954 – the year in which London County Council unveiled a commemorative blue plaque at Wilde's (and Holland's) family home in Tite Street – Holland published his moving memoir *Son of Oscar Wilde*. These publications – and still more the publication in 1962 of Wilde's surviving correspondence, skilfully edited by Rupert Hart-Davis, including a full, accurate transcription of his prison letter to Douglas – helped bring about a sea-change in understanding. This change owes something too to the work of the scholar and politician H. Montgomery Hyde, who in 1948 published a sympathetic, scholarly account of Wilde's criminal trials (still in print today), followed in 1963 by an equally sympathetic biographical account of Wilde's conviction and years of imprisonment. Wilde's late twentieth-century redemption owes much too to works of popular culture such as Albert Lewin's film adaptation of *The Picture of Dorian Gray* (1945), Anthony Asquith's 1952 film adaptation of *The Importance of Being Earnest* and Micheál Mac Liammóir's one-man stage show *The Importance of Being Oscar* (1960, reprised and updated repeatedly throughout the 1960s and broadcast by the BBC), as well as two sympathetic film adaptations of Wilde's life that appeared in 1960, *The Trials of Oscar Wilde* and *Oscar Wilde*, featuring such renowned British actors as Peter Finch, Ralph Richardson, Robert Morley and James Mason.

By the late 1960s Wilde was an iconic symbol for the emerging gay rights movement and a figurehead for all those oppressed and imprisoned through the unjust anti-homosexuality laws that were now beginning to be overturned. Untrammelled by the prejudices of early generations, scholars from the 1960s onwards began assessing more objectively Wilde's relations not merely to Victorian culture but also to the world in which we live today.

As Wilde himself put it in *De profundis*, 'I was a man who stood in symbolic relations to the art and culture of my age.' That Wilde stood in a critical relation to the art and culture of his day is clear from the explicit condemnation of his fellow Victorians in 'The Soul of Man under Socialism', as well as from the barely concealed critique of the social comedies, the fairy tales and *The Ballad of Reading Gaol*. Often understood as the spokesman for a narrow, self-involved 'art for art's sake', Wilde was one of the most social – and sociable – of Victorian intellectuals, always conscious of the effects of his language on audiences that were diverse in nature and whose ideological make-up he knew only too well. His social comedies and fictions held up a mirror to their early audiences, exposing the limitations of their desire for polished entertainments while eliciting laughter at the artifice of Victorian public life. More broadly, he exposed the artistic foundations on which the edifice of Victorian meaning was built. 'In matters of grave importance, style, not sincerity, is the gravest thing,' he famously wrote, and 'it is style that makes us believe in a thing – nothing but style.'[7] With their gilt-stamped bindings and elaborate designs, the exquisitely wrought editions of his writings published in Wilde's own lifetime constitute what the French philosopher Gilles Deleuze calls 'little non-signifying machines' and reveal as much about their readers as they do about 'the text itself'.[8] More than any other Victorian, Wilde was conscious that his art and his very self were 'aesthetic' constructs, and he looked forward to strains in Modernism in which critical self-consciousness, commodification and the larger 'business' of art become the very subject of the artwork.

In this regard, his dialogues and essays – four of them gathered into the aptly named *Intentions* – display the richness and originality of his thought. In 'The Decay of Lying' and 'The Critic as Artist', as we have seen, Wilde overthrew the tenets of realism, sincerity and truthfulness that had dominated judgements about Victorian literature and art, replacing them with a fresh and wholly original attention to style, linguistic construction and art's affect. In 'Pen, Pencil, and Poison', he emancipated aesthetic judgement from its moralistic Victorian straitjacket, flaunting Wainewright's criminality so as to accentuate the separation of aesthetic concerns from ethical and biographical ones. His prose criticism is saturated by a desire to overturn accepted truisms in favour of their subversive opposites, and Wilde's symbolic relations with Victorian culture are never more vividly on display than in his paradoxes. The Preface to *The Picture of*

Dorian Gray was a model for such important twentieth-century artistic manifestos as Marinetti's *Manifesto of Futurism*, Tristan Tzara's 'Dada Manifesto 1918' and Gilbert and George's 'Laws of Sculptors'. Considered in the wider context of Wilde's life and work, it is difficult not to associate the centrality of the Wildean paradox with his broader subversion of the dominant strains in Victorian life. *The Picture of Dorian Gray*, in particular, represents a full-bore assault on the repressive hypocrisy and false piety of Victorian Britain in favour of an unapologetic acknowledgement of sexual desire, a 'New Hedonism' and a frank recognition – expressed in the very fabric of Wilde's language – of the power of the human senses.

When Wilde says he was a man who stood in symbolic relations to the art and culture of his age, however, he means more than this. His whole life was a provocation, and in his personal appearance, behaviour and wit he turned himself into a mythic figure in his own lifetime while obliging his fellow Victorians to rethink the things they held dearest. Not least was the provocation he offered to Victorian notions of masculinity and heterosexuality, in part by self-conscious displays of what Thomas Wentworth Higginson called 'unmanliness', while he also blurred the traditional boundaries between masculine and feminine. We can see this in his personal appearance and behaviour no less than in his preoccupation with cross-dressing in 'The Portrait of Mr W. H.' or the subtle androgyny of *The Importance of Being Earnest.* Although censored by its editor before publication, *The Picture of Dorian Gray* was immediately and widely recognized to be a sexually subversive work, and it became a rallying text for generations of homosexual men whose lives and experiences had been largely unrepresented in the annals of fiction. 'Here are . . . the heart of vices/ and sweet sins,' wrote the homosexual poet (and cousin of Lord Alfred Douglas) Lionel Johnson, shortly after Wilde had given him a copy of the novel; 'In the heavens and in the depths,/ Be to you, who perceive so much,/ Glory of all glories,' Johnson wrote to Wilde in verse.[9] After the publication of *Dorian Gray*, as Richard Ellmann has written, 'Victorian literature had a different look.'[10]

From the period he spent as editor of *Woman's World* onwards, Wilde was a liberatory figure for many women too. As the scholar Margaret Stetz has written, his Aestheticism embraced 'a wholehearted concern with the condition and details of modern women's lives', and in his day Wilde 'was an important ally of feminists and of working women in general, as well as an advocate for women in the arts in particular'.[11] He gave eloquent expression to the sexual double standard in his Society comedies, he lent his voice to the cause of female self-expression in his lectures and essays, and he wrote timeless, powerful roles for Victorian actresses in plays such as *Salome*, *The Importance of Being Earnest*, *An Ideal Husband* and even the early failure *Vera; or, The Nihilists.*

If Wilde helped advance the overthrow of Victorianism, he was also a man who had much in common with our own times. In combination with his personal style, his criminal trials and conviction cemented the twentieth-century notion of 'the homosexual', and his proud defence from the dock of 'the love that dare not speak its name' constitutes an epochal moment in the history of modern homosexuality. The novelist Paul Russell calls Wilde 'the world's first modern homosexual' and ranks him as the third most important homosexual in history, after Socrates and Sappho.[12] 'The self he brought to trial crystallized gay identity in ways we are still living with,' writes Russell, and after his brilliant catastrophe, 'neither the public discourse of homosexuality nor the private course of [queer] identity could ever be the same again.'[13] Wilde was a key figure in 'the formation of a nascent twentieth-century homosexual taste', agrees the scholar Stefano Evangelista, and his name 'is "invisibly inscribed" in the writings of such giants of twentieth-century literature as Marcel Proust and Thomas Mann, who are fascinated by the emotional possibilities of homoerotic desire'.[14]

More than a decade before his criminal trials, Wilde was also the first global celebrity, a precursor to Andy Warhol, Madonna and numerous others of our own day whose cultural 'image' goes far before them. In his careful exploitation of the popular press to cement such an image, together with his use of still-new telegraphic and photographic media to disseminate his portrait and witticisms, both before and during his American tour of 1882, he anticipated the promotional management of such modern-day 'stars' as Elvis Presley, Marilyn Monroe and The Beatles. His insistence on style and beauty was a rebuke to the mercantilism and utilitarianism of his age, but equally it democratized art, using the press as its medium, bringing art into the quotidian world in a way that made it approachable and achievable by anyone with a fashion sense. Indeed, as we've seen, in his careful promotion of new standards and materials for 'dress' among both men and women, Wilde invented the very notion of 'fashion sense' as we presently understand it.

With his well-reasoned defences of individual 'personality', personal rights and creative self-invention, finally, as well as with his reminder that 'to love oneself is the beginning of a lifelong romance,' Wilde ushered into being an era in which one's personal identity or individuality mattered more than class, ethnic, religious or national affiliation. His ideas have long been recognized to have had close affinities with anarchist thought, and he was both a friend and admirer of Peter Kropotkin, the father of modern anarchism. In his defence of individual and artistic freedoms, however, and in his recognition that 'a man . . . may commit a sin against society, and yet realise through that sin his own perfection,' Wilde anticipates the modern notion of subcultural and transgressive identity. In 1964 Susan Sontag saw him as the embodiment and fountainhead of the modern notion of camp, queering the staid aesthetic formulas of an older generation and setting a precedent for later self-ironizing movements in both popular and 'high' culture, including Art Nouveau, the songs of Tin Pan Alley, Hollywood musicals of the 1930s, *The Maltese Falcon*, the operas of Richard Strauss and even The Beatles (who featured Wilde on the cover of *Sgt. Pepper's Lonely Hearts Club Band*). With his paradoxes and irony, he was certainly a precursor to postmodernism and deconstruction, exposing the binary logic and logocentrism at the heart of authoritative thinking; although he is not known to have read Nietzsche, he echoed his great German contemporary in seeing 'beyond good and evil', and he anticipated Wittgenstein and Derrida in viewing language as the basis, not the servant, of thought.

Today Wilde's witticisms are legendary, and the dialogue of his fictions and plays continues to sparkle. He developed lines of thought that shocked the Victorians but which we now take for granted, only to expose their whimsicality with a flourish and explode them like fireworks. He would have agreed with Hamlet that 'the play's the thing.' Ideas were fundamentally performative entities, for Wilde, as was the individual self. His work stands behind not merely Proust and Mann but also such exemplary modern figures as James Joyce, E. M. Forster, Jorge Luis Borges, John Cowper Powys, Noel Coward, Jean Cocteau, Frank Lloyd Wright, Groucho Marx, Winston Churchill, Roland Barthes, Susan Sontag and the musicians Morrissey, David Bowie and Bob Dylan.

But Wilde's greatest invention was himself, and Wilde today embodies the very ideas of wit, beauty and style. In his final exile, deprived of money, an assured audience and the company of those he loved, he nevertheless maintained a threadbare majesty. Even the onset of fatal illness was an opportunity for morbid wit and poetry ('my throat is a lime kiln, my brain a furnace, and my nerves a coil of angry adders'). He could laugh in the very face of death, as his legendary final witticisms indicate: 'I am dying as I lived – above my means,' 'I am fighting a duel to the death with my wallpaper and one of us has to go,' 'I shall never outlive the century . . . the English people would not stand it.' If life and worldly success are finite, Wilde tells us, human invention, like laughter, is limitless. Wilde the man died more than a century ago, but his wit, laughter and wisdom continue ringing out in the world we inhabit today.

References

Introduction

1 *The Complete Letters of Oscar Wilde*, ed. Merlin Holland and Rupert Hart-Davis (New York, 2000), p. 652.
2 *The Annotated Prison Writings of Oscar Wilde*, ed. Nicholas Frankel (Cambridge, MA, 2018), p. 173.

ONE: The Birth of 'Oscar Wilde'

1 Richard Ellmann, *Oscar Wilde* (New York, 1988), p. 10.
2 *The Annotated Prison Writings of Oscar Wilde*, ed. Nicholas Frankel (Cambridge, MA, 2018), p. 147.
3 Ellmann, *Oscar Wilde*, p. 13.
4 *The Complete Letters of Oscar Wilde*, ed. Merlin Holland and Rupert Hart-Davis (New York, 2000), p. 54.
5 Quoted in Davis Coakley, *Oscar Wilde: The Importance of Being Irish* (Dublin, 1995), p. 161.
6 Quoted ibid., pp. 89–90.
7 Ian Gibson, *Samuel Beckett* (London, 2009), pp. 26–9. See also Coakley, *Oscar Wilde: The Importance of Being Irish*, pp. 76–85.
8 Purser, quoted in Ellmann, *Oscar Wilde*, p. 23.
9 *Complete Letters*, ed. Holland and Hart-Davis, p. 562.
10 In his Acknowledgements to the first edition of *Social Life in Greece*, Mahaffy thanks Wilde for having 'made improvements and corrections all through the book'.
11 Wilde, 'Aristotle at Afternoon Tea', signed review of Mahaffy's *The Principles of the Art of Conversation*, *Pall Mall Gazette*, 16 December 1887.
12 See Ellmann, *Oscar Wilde*, p. 67.
13 *Complete Letters*, ed. Holland and Hart-Davis, p. 45.

14 Quoted in Charles Ricketts, *Oscar Wilde: Recollections* (1932), in Charles Ricketts, *Everything for Art: Selected Writings*, ed. Nicholas Frankel (High Wycombe, 2014), p. 235.
15 *Complete Letters*, ed. Holland and Hart-Davis, p. 43.
16 By altering 'a little child' to 'the young boy-priest' and 'these sweet and honied hours' to 'those sweet Hellenic hours', in the version printed in *Poems* (1881), Wilde underscored his gradual alienation from Catholicism in favour of Hellenism.
17 David Hunter-Blair, 'Oscar Wilde as I Knew Him' (1939), reprinted as 'Oscar Wilde at Magdalen College Oxford', in *Oscar Wilde: Interviews and Recollections*, ed. E. H. Mikhail, 2 vols (London, 1979), vol. I, p. 9.
18 The exceptions are *Ravenna*, Wilde's first English publication, published by the Oxford bookseller Thomas Shrimpton in 1878 (Shrimpton routinely published the annual Newdigate Prize poem for distribution locally); also three poems (Wilde's first American publications) that appeared in 1876 and 1877 in the Boston *Pilot*, whose editor, John Boyle O'Reilly, an Irish Fenian, was a friend of Wilde's mother.
19 Ellmann, *Oscar Wilde*, p. 38.
20 Coulson Kernahan, from *In Good Company* (London, 1917), reprinted as 'Oscar Wilde', in *Oscar Wilde: Interviews and Recollections*, ed. Mikhail, vol. II, p. 308.

TWO: The Poetry of Englishness

1 The exception was the sonnet 'Ave! Maria', published over the old signature O. F. O'F. W. W. in *Kottabos*, the magazine of his alma mater, Trinity College, in Michaelmas Term 1879. Earlier in the same year Wilde had also published 'La Belle Marguerite: Ballade du Moyen Age' in *Kottabos*, again over his full signature initials. Since this poem appeared in the Hilary Term of 1879, however, it probably predated Wilde's first publication in English journals.
2 *The Complete Letters of Oscar Wilde*, ed. Merlin Holland and Rupert Hart-Davis (New York, 2000), p. 29.
3 Ibid., p. 71.
4 Davis Coakley, *Oscar Wilde: The Importance of Being Irish* (Dublin, 1995), p. 178.
5 *Oscar Wilde in America: The Interviews*, ed. Matthew Hofer and Gary Scharnhorst (Urbana and Chicago, IL, 2010), pp. 43

and 103. Had he remained in Ireland, he added, his 'career would have been a political one'.

6 Quoted in 'Stuart Mason' [Christopher Millard], *Bibliography of Oscar Wilde* (London, 1914), p. 226.

7 'Phèdre' constitutes an exception, since it only acquired this title (after the title role in Racine's play, which Wilde had seen Bernhardt perform in June 1879) on being republished in *Poems* in 1881. On its first publication, in *The World*, in June 1879, this sonnet had been titled 'To Sarah Bernhardt'.

8 'Sen Artysty' appeared in the Christmas annual *The Green Room*, edited by the drama critic Clement Scott.

9 Quoted in Richard Ellmann, *Oscar Wilde* (New York, 1988), p. 128.

10 Langtry, 'The Oscar I Knew' (1925), reprinted in *Oscar Wilde: Interviews and Recollections*, ed. E. H. Mikhail, 2 vols (London, 1979), vol. II, p. 258.

11 See John Cooper, 'The Cello Coat' and 'Cello Encore', https://oscarwildeinamerica.blog. Until recently it was thought that Wilde wore the cello coat to the opening of the Grosvenor Gallery in 1877. However, Cooper has convincingly shown that Wilde can't have designed and worn it until 1885.

12 Quoted in 'Mason', *Bibliography*, pp. 232 and 291.

13 *Complete Letters*, ed. Holland and Hart-Davis, p. 390.

14 See Chapter One, n. 18 above.

15 *Oscar Wilde: The Critical Heritage*, ed. Karl Beckson (London, 1970), pp. 34, 42 and 54.

16 Quoted in Ellmann, *Oscar Wilde*, p. 146.

17 Unsigned review of Wilde's *Poems*, *The Nation*, 14 August 1881, p. 101.

18 Matthew Arnold, *Culture and Anarchy* (1869), ed. J. Dover Wilson (1935; reprinted Cambridge, 1981), p. 54.

19 Matthew Arnold, 'The Study of Poetry', in *Selected Poems and Prose*, ed. Miriam Allott (London, 1978), p. 241.

20 Matthew Arnold, 'The Incompatibles' (1881), repeated in *English Literature and Irish Politics*, vol. IX of *The Complete Prose Works of Matthew Arnold*, ed. R. H. Super (Ann Arbor, MI, 1973), pp. 262–71.

21 *Oscar Wilde in America: The Interviews*, ed. Hofer and Scharnhorst, pp. 18 and 24.

22 *Complete Letters*, ed. Holland and Hart-Davis, p. 117.

23 Quoted in 'Mason', *Bibliography*, p. 254.

24 Quoted in Ellmann, *Oscar Wilde*, p. 152.

THREE: 'Nothing to Declare Except My Genius'

1 Nathan's, established in 1790, was one of London's leading theatrical costume suppliers. Lajos Kossuth (1802–1894), the Hungarian revolutionary who resided in London for a while, was almost as famous for his revolutionary headgear as for his politics. Mr Mantalini, the husband of a milliner in Dickens's *Nicholas Nickleby*, is distinguished by his gorgeous morning gown.
2 *The Complete Letters of Oscar Wilde*, ed. Merlin Holland and Rupert Hart-Davis (New York, 2000), p. 785.
3 No corroborating witness to Wilde's answer was ever found, and it is likely that this famous quip is apocryphal.
4 *Complete Letters*, ed. Holland and Hart-Davis, p. 124.
5 *Oscar Wilde in America: The Interviews*, ed. Matthew Hofer and Gary Scharnhorst (Urbana and Chicago, IL, 2010), p. 136.
6 Ibid., p. 262.
7 Quoted in Robert D. Pepper, Introduction to Wilde, *Irish Poets and Poetry of the Nineteenth Century*, ed. Robert D. Pepper (San Francisco, CA, 1972), p. 8.
8 'Oscar Wilde in New York' (1911), reprinted in *Oscar Wilde: Interviews and Recollections*, ed. E. H. Mikhail, 2 vols (London, 1979), vol. I, p. 101.
9 Mary Blanchard, *Oscar Wilde's America: Counterculture in the Gilded Age* (New Haven, CT, 1998), pp. xiii–xv.
10 See John Cooper, '"A Picturesque Subject Indeed": The Sarony Photographs of Oscar Wilde', *The Wildean*, 55 (July 2019), p. 20.
11 Blanchard, *Oscar Wilde's America*, p. 3.
12 Thomas Wentworth Higginson, 'Unmanly Manhood' (1882), reprinted in *Oscar Wilde: The Critical Heritage*, ed. Karl Beckson (London, 1970), p. 51.
13 Quoted in Blanchard, *Oscar Wilde's America*, p. 13.
14 Roy Morris Jr., *Declaring His Genius: Oscar Wilde in North America* (Cambridge, MA, 2013), p. 205.
15 *Oscar Wilde in America: The Interviews*, ed. Hofer and Scharnhorst, p. 140.
16 See John Cooper, 'Oscar Wilde in America: A Selected Resource of Oscar Wilde's Visits to America', www.oscarwildeinamerica.org.
17 *Oscar Wilde in America: The Interviews*, ed. Hofer and Scharnhorst, pp. 13, 17 and 31.

18 See Pepper, Introduction to Wilde, *Irish Poets and Poetry of the Nineteenth Century*, p. 14.

FOUR: 'Married . . . in Consequence of a Misunderstanding': London 1883–6

1 Robert H. Sherard, *The Real Oscar Wilde* (London, 1916), p. 200.
2 Richard Ellmann, *Oscar Wilde* (New York, 1988), pp. 208–9. These plans for a 'dream theater' ultimately came to nothing.
3 Quoted in 'Stuart Mason' [Christopher Millard], *Bibliography of Oscar Wilde* (London, 1914), p. 258.
4 In 1879, three years after the death of Wilde's father, his impecunious mother, Lady Wilde, moved to London and started a weekly literary salon. Wilde is known to have given his mother financial support. He also attended her salon regularly when settled in London.
5 Shortly after completing the play, Wilde had twenty copies of an acting edition privately printed and copyrighted in London. This edition dates the play's completion to 'March 15, 1883, A.D.', and its title page states – in counterpoint to the play's subtitle, 'A Tragedy of the XVI Century' – that it was 'written in Paris in the XIX Century'. The edition is now exceedingly rare: only five copies are known to exist.
6 Max Beerbohm, letter to Ada Leverson, 20 May 1916, Max Beerbohm Collection 2.4, Harry Ransom Center, University of Texas at Austin.
7 Wilde, 'A Note on Some Modern Poets', in *The Artist as Critic: Critical Writings of Oscar Wilde*, ed. Richard Ellmann (New York, 1969), p. 91.
8 Sherard, *The Real Oscar Wilde*, p. 155. In an unpublished letter written 54 years after the event, Sherard recounts this incident more salaciously: 'One evening in 1883 he admitted that Priapus was calling and left me to go to the Eden Music Hall . . . It was . . . the place to pick up the better class whores. Oscar there picked up Marie Aguétant' (Sherard to A.J.A. Symons, 31 May 1937, British Library Add. MS 81730).
9 W. E. Henley, 'The Sphinx up to Date', unsigned review of Wilde's *The Sphinx*, *Pall Mall Gazette*, 9 July 1894; reprinted in *Oscar Wilde: The Critical Heritage*, ed. Karl Beckson (London, 1970), p. 168.

10 Elaborately decorated and illustrated by the artist Charles Ricketts, who was responsible for the striking typography too, the book incorporated three differently coloured inks and was printed throughout in tiny uppercase letters, except for a series of large hand-drawn illuminated capitals printed in green. A digital facsimile of the first edition of *The Sphinx* was published by Rice University Press in 2010 and can be freely accessed online, along with accompanying critical commentary and contextual materials, at https://cnx.org. See too my *Oscar Wilde's Decorated Books* (Ann Arbor, MI, 2000), pp. 155–75.

11 Wilde's invitation to lecture to Royal Academy students elicited both jealousy and assistance from the painter James Abbott McNeill Whistler. In his lecture Wilde praised Whistler effusively as 'the greatest artist of the day' and as a man 'who unites in himself all the qualities of the noblest art', and the lecture owes a great deal to Whistler's ideas. The event lay at the root of the charges of plagiarism and humbuggery that Whistler would level at Wilde later in the 1880s.

12 Quoted in Ellmann, *Oscar Wilde*, p. 234.

13 *The Complete Letters of Oscar Wilde*, ed. Merlin Holland and Rupert Hart-Davis (New York, 2000), p. 676. Some of this income derived from a trust fund of £5,000 created by Constance's doting grandfather to help set the newlyweds on their feet. But Constance also brought a substantial individual income to the marriage, which was set to rise considerably upon the death of her mother. During his bankruptcy proceedings, in 1895, Wilde declared the income from his marriage settlement to be 'about £800 a year'. Donald Mead suggests that it was probably closer to £750 a year, equivalent to roughly £75,000 per annum today. See his 'Heading for Disaster: Oscar's Finances', *The Wildean*, 45 (July 2014), p. 60.

14 *Complete Letters*, ed. Holland and Hart-Davis, pp. 241–2. Wilde speaks entirely platonically to Constance in this letter, saying 'your bodily presence here would not make you more real' and 'the air is full of the music of your voice, my soul and body seem no longer mine, but mingled in some exquisite ecstasy with yours.'

15 Ellmann, *Oscar Wilde*, p. 253. Huysmans's novel is an imaginative study in self-conscious perversity, sexual and otherwise, and years later it was described by Arthur Symons as the very 'breviary of the Decadence'. It exerted a strong influence on Wilde's mind

and it stands behind the 'poisonous' French novel that exerts such a powerful influence over the eponymous hero of Wilde's own novel *The Picture of Dorian Gray*.

16 Robert H. Sherard, *Oscar Wilde: The Story of an Unhappy Friendship* (London, 1905), pp. 94–5. It is possible that Sherard misdates these oft-cited recollections of Wilde's Paris slumming. Sherard begins these recollections by saying 'I *think* it was during his stay in Paris at this time that he visited,' and so on (my italics), and he also states more categorically that 'the American, Stuart Merrill, . . . was one of the party.' However, Wilde did not meet Merrill until 1890. It seems likely that Sherard is confusing Wilde's honeymoon with one of Wilde's later stays in Paris, in 1891, when Wilde saw much of Merrill and Sherard, among others.

17 *The Autobiography of Lord Alfred Douglas* (London, 1929), pp. 59–60.

18 Ellmann, *Oscar Wilde*, p. 236.

19 Wilde had been married to Constance for a full year when 'Roses and Rue' first appeared, although the poem had existed for some years before this in manuscript form under the title 'To L. L.'

20 Franny Moyle, *Constance: The Tragic and Scandalous Life of Mrs Oscar Wilde* (London, 2012), p. 81.

21 See Robert H. Sherard, *The Life of Oscar Wilde* (London, 1906), pp. 255–7; also Ellmann, *Oscar Wilde*, p. 249.

22 See Moyle, *Constance*, p. 85; also John Cooper, 'Constance Wilde's Dress', in his very useful *Oscar Wilde on Dress* (Philadelphia, PA, 2013), unpaginated.

23 Moyle, *Constance*, p. 73.

24 Quoted in Ellmann, *Oscar Wilde*, p. 251.

25 Vyvyan Holland, *Son of Oscar Wilde* (1954; Oxford, 1988), p. 44. This room seemed very dark and gloomy by comparison with the bright hues of other rooms, says Holland, and it was filled with divans, ottomans, Moorish hangings and lanterns.

26 While no information survives to indicate how 'Shakespeare and Stage Costume' came to be published in *Nineteenth Century*, the essay is closely related to the short essay 'Shakespeare on Scenery' that Wilde published in the short-lived *Dramatic Review* two months earlier, in March 1885. In the same month he was approached by the editor of the prestigious *Fortnightly Review*, leading him to promise 'the article I could have ready for your May number' (*Complete Letters*, ed. Holland and Hart-Davis,

p. 253). In the event, the *Fortnightly* would not publish anything by Wilde until 'Pen, Pencil, and Poison', in January 1889, by which time it was under a new editor.

27 'Shakespeare and Stage Costume', *Nineteenth Century*, XVII (May 1885), p. 801.

28 See Nicholas Frankel, 'On the Whistler-Ruskin Trial', *BRANCH: Britain, Representation, and Nineteenth-century History*, www.branchcollective.org.

29 Partridge, unpublished letter to Hesketh Pearson, 30 September 1943, Hesketh Pearson Collection, Harry Ransom Center, University of Texas at Austin.

30 Quoted in Moyle, *Constance*, p. 124.

31 Lord Alfred Douglas once described his early sexual relations with Wilde as 'simply what is euphemistically called "the sort of nonsense that goes on between schoolboys"', and it is more than likely that Wilde shared the same view (Douglas, letter to Frank Harris, 22 March 1925, Harry Ransom Center, University of Texas at Austin).

32 Molly Whittington-Egan, *Frank Miles and Oscar Wilde: 'Such White Lilies'* (High Wycombe, 2009), p. 42.

33 Joseph Bristow, 'Oscar Wilde, Ronald Gower, and the Shakespeare Monument', *Études anglaises*, LXIX/1 (2016), p. 15.

FIVE: The Rhythmical Value of Prose: Wilde's Career in Fiction

1 The Criminal Law Amendment Act 1885 (48 and 49 Vict. c.69), Sec. 11.

2 Richard Ellmann, *Oscar Wilde* (New York, 1988), pp. 278 and 299.

3 See Joan Navarre, 'Oscar Wilde, Edward Heron-Allen, and the Palmistry Craze of the 1880s', *English Literature in Transition, 1880–1920*, LIV/2 (2011), pp. 177–9.

4 Merlin Holland, *The Wilde Album* (New York, 1998), p. 127, quoted in Navarre, 'Oscar Wilde, Edward Heron-Allen, and the Palmistry Craze', p. 183, n. 19.

5 Alexander Galt Ross, unsigned review of *The Happy Prince and Other Tales*, *Saturday Review*, 20 October 1888; reprinted in *Oscar Wilde: The Critical Heritage*, ed. Karl Beckson (London, 1970), p. 61.

6 Perry Nodelman, 'The Young Know Everything: Oscar Wilde's Fairy Tales as Children's Literature', in *Oscar Wilde and the*

Cultures of Childhood, ed. Joseph Bristow (Cham, Switzerland, 2017), pp. 189–90.

7 *The Complete Letters of Oscar Wilde*, ed. Merlin Holland and Rupert Hart-Davis (New York, 2000), p. 355. See too Wilde's comment to Amélie Rives Chanler that his fairy tales were 'an attempt to mirror modern life in a form remote from reality – to deal with modern problems in a mode that is ideal and not imitative'. *Complete Letters*, ed. Holland and Hart-Davis, p. 388.

8 In the Bible, the field of the fullers was beyond Jerusalem's walls.

9 *Complete Letters*, ed. Holland and Hart-Davis, p. 402.

10 Horst Schroeder, *Oscar Wilde, The Portrait of Mr W. H.: Its Composition, Publication, and Reception* (Braunschweig, Germany, 1984), pp. 14–15.

11 J. M. Stoddart, letter to Craige Lippincott, 10 April 1890, quoted in Textual Introduction to *The Picture of Dorian Gray: An Annotated, Uncensored Edition*, ed. Nicholas Frankel (Cambridge, MA, 2011), p. 45.

12 See *The Picture of Dorian Gray: An Annotated, Uncensored Edition*, ed. Frankel, pp. 60–61, n. 23.

13 Ibid., pp. 42–5.

SIX: Paradox and Perversity: Wilde as a Subversive Thinker

1 'It is Art, and Art only, that reveals us to ourselves,' Wilde wrote around this time in the expanded version of 'The Portrait of Mr W. H.' (*The Short Stories of Oscar Wilde: An Annotated Selection*, ed. Nicholas Frankel (Cambridge, MA, 2020), p. 312). Similarly, he writes in 'The Decay of Lying' that 'the true disciples of the great artist are . . . those who become like his works of art' and, in 'The Critic as Artist', that 'it is through Art, and through Art only, that we can realise our perfection.'

2 Oscar Wilde, 'Aristotle at Afternoon Tea', signed review of Mahaffy, *The Principles of the Art of Conversation*, *Pall Mall Gazette*, 16 December 1887.

3 See *William Morris on Art and Socialism*, ed. Norman Kelvin (New York, 1999); also Marx, *Economic and Philosophical Manuscripts of 1844*, ed. and trans. Martin Milligan (1961; reprinted New York, 2007).

4 For Wilde's expansive concept of artistry and his important comment that 'there are not many arts, but one art merely

– poem, picture and Parthenon, sonnet and statue – all are in their essence the same, and he who knows one knows all', see Chapter Four.

5 See, for instance, Thomas Hardy's essay 'Candour in English Fiction' (1890), in which Hardy complained that 'the patrons of literature – no longer Peers with a taste – acting under the censorship of prudery, rigorously exclude from the pages they regulate subjects that have been made . . . the bases of the finest imaginative compositions since literature rose to the dignity of art.'

6 *The Complete Letters of Oscar Wilde*, ed. Merlin Holland and Rupert Hart-Davis (New York, 2000), p. 439.

7 Ibid., p. 585. After his comments on his own novel, Wilde added the following: 'I . . . go to St. James's Place, number 10, where I have rooms every day at 11.30. Come on Tuesday about 12.30, will you? But perhaps you are busy? Still, we can meet, surely, some day. Your handwriting fascinates me, your praise charms me.'

8 Jonathan Dollimore, *Sexual Dissidence: Augustine to Wilde, Freud to Foucault* (Oxford, 1991), p. 16.

9 Ernest Newman, 'Oscar Wilde: A Literary Appreciation' (1895), reprinted as 'Ernest Newman on Wilde's Genius for Paradox', in *Oscar Wilde: The Critical Heritage*, ed. Karl Beckson (London, 1970), p. 203.

10 *The Real Trial of Oscar Wilde*, introduction and commentary by Merlin Holland (New York, 2004), pp. 73–5.

SEVEN: Drama as a Mode of Personal Expression

1 Peter Raby, 'Wilde's Comedies of Society', in *The Cambridge Companion to Oscar Wilde* (Cambridge, 1997).

2 W. Macqueen-Pope, quoted in Regenia Gagnier, *Idylls of the Marketplace: Oscar Wilde and the Victorian Public* (Palo Alto, CA, 1986), p. 107.

3 A. B. Walkley, signed review of *Lady Windermere's Fan* (1892), reprinted in *Oscar Wilde: The Critical Heritage*, ed. Karl Beckson (London, 1970), pp. 119–20.

4 Gagnier, *Idylls of the Marketplace*, p. 108.

5 See Thorstein Veblen, *The Theory of the Leisure Class* (New York, 1899).

6 Ibid., pp. 9 and 109.

7 Camille Paglia, *Sexual Personae* (New Haven, CT, 1990), pp. 531–2.

8 *The Short Stories of Oscar Wilde: An Annotated Selection*, ed. Nicholas Frankel (Cambridge, MA, 2020), p. 296.
9 Terence Brown, 'The Plays: Introduction', in *The Complete Works of Oscar Wilde*, introduction by Merlin Holland, 5th edn (London, 2003), pp. 354–5.
10 Timothy D'Arch Smith, *Bunbury: Two Notes* (Bacary, France, 1998); and Joel Fineman, 'The Significance of Literature: *The Importance of Being Earnest*' (1980), reprinted in *Critical Essays on Oscar Wilde*, ed. Regenia Gagnier (New York, 1991), p. 113.
11 *The Complete Letters of Oscar Wilde*, ed. Merlin Holland and Rupert Hart-Davis (New York, 2000), p. 601; Peter Raby, 'Wilde, and How to Be Modern', in *Wilde Writings, Contextual Conditions*, ed. Joseph Bristow (Toronto, 2003), p. 152.
12 When Wilde dined with Fort in December 1891, during the composition of *Salome*, Fort had already staged plays by Rachilde, Maeterlinck and de Banville, as well as Shelley's reputedly unperformable *The Cenci*, Mallarmé's symbolist poem 'L'Après-midi d'un faune' and a dramatic adaptation of The Song of Songs. Fort's admiration for Wilde is well known, and in 1900 Fort would be one of just a handful of mourners to attend Wilde's funeral.
13 *Complete Letters*, ed. Holland and Hart-Davis, p. 499.
14 See Linda Zatlin, 'Wilde, Beardsley, and the Making of *Salome*', *Journal of Victorian Culture*, v/2 (2000), pp. 341–57; also Ian A. Macdonald, 'Oscar Wilde as a French Writer: Considering Wilde's French in *Salomé*', in *Refiguring Oscar Wilde's Salome*, ed. Michael Y. Bennett (Amsterdam and New York, 2011), pp. 1–19.
15 For Ricketts's account of how, at Wilde's request and with input from Wilde himself, he sketched out a plan for staging *Salome* in Paris in late 1891 or early 1892, see 'On Wilde's *Salome*', in Charles Ricketts, *Everything for Art: Selected Writings*, ed. Nicholas Frankel (High Wycombe, 2014), pp. 259–60.
16 Wilde's inscription in a presentation copy of the French first edition, *Salomé: Drame en un acte*, given to Beardsley in 1893, quoted in my *Oscar Wilde's Decorated Books* (Ann Arbor, MI, 2000), p. 80. The phrase 'subtle and fantastic decorator', Wilde's own description of Ricketts, is from a letter by Wilde to the editor of *The Speaker* (*Complete Letters*, ed. Holland and Hart-Davis, p. 501).
17 The play was performed only once on stage in Wilde's lifetime – in Paris in 1896, under the direction of the avant-garde theatre

director Aurélien-Marie Lugné-Poe, while the play's author was incarcerated in England. However, Wilde tried to get the play staged in Italy shortly after his release from prison, with Eleonora Duse in the title role. See Nicholas Frankel, *Oscar Wilde: The Unrepentant Years* (Cambridge, MA, 2017), pp. 150–51.
18 Charles Ricketts, *Oscar Wilde: Recollections* (1932), in Ricketts, *Everything for Art*, p. 247.
19 Ricketts, 'On Wilde's *Salome*', p. 260.
20 Translated from the French and quoted in Richard Ellmann, *Oscar Wilde* (New York, 1988), p. 375.
21 Joseph Donohue, *Introduction to Salomé: A Tragedy in One Act*, trans. Joseph Donohue (Charlottesville, VA, 2011).
22 Coulson Kernahan, *In Good Company* (London, 1917), p. 223.

EIGHT: 'A Poet Who Loves Boys'

1 Alfred Douglas, *Oscar Wilde: A Summing-Up* (London, 1940), pp. 95–6.
2 Quoted in Neil McKenna, *The Secret Life of Oscar Wilde* (New York, 2005), p. 111.
3 Quoted ibid., p. 98; Matthew Sturgis, *Oscar: A Life* (London, 2018), p. 371.
4 McKenna, *The Secret Life*, p. 90; Sturgis, *Oscar*, pp. 370–71.
5 McKenna, *The Secret Life*, p. 88.
6 Richard Ellmann, *Oscar Wilde* (New York, 1988), p. 307.
7 H. Montgomery Hyde, *The Trials of Oscar Wilde*, 2nd edn (New York, 1973), pp. 125 and 202–3.
8 Sturgis, *Oscar*, p. 420.
9 *The Complete Letters of Oscar Wilde*, ed. Merlin Holland and Rupert Hart-Davis (New York, 2000), p. 795.
10 *The Autobiography of Lord Alfred Douglas* (London, 1929), pp. 75 and 86.
11 Douglas, unpublished letter to Frank Harris, 22 May 1925, Harry Ransom Center, University of Texas at Austin.
12 McKenna, *The Secret Life*, p. 188.
13 *The Real Trial of Oscar Wilde*, introduction and commentary by Merlin Holland (New York, 2004), p. 111.
14 Quoted in Ellmann, *Oscar Wilde*, p. 394.
15 *The Annotated Prison Writings of Oscar Wilde*, ed. Nicholas Frankel (Cambridge, MA, 2018), p. 141.
16 *Complete Letters*, ed. Holland and Hart-Davis, p. 1019.

NINE: Prisoner c.3.3.

1 Douglas, quoted in Richard Ellmann, *Oscar Wilde* (New York, 1988), p. 404.
2 *The Annotated Prison Writings of Oscar Wilde*, ed. Nicholas Frankel (Cambridge, MA, 2018), p. 77.
3 Matthew Sturgis, *Oscar: A Life* (London, 2018), p. 501.
4 Quoted in Ellmann, *Oscar Wilde*, pp. 417–18.
5 Ibid.
6 Sturgis, *Oscar*, p. 507.
7 Quoted in Ellmann, *Oscar Wilde*, p. 420.
8 Ibid.
9 *Annotated Prison Writings*, ed. Frankel, pp. 115 and 119.
10 The sexual excess of this vacation is evoked more fully in the writings of André Gide, who ran into them during their stay. In *Oscar Wilde* (1900), Gide says merely that Wilde set out to 'demoralize' Algiers and was 'preceded, escorted, [and] followed by an extraordinary band of ragamuffins'. In *If It Die* (1920), Gide describes more explicitly how Wilde encouraged him to act on his homosexual desires and arranged for Gide to spend a night with a young man to whom he was attracted.
11 See *The Real Trial of Oscar Wilde*, introduction and commentary by Merlin Holland (New York, 2004). For a transcript of Wilde's two criminal trials for gross indecency, see Joseph Bristow, *Oscar Wilde on Trial: The Criminal Proceedings, from Arrest to Imprisonment* (New Haven, CT, 2021).
12 *Annotated Prison Writings*, ed. Frankel, p. 177.
13 Quoted in H. Montgomery Hyde, *The Trials of Oscar Wilde*, 2nd edn (New York, 1973), p. 145.
14 *The Illustrated Police Budget*, 13 April 1895, reprinted in *The Oscar Wilde File*, compiled by Jonathan Goodman (London, 1989), p. 84.
15 *The Complete Letters of Oscar Wilde*, ed. Merlin Holland and Rupert Hart-Davis (New York, 2000), p. 652.
16 Quoted in Hyde, *The Trials of Oscar Wilde*, p. 201.
17 Linda Dowling, *Hellenism and Homosexuality in Victorian Oxford* (Ithaca, NY, 1994), p. 2.
18 Sean McConville, *English Local Prisons, 1860–1900: Next Only to Death* (London and New York, 1995), p. 187; McConville, 'The Victorian Prison: England, 1865–1965', in *The Oxford History of the Prison*, ed. N. Morris and D. J. Rothman (New York, 1998),

p. 147. Many of the prisons built to facilitate the harsh regime under which Wilde was punished are still in use today, and as McConville observes, twentieth- and twenty-first-century imprisonment in England 'has been marked by a tenacious Victorian inheritance' ('The Victorian Prison', p. 154).

19 *Complete Letters*, ed. Holland and Hart-Davis, p. 754.
20 *Annotated Prison Writings*, ed. Frankel, p. 47.
21 Quoted in Frankel, Introduction to *Annotated Prison Writings*, ed. Frankel, p. 7.
22 *Complete Letters*, ed. Holland and Hart-Davis, p. 782.
23 *Annotated Prison Writings*, ed. Frankel, p. 135.
24 Ibid., pp. 145–7.

TEN: Sebastian Melmoth

1 *The Complete Letters of Oscar Wilde*, ed. Merlin Holland and Rupert Hart-Davis (New York, 2000), pp. 864 and 1169.
2 Thomas Mann, *Death in Venice and Seven Other Stories*, trans. H. T. Lowe-Porter (New York, 1989), p. 11.
3 Wilde invokes Reni's painting frequently in his writings. In 'The Tomb of Keats', one of his earliest prose publications, he says that while standing over the grave of John Keats, in Rome, 'the vision of Guido's St. Sebastian came before my eyes . . . a lovely brown boy, with crisp, clustering hair and red lips, bound by his evil enemies . . . and though pierced by arrows, raising his eyes with divine, impassioned gaze towards the Eternal Beauty of the opening heavens.'
4 *Complete Letters*, ed. Holland and Hart-Davis, p. 847.
5 Ibid., p. 873.
6 *The Annotated Prison Writings of Oscar Wilde*, ed. Nicholas Frankel (Cambridge, MA, 2018), p. 313.
7 Jack London, *The People of the Abyss* (1903), quoted in *Annotated Prison Writings*, ed. Frankel, p. 298, n. 12.
8 The addition of Wilde's name, in brackets, to the title page of the seventh edition of *The Ballad of Reading Gaol*, fifteen months after the appearance of the first edition, constitutes an important exception.
9 *Complete Letters*, ed. Holland and Hart-Davis, p. 865.
10 Quoted in Nicholas Frankel, *Oscar Wilde: The Unrepentant Years* (Cambridge, MA, 2017), p. 103.
11 *Complete Letters*, ed. Holland and Hart-Davis, p. 898.

12 *The Autobiography of Lord Alfred Douglas* (London, 1929), p. 152.
13 *Complete Letters*, ed. Holland and Hart-Davis, p. 942.
14 Ibid., p. 948.
15 Ibid., p. 947.
16 Ibid., p. 1185.
17 Quoted in Frankel, *Oscar Wilde: The Unrepentant Years*, p. 192.
18 Ibid., p. 200.
19 Arthur Symons, signed review of *The Ballad of Reading Gaol*, *Saturday Review*, 12 March 1898, reprinted in *Oscar Wilde: The Critical Heritage*, ed. Karl Beckson (London, 1970), p. 221.
20 Unsigned review of *The Ballad of Reading Gaol*, *The Academy*, 26 February 1898, reprinted in *Oscar Wilde: The Critical Heritage*, ed. Beckson, p. 211.
21 *Complete Letters*, ed. Holland and Hart-Davis, p. 1025.
22 Jorge Luis Borges, 'A Poem by Oscar Wilde', trans. Suzanne J. Levine, *Southern Cross Review*, 64 (May 2009), https://southerncrossreview.org; John Cowper Powys, *Suspended Judgements: Essays on Books and Sensations* (London, 1916), p. 406.
23 *Annotated Prison Writings*, ed. Frankel, p. 305.
24 Quoted ibid., p. 372.
25 Quoted in Frankel, *Oscar Wilde: The Unrepentant Years*, p. 206.
26 *Complete Letters*, ed. Holland and Hart-Davis, p. 1169.
27 Vincent O'Sullivan, *Aspects of Wilde* (New York, 1936), p. 50; Alfred Douglas, *Oscar Wilde and Myself* (New York, 1914), p. 134.
28 Wilde, 'A Few Maxims for the Instruction of the Over-educated', *Saturday Review*, 17 November 1894; reprinted in *The Letters of Oscar Wilde*, ed. Rupert Hart-Davis (London, 1962), Appendix B, p. 869. For details of the dubious schemes into which Wilde entered in order to raise much-needed cash, see Frankel, *Oscar Wilde: The Unrepentant Years*, pp. 239–40, 251 and 274–5.
29 Henri Mazel and Ernest La Jeunesse, both quoted in Frankel, *Oscar Wilde: The Unrepentant Years*, p. 271; *Complete Letters*, ed. Holland and Hart-Davis, p. 1196.
30 Richard Ellmann, *Oscar Wilde* (New York, 1988), p. 584.
31 Quoted in Frankel, *Oscar Wilde: The Unrepentant Years*, p. 355, n. 63; for Ross's account of Wilde's death, see Frankel, *Oscar Wilde: The Unrepentant Years*, pp. 283–4, and *Complete Letters*, ed. Holland and Hart-Davis, p. 1220.

EPILOGUE: 'A Man Who Stood in Symbolic Relations to . . . My Age'

1 Quoted in Nicholas Frankel, *Oscar Wilde: The Unrepentant Years* (Cambridge, MA, 2017), pp. 295–6.
2 *The Complete Letters of Oscar Wilde*, ed. Merlin Holland and Rupert Hart-Davis (New York, 2000), p. 780; quoted in *The Annotated Prison Writings of Oscar Wilde*, ed. Nicholas Frankel (Cambridge, MA, 2018), p. 35.
3 R. B. Cunningham-Graham, 'Vox Clamantis' (1905), reprinted in *Oscar Wilde: The Critical Heritage*, ed. Karl Beckson (London, 1970), p. 256.
4 Gosse, letter to Robert Ross, reprinted in *Oscar Wilde: The Critical Heritage*, ed. Beckson, p. 243.
5 Beerbohm, 'A Lord of Language' (1905), reprinted in *Oscar Wilde: The Critical Heritage*, ed. Beckson, p. 250.
6 Housman, letter to Robert Ross, reprinted in *Oscar Wilde: The Critical Heritage*, ed. Beckson, p. 243.
7 *The Annotated Importance of Being Earnest*, ed. Nicholas Frankel (Cambridge, MA, 2015), p. 217; 'The Decay of Lying', in *Criticism: Historical Criticism, Intentions, The Soul of Man*, ed. Josephine M. Guy, vol. IV of *The Complete Works of Oscar Wilde* (Oxford, 2007), p. 99.
8 A book is 'a little non-signifying machine', writes Deleuze, 'and the only question is "Does it work, and how does it work?"' ('Letter to a Harsh Critic', in *Negotiations: 1972–1990*, trans. Martin Joughin (New York, 1995), p. 8).
9 These lines are from Ian Fletcher's translation of Johnson's Latin poem 'In honorem Doriani creatorisque eius', quoted in *The Picture of Dorian Gray: An Annotated, Uncensored Edition*, ed. Nicholas Frankel (Cambridge, MA, 2011), p. 75, n. 20.
10 Richard Ellmann, *Oscar Wilde* (New York, 1988), p. 314.
11 Margaret D. Stetz, 'The Bi-social Oscar Wilde and "Modern" Women', *Nineteenth-century Literature*, LV/4 (March 2001), pp. 524 and 537.
12 Paul Russell, *The Gay 100: A Ranking of the Most Influential Gay Men and Lesbians, Past and Present* (New York, 1995), p. 10.
13 Ibid.
14 Evangelista, Introduction to *The Reception of Oscar Wilde in Europe*, ed. Stefano Evangelista (London, 2010), p. 18.

Select Bibliography

Editions

The Annotated Importance of Being Earnest, ed. Nicholas Frankel (Cambridge, MA, 2015)

The Annotated Prison Writings of Oscar Wilde, ed. Nicholas Frankel (Cambridge, MA, 2018)

The Complete Letters of Oscar Wilde, ed. Merlin Holland and Rupert Hart-Davis (New York, 2000)

Criticism: Historical Criticism, Intentions, The Soul of Man, ed. Josephine M. Guy, vol. IV of *The Complete Works of Oscar Wilde* (Oxford, 2007)

In Praise of Disobedience: The Soul of Man under Socialism and Other Works, introduction by Neil Bartlett (London, 2018)

Journalism, ed. John Stokes and Mark Turner, vol. VI and VII of *The Complete Works of Oscar Wilde* (Oxford, 2013)

The Picture of Dorian Gray: An Annotated, Uncensored Edition, ed. Nicholas Frankel (Cambridge, MA, 2011)

Salome, illus. Aubrey Beardsley (New York, 1967)

Salome, ed. Kimberly Stern (Peterborough, ON, 2015)

The Short Stories of Oscar Wilde: An Annotated Selection, ed. Nicholas Frankel (Cambridge, MA, 2020)

The Sphinx, with Decorations by Charles Ricketts, ed. Nicholas Frankel (Houston, TX, 2010). Available online at: https://cnx.org (accessed 17 July 2020)

Biographical

Bristow, Joseph, *Oscar Wilde on Trial: The Criminal Proceedings, from Arrest to Imprisonment* (New Haven, CT, 2021)

Ellmann, Richard, *Oscar Wilde* (New York, 1988)

Fitzsimons, Eleanor, *Wilde's Women: How Oscar Wilde Was Shaped by the Women He Knew* (London, 2015)
Frankel, Nicholas, *Oscar Wilde: The Unrepentant Years* (Cambridge, MA, 2017)
Holland, Merlin, intro. and commentary, *The Real Trial of Oscar Wilde* (New York, 2004); published in the UK as *Irish Peacock and Scarlet Marquess: The Real Trial of Oscar Wilde* (London, 2003)
—, *The Wilde Album* (New York, 1998)
McKenna, Neil, *The Secret Life of Oscar Wilde* (New York, 2005)
Mendelssohn, Michèle, *Making Oscar Wilde* (Oxford, 2018)
Mikhail, E. H., ed., *Oscar Wilde: Interviews and Recollections*, 2 vols (London, 1979)
Morris, Roy Jr, *Declaring His Genius: Oscar Wilde in North America* (Cambridge, MA, 2013)
Stern, Kimberly J., *Oscar Wilde: A Literary Life* (Cham, Switzerland, 2019)
Sturgis, Matthew, *Oscar: A Life* (London, 2018)

Bibliographical

Beckson, Karl, ed., *Oscar Wilde: The Critical Heritage* (London, 1970)
Goodman, Jonathan, compiler, *The Oscar Wilde File* (London, 1989)
Hofer, Matthew, and Gary Scharnhorst, eds, *Oscar Wilde in America: The Interviews* (Urbana and Chicago, IL, 2010)
Mason, Stuart [Christopher Millard], *Bibliography of Oscar Wilde* (London, 1914)
'Oscar Wilde in America: A Selected Resource of Oscar Wilde's Visits to America', www.oscarwildeinamerica.org

Critical

Bashford, Bruce, *Oscar Wilde: The Critic as Humanist* (Madison, NJ, 1999)
Blanchard, Mary, *Oscar Wilde's America: Counterculture in the Gilded Age* (New Haven, CT, 1998)
Boker, Uwe, Richard Corballis and Julie A. Hibbard, eds, *The Importance of Reinventing Oscar: Versions of Wilde during the Last 100 Years* (Amsterdam and New York, 2002)
Bristow, Joseph, ed., *Oscar Wilde and Modern Culture: The Making of a Legend* (Athens, OH, 2008)

—, ed., *Wilde Writings: Contextual Conditions* (Toronto, 2003)
—, and Rebecca N. Mitchell, *Oscar Wilde's Chatterton: Literary History, Romanticism, and the Art of Forgery* (New Haven, CT, 2015)
Brown, Julia Prewitt, *Cosmopolitan Criticism: Oscar Wilde's Philosophy of Art* (Charlottesville, VA, 1997)
Danson, Lawrence, *Wilde's Intentions: The Artist in His Criticism* (Oxford, 1997)
Dellamora, Richard, *Masculine Desire: The Sexual Politics of Victorian Aestheticism* (Chapel Hill, NC, 1990)
Dollimore, Jonathan, *Sexual Dissidence: Augustine to Wilde, Freud to Foucault* (Oxford, 1991)
Eltis, Sos, *Revising Wilde: Society and Subversion in the Plays of Oscar Wilde* (Oxford, 1996)
Evangelista, Stefano, *The Reception of Oscar Wilde in Europe* (London, 2010)
Fortunato, Paul L., *Modernist Aesthetics and Consumer Culture in the Writings of Oscar Wilde* (New York, 2007)
Frankel, Nicholas, *Oscar Wilde's Decorated Books* (Ann Arbor, MI, 2000)
Gagnier, Regenia, *Idylls of the Marketplace: Oscar Wilde and the Victorian Public* (Palo Alto, CA, 1986)
Guy, Josephine M., and Ian Small, *Oscar Wilde's Profession: Writing and the Culture Industry in the Late Nineteenth Century* (Oxford, 2000)
—, *Studying Oscar Wilde: History, Criticism, and Myth* (Greensboro, NC, 2006)
McCormack, Jerusha, ed., *Wilde the Irishman* (New Haven, CT, 1998)
Mackie, Gregory, *Beautiful Untrue Things: Forging Oscar Wilde's Extraordinary Afterlife* (Toronto, 2019)
Markey, Anne, *Oscar Wilde's Fairy Tales: Origins and Contexts* (Dublin, 2011)
Mendelssohn, Michèle, *Henry James, Oscar Wilde, and Aesthetic Culture* (Edinburgh, 2007)
Nunokawa, Jeff, *Tame Passions of Wilde: The Styles of Manageable Desire* (Princeton, NJ, 2003)
Pine, Richard, *The Thief of Reason: Oscar Wilde and Modern Ireland* (Dublin, 1995)
Powell, Kerry, *Acting Wilde: Victorian Sexuality, Theatre, and Oscar Wilde* (Cambridge, 2009)

—, *Oscar Wilde and the Theatre of the 1890s* (Cambridge, 1990)
—, and Peter Raby, eds, *Oscar Wilde in Context* (Cambridge, 2013)
Raby, Peter, ed., *The Cambridge Companion to Oscar Wilde* (Cambridge, 1997)
Riley, Kathleen, et al., eds, *Oscar Wilde and Classical Antiquity* (Oxford, 2018)
Roden, Frederick S., ed., *Critical Insights: Oscar Wilde* (Ipswich, MA, 2019)
—, ed., *Palgrave Advances in Oscar Wilde Studies* (New York, 2004)
Sammells, Neil, *Wilde Style: The Plays and Prose of Oscar Wilde* (Harlow, 2000; Abingdon and New York, 2014, reprinted 2017)
Sinfield, Alan, *The Wilde Century* (1994)
Sloan, John, *Oscar Wilde*, Authors in Context series (Oxford, 2009)
Smith, Phillip E., II, ed., *Approaches to Teaching the Works of Oscar Wilde* (New York, 2008)
—, and Michael S. Helfand, eds, *Oscar Wilde's Oxford Notebooks: A Portrait of Mind in the Making* (Oxford, 1989)
Tanitch, Robert, *Oscar Wilde on Stage and Screen* (London, 1999)
Whiteley, Giles, *Oscar Wilde and the Simulacrum: The Truth of Masks* (Abingdon and New York, 2015)
Williams, Kristian, *Resist Everything Except Temptation: The Anarchist Philosophy of Oscar Wilde*, foreword by Alan Moore (Chico, CA, and Edinburgh, 2020)
Willoughby, Guy, *Art and Christhood: The Aesthetics of Oscar Wilde* (Rutherford, NJ, 1993)
Wood, Julia, *The Resurrection of Oscar Wilde: A Cultural Afterlife* (Cambridge, 2007)
Wright, Thomas, *Oscar's Books: A Journey around the Library of Oscar Wilde*, e-book (London, 2013); published in USA as *Built of Books: How Reading Defined the Life of Oscar Wilde* (New York, 2009)

Acknowledgements

I am immensely grateful to Vivian Constantinopoulos, editorial director at Reaktion Books, for the patience, wisdom and understanding with which she guided this book through its long gestation. I am grateful, too, to Merlin Holland, Wilde's grandson, for kind permission to reprint extracts from Wilde's letters and *De profundis*; also to the dean of the College of Humanities and Sciences and the Chair of the Department of English, Catherine Ingrassia, at Virginia Commonwealth University (VCU), for supporting the book's completion in late 2019 through the award of a semester's research leave. Many individuals at Reaktion calmly and expertly oversaw the book's production in the midst of the COVID-19 crisis of 2020, not least Martha Jay, Phoebe Colley and Alex Ciobanu. My thanks to them, and also to the staff of the Interlibrary Loan Office at VCU's Cabell Library, for performing wonders in challenging and exceptional circumstances. My largest debt is to my wife, Susan, and my sons Max, Theo and Oliver, who have lived with Oscar Wilde for many years now. Without their love and support, I would not have been able to complete this book.

Photo Acknowledgements

The author and publishers wish to express their thanks to the below sources of illustrative material and/or permission to reproduce it. Some locations of artworks are also given below, in the interest of brevity:

British Library, London: pp. 53, 197, 233; from Lord Alfred Douglas, *Oscar Wilde and Myself* (New York, 1914), photo Wellcome Library, London: p. 194; The Furió Collection: p. 43; from *Irish Fireside* (supplement), v/115 (2 September 1885): p. 20; Library of Congress, Prints and Photographs Division, Washington, DC: pp. 8, 58, 62, 64, 72, 77, 78, 79; photo Luke McKernan (CC BY-SA 2.0): p. 250; Mark Samuels Lasner Collection, University of Delaware Library, Museums and Press, Newark: pp. 132, 193; The Metropolitan Museum of Art, New York: pp. 47, 75; Musei di Strada Nuova, Palazzo Rosso, Genoa: p. 227; National Library of Ireland on The Commons: pp. 18, 26; National Portrait Gallery, London: p. 189; from Robert Harborough Sherard, *The Life of Oscar Wilde* (New York, 1907), photos The New York Public Library: pp. 51, 220; from Robert Harborough Sherard, *The Real Oscar Wilde* (London, 1916): pp. 29, 109; Special Collections, University of Virginia Library, Charlottesville: pp. 104, 105, 137; from Oscar Wilde, *The Harlot's House and Other Poems* (New York, 1929): p. 96; William Andrews Clark Memorial Library, UCLA College, Los Angeles: p. 244.

Index

Page numbers in *italics* denote illustrations